T0037168

20 GOTO 10

20 GOTO 10

10101001 FACTS ABOUT RETRO COMPUTERS

Steven Goodwin

unbound

First published in 2023

Unbound
c/o TC Group, 6th Floor Kings House, 9–10 Haymarket,
London, United Kingdom, SW1Y 4BP

www.unbound.com

Typeset by Patty Rennie

A CIP record for this book is available from the British Library

ISBN 978-1-80018-274-5 (hardback)
ISBN 978-1-80018-275-2 (ebook)

Printed in Great Britain by Clays Ltd, Elcograf S.p.A.

MIX
Paper from
responsible sources
FSC® C018072

In Memoriam

Jack Tramiel
13 December 1928–8 April 2012

Sir Clive Sinclair
30 July 1940–16 September 2021

Jay Miner
31 May 1932–20 June 1994

Steve Jobs
24 February 1955–5 October 2011

Artwork by Justyna Graphics

For Lily,
'Woo hoo!'

Contents

WARNING!

Do not read this book from the start until it terminates! These pages contain many different versions of computing history. From time to time, as you read along, you will discover the origin of how one piece of technology connects to another via a simple number. You must then make a choice – either you can continue reading, or you can get distracted by this other number. After you make your choice, turn to that section and keep reading until you are ready to make another choice.

Your success in understanding retro computers lies in your ability to see how individual numbers form a coherent whole, like a matrix of green-on-black characters falling downwards on a screen, and to recall from memory the product number of a Commodore 64 disk drive, the *FX instruction to disable the ESCAPE key on an Acorn BBC Micro, or the infinite lives POKE for *Jet Set Willy* on the Sinclair ZX Spectrum!

Think carefully before you make each move, as you could just as easily discover a radio station which broadcasts software over the air as you could know the speed of a cassette tape, or learn the instruction code which does nothing on an antique processor.

Good luck!

Preface

My love of retro computers began when they were called, simply, computers. In 1983 my family bought a Sinclair ZX81 Starter Pack, since I had shown an interest in the single BBC Micro computer at school, and it seemed like a good way to help my sister and me with our schoolwork. But it wasn't. The family quickly became disinterested with the machine and so the most complex piece of technology in the house got relegated to 'that thing Steven plays with after school'.

But I loved learning about the underlying mechanics of the machine. BASIC. Machine code. Hardware interfaces. Everything. I borrowed every library book, and read every magazine, about it. Then I'd borrow library books about every *other* computer, and learn how to port their programs to *my* machine (since it was now accepted that the *family* computer was living with me!). I later bought a Dragon 32, a Sinclair Spectrum, a Tatung Einstein, an Apple II and anything else on sale at the local car boot sale. I learned to program them all. So different, yet so similar.

By the time I began to volunteer at the Centre for Computing History I had amassed a breadth of knowledge across many machines, but rarely any significant depth. I enjoyed writing books because they required me to research deep topics, but I couldn't find any justification for writing about retro computers because so many blogs had already done it. So, in 2014, for fun, I made notes of amusing anecdotes about the technology, the games, and the people.

Over the next few years I collected stories from retrocomputing festivals, friends, and the web. As my collection grew I needed a method to organise them. As an accidental taxonomist I wasn't skilled enough to create a cataloguing system where I could retrieve each story as deftly as possible. But I had noted that they all had a number. Pop!

A year or two after this I made the connection that some numbers had multiple entries, and some near-identical topics had different numbers. Pop!

Then, on realising that everyone has attempted to write one BASIC program in their life, I found it made sense to connect each entry through GOTO statements, which redirect a BASIC program to a new line number, and treat each section as if it were a line of code. Pop!

From that, the title *20 GOTO 10* was obvious to me, and the last piece of the puzzle fell into place. The project had moved from anecdotes to anecdata!

This, then, is a book of breadth. Its value, I hope, lies in the range of topics presented, across machines that were both superstars and also-rans. A curated set of stories that focuses more on the connections between the parts of history than on retelling geek folklore. If you've come for the history of the Commodore 64, I hope you'll stay for the tale about Amstrad and Spanish tax law, and discover why random numbers aren't random.

In 2021 Unbound and I discussed the project and formulated a plan to take the book to the masses via crowdfunding. This endeavour became more about 'us' rather than 'me', with each supporter being able to suggest topics, express preferences, and be involved in the process. It's a community, and one of which you are now part.

The book was finished in 2022 with all references relative to then. If you're reading this in 2032 please consider that what you regard as retro in your time is probably very different from what we do. And if you're reading this in 3022 with a holographic mind link whilst sat in a space station around Saturn and have discovered time travel, please come back and say hello – I'd love to know what the computing industry has in store!

The game

20 GOTO 10 is a book of numbers that describe the many facets of computing history, focusing on the golden age of old computers and retro games and consoles of the 1980s and 90s. It covers the hardware, software, and social history of the era, showing how they're linked through numbers such as 48K, C15, and 35899. Given that this book contains a range of entries, of varying geekery and complexity, I will explain everything from first principles so you can get up to speed as quickly as possible. If there are any terms you've missed, then Appendix 0 should help.

Had this book been written in the last century we wouldn't have been able to include some of the material presented here. Many machines, especially the early game consoles, could not be programmed or understood by the enthusiast. If you wanted to develop for the Nintendo Game Boy, for example, you had to be a registered developer with Nintendo by being noteworthy, talented, and (most importantly) rich! In return you'd get confidential documents on how the machine worked, and the necessary tools to program it. Since then, many developers from around the world have reverse engineered and documented these systems so that anyone can now understand and build games for them, and so we shall expose some of their secrets here. (Similarly, mass communication has enabled many historical oddities to be rescued from obscurity, so we'll show them some love, too.)

Each entry starts with a number, and by choosing a related number you'll create a unique adventure through the book and into a web of forgotten geek lore and incredible facts. With luck, you'll find a way to arrive at the number used to grant infinite lives in *Jet Set Willy* on the Sinclair ZX Spectrum. This is your goal!

Some of the more technical entries are marked with an icon 🖥 indicating that a basic understanding of programming and numbers will be helpful here, although it is not essential. If this were a role-playing game, you'd likely roll 1D6 and add it to your strength for any such section you successfully complete! (Or just skip to the end of the entry and continue as normal! It's not like I can check up on you!)

While most entries lead to a new part of history, there are some one-way tracks and some dead ends. If you reach one of these, the game is over and you should start over. These dead ends are subtly signposted as topics which indicate the death of the retro era, or your personal association with it.

There are isolated sections which don't connect to the main text. These are secret Easter eggs for you to discover at your leisure.

Also, to show love of 1980s computer magazines, there is a small game for you to type in littered throughout the book. It is written in BASIC for the Acorn BBC Micro. (But it won't be an authentic type-in experience... this program will actually work!)

How to play

After finding a starting point (see below), read the section and determine a suitable course of action. Unless you've reached a dead end, each section ends with one or more GOTO statements indicating the next section name and a REMark indicating its subject.

```
GOTO 6 : REM Kings Parade, Cambridge
GOTO 672 : REM 1K Chess
```

Choose one of these numbers and turn to that entry as indicated by the heading. Your decision is final. There's no turning back!

Each section is related, either through topic, manufacturer, or some esoteric connection. Sometimes that relation is simply the coincidence of it having the same number.

Occasionally, there are GOSUB statements. These reference footnotes for incidental information, slightly askew to the main text. If you wish to follow that route, make a note of the current entry number and read the new section. After finishing it, you'll see the keyword RETURN, at which point you should turn back to the entry from which you came.

Where to start?

Given that the set of numbers has no beginning and no end, there is no predetermined 'first page'. Begin where you like. Start with the first entry, the last one, or flick through the book and ask someone to say 'stop' when they get the urge!

If all that seems a trifle random, then I offer a few suggestions:

What do you consider retro? Jump to the first product which applies.

```
IF CHROMEBOX THEN
    GOTO 2012 : REM The year 2012
```

```
IF MICROSOFT_XBOX THEN
    GOTO 2002 : REM The year 2002

IF WOLFENSTEIN_3D THEN
    GOTO 1992 : REM The year 1992

IF SINCLAIR_ZX_SPECTRUM THEN
    GOTO 1982 : REM The year 1982
```

Or: which area most intrigues you?

```
IF PROCESSORS THEN
    GOTO 4 : REM Peripherals for processing

IF KEYBOARDS THEN
    GOTO 40 : REM Keyboards

IF AUDIO THEN
    GOTO 6581 : REM Sound generation

IF DISPLAYS THEN
    GOTO 2455992 : REM The Cathode Ray Tube
```

Curious about the title? If so, start with the following.

```
GOTO 10 : REM PRINT "Always get someone to cheque your work. ";
```

0 : False

Given that all modern computers work with binary – a series of 0s and 1s – it's no surprise that we start here. Beginning in 1847, when the inventor of Boolean logic, George Boole, wrote *The Mathematical Analysis of Logic*, 0 is treated as a false condition in almost all programming languages, with this simple yes/no state requiring only one bit of storage.

Literally.

This 'bit', short for 'binary digit', is the smallest amount of data a computer can process. Generally speaking, eight of these bits represent one 'byte'. However, since the architecture doesn't allow the CPU to retrieve a single bit from memory, every machine always gets a whole byte of them as one operation, and ignores what it doesn't need. Such computers are known as 8-bit machines, and are the most common variety from the retro era of the 1970s and 1980s. Later on, machines gained more bits than you could shake a slinky at, as 16, 32, and even 64 bits became the norm. To avoid confusion with the byte, these quantities are known as 16-bit words, 32-bit words, and so on. The 'word size' refers to the quantity of data bits that can be transferred, as a unit, by the computer.

```
GOTO 0 : REM First!
GOTO 0 : REM NOP
GOTO 0 : REM CC
GOTO 0 : REM Dewey Decimal Classification
GOTO 0 : REM Abbreviations
GOTO 1 : REM True
```

0 : First!

Computers count from zero. It is the most natural place to start since, no matter how many bits constitute a byte, the lowest number is always a row of zeros. Humans generally only start counting from zero when measuring their age. (The day on which they're born is the zeroth birthday while their second birthday, on average 365.2425 days later, is their first, and so on!) Computers will even pass on the zero index concept when labelling the first disc: in a Commodore Amiga as DF0, or as Drive 0 on the BBC Micro.

When a computer is first switched on, the processor needs to start executing instructions. On the Zilog Z80 CPU, the first place they are looked for is in memory location zero. That might appear to be the most logical thing to do, but it is an anomaly amongst processors. Others, like the MOS 6502 and Motorola 6809, first request two bytes from the upper part of memory (addresses $FFFC/$FFFD for the 6502 and $FFFE/$FFFF for the 6809) and jump to the location which those bytes specify. Which of these two approaches is correct would be an ecumenical matter, but it gives designers *using* the chip more scope as to where in memory they can place their program instructions. With the 6502, there's a technical benefit to *not* starting execution at address 0. It is known as the zero page.

The zero page is a set of addresses at the very bottom of memory, from 0 to 255. Any one of these addresses can be accessed with a special set of instructions that take less memory. Loading data from location $00020 could be changed from:

```
AD 20 00    lda $0020
```

to

```
A5 20       lda $20
```

This saves one byte of space and the amount of time that would normally be used to fetch that extra byte from memory when the instruction is executed. (The specific amount of time is called a 'cycle', the duration of which varies according to the speed of the machine.) Both are savings worth having, so naturally these 256 bytes are at a premium and usually used by the most common variables of the software (such as the BASIC ROM).

One quirk of using a zero page in this way is that because *only* the first 256 bytes are available, any attempt to use memory beyond the 0–255 limit gets wrapped back to the start. This shows up in a 6502 addressing mode called 'zero-page indexed' which has instructions like:

```
B5 20       lda $20,X
```

Here, data is loaded from the memory location determined by adding the value of register X to the number $20. But if the total of $20 + X is 256, then the address of 256 would wrap around, and it would load data from address 0 instead. If the total is 257, it would load from address 1. And so on. Although this is a feature of the

2

chip, and covered by the documentation, it is something that catches out developers who are all to ready to scream, 'Bug!'

(Speaking of bugs, the 1995 game *Grand Prix Manager*, developed by Edcom and released by MicroProse, had a case where Damon Hill would suffer more incidents than every other driver combined. This occurred because he was the first driver in the game, and the 'which driver gets affected by an incident' code was broken and often produced zero!)

```
GOTO 0 : REM False
GOTO 0 : REM NOP
GOTO 0 : REM CC
GOTO 0 : REM Dewey Decimal Classification
GOTO 0 : REM Abbreviations
GOTO 1 : REM First!
GOTO 2 : REM First!
GOTO 256 : REM Nintendo Game Boy Boot ROM
```

O : NOP

On computers using the Zilog Z80 microprocessor, like the Sinclair ZX81 and ZX Spectrum, an instruction byte of zero represented a null operation, or 'no operation' (NOP), where nothing happened. It was often used as padding so new instructions could be added later by overwriting these NOPs, or to replace existing instructions which did something untoward. (Later processors would use NOP to synchronise instruction pipelines.) When a computer game used a DEC (i.e., decrement) instruction to reduce the number of lives a player had, it was not unusual for magazines to publish POKEs which would replace that instruction with an NOP so that lives were never lost. (An alternate method was to change the first instruction of the 'check if the player collided with an enemy' routine to RETURN, bypassing all the 'did they die' logic. This created an immunity, rather than infinite lives. A subtle difference.)

Sometimes, programmers would add NOP instructions to make their own (real-world) lives easier. For example, when writing assembly without an assembler you needed to manually convert mnemonics such as LDA and JMP into their CPU instruction equivalents (say: 0x86 or 0x0E). Since every instruction could be of a different length, you needed to (manually) calculate the size of each section of code, to know how many bytes your program needed to jump forwards, or backwards, to avoid that section. And naturally, every time you changed anything in that section of code, the size might change, so you'd need to calculate a new total size.

Jumping forward is easy – simply add the number onto the current program counter. But computers that stored their numbers using 2s complement would not understand a jump backwards of -1 unless you wrote it as 255, while a jump back of two instructions was 254, and so on. Calculating the exact number by hand was tricky to get right, especially as it was easy to forget to jump back over the jump instruction itself. So some developers would write several NOP instructions at the start of their code and jump back to somewhere they thought was 'about right', knowing that even if they made a mistake, the computer would execute an NOP (which did nothing, and therefore did nothing bad) rather than a bogus instruction that might damage the program.

Regardless of the processor, the NOP instruction was almost always a single byte in length, even when it was not represented by a zero.

```
GOTO 0 : REM False
GOTO 0 : REM First!
GOTO 0 : REM CC
GOTO 0 : REM Dewey Decimal Classification
GOTO 0 : REM Abbreviations
GOTO 2 : REM 2's complement
GOTO 35899 : REM PEEK and POKE
```

0 : CC

From Bill Gates' infamous 1976 'Open Letter to Hobbyists' to Richard Stallman's commitment to free software with the release of the GNU General Public License in 1989, the relationship between copyright and software is legally clear, yet ethically fraught. To combat this, a number of developers have released software into the public domain, free from licensing issues.

During the 1990s public domain software flourished, with libraries accumulating work from various sources – often the authors themselves – and compiling them onto disks, each one becoming part of that library's 'collection'. Each disc would then be sold via mail order at a nominal fee (50p–£1, often with the phrase, 'Please rush me') along with whatever P&P and minimum order costs applied. Depending on the popularity of the machine, you might have only a few libraries (APDL for the Archimedes PD library), whereas others, notably the Amiga, would have many. But, since there was no copyright to contend with, anyone could buy PD discs from one library and sell them on. Some, like Fred Fish, compiled over a thousand discs which found their way around the world, by post, like a viral meme. While the software was, generally, of better quality than that which you'd find printed in a magazine, each had the distinct advantage of not needing to be typed in!

While you could argue that the law will never move as fast as the technology it is trying control, the phrase 'public domain' does not carry the same legal meaning in all jurisdictions. Therefore, Creative Commons have created a license called the CC0 which can be applied to all new media intended to be released as public domain, and which has the legal strength to apply your intention as widely as possible, including locations where the term 'public domain' is not acknowledged. As a license, it is not limited to software; music, such as the *Open Goldberg Variations*, has also been released using it.

```
GOTO 0 : REM False
GOTO 0 : REM First!
GOTO 0 : REM Dewey Decimal Classification
GOTO 0 : REM NOP
GOTO 0 : REM Abbreviations
```

0 : Dewey Decimal Classification

Far be it from us to believe that computers are the beginning of all life, but the numbering system used to classify library books by subject matter places 'computing' between 000 and 006. Starting at zero, just like computers should!

```
GOTO 0 : REM False
GOTO 0 : REM First!
GOTO 0 : REM NOP
GOTO 0 : REM CC
GOTO 0 : REM Abbreviations
```

0 : Abbreviations

The number zero (0) could legally be represented as a single dot (.) on the Sinclair ZX81 as a shortened form of 0.0. This reduced the memory used from seven bytes to one. Another abbreviation was to write 40000 as 4E4, because the ZX81 supported scientific notation; this was often used in PAUSE statements, since any number larger than 32767 constituted 'forever' and 4E4 audibly sounds a little like 'forever'.

The single dot was also used as an abbreviation within the BBC Micro's operating system, MOS. It could be added after any number of letters, to invoke the first command which matched. So *L. would be equivalent to *LOAD, rather like adventure games allowing you to replace NORTH with simply N. The default command, if no letters were provided, matched the command *CAT to show the directory listing of a disc. This was of great convenience since

*.

were on adjacent keys on the bottom right of the keyboard.

Pronounced 'stardot', this combination lives in Acorn lore as the name of a prominent online forum.

```
GOTO 0 : REM False
GOTO 0 : REM First!
GOTO 0 : REM NOP
GOTO 0 : REM CC
GOTO 0 : REM Dewey Decimal Classification
GOTO 3 : REM Optimising for size
GOTO 49 : REM Optimising for speed
```

1 : I'd buy that for a dollar

In most law, a contract can only exist if something is given up by both sides, even if that something is of nominal value. (Traditionally this was a peppercorn, as in 'peppercorn rent'.) In the tech world, that nominal amount is a dollar. But what can you get for $1? One dollar can buy you a Silicon Valley CEO for a year, like Steve Jobs, Elon Musk or Mark Zuckerberg, who will gain stock, health plans, or other benefits in lieu. It also bought the entire rights to Apple's MacBASIC.

In 1985 the contract for Applesoft BASIC, written by Microsoft for the Apple II, was up for renewal. Given that the Macintosh hadn't yet taken hold of the market, Applesoft Basic was a necessary part of the Apple II offering. (Especially given that it supported floating point numbers, which Apple's own BASIC didn't.) Bill Gates added a stipulation that if Microsoft continued to provide Applesoft BASIC, he would want MacBASIC to be scrapped. The Apple CEO, John Sculley, couldn't cancel the project in such an obvious way. Instead he could sabotage it – by selling MacBASIC to Microsoft for $1, who then cancelled it.

```
GOTO 1 : REM First!
GOTO 1 : REM REM Captain Blood Kill 5 Duplicate Planet Find?
GOTO 1 : REM True
GOTO 9 : REM Nine Tiles
GOTO 10 : REM New pence
GOTO 256 : REM The $2.56 reward program
```

1 : First!

One question the uninitiated will ask in any field of endeavour is, 'What was the first…?' Or: 'What was the best…?' As always, the answer is: 'It depends.'

We can commit to some well-known milestones, such as the first computer to sell a million units (the Commodore VIC-20), or the first company to hit the $1 billion mark for annual sales (Apple), but everything else is a matter of framing. How do you define computer?

Until perhaps as late as the 1960s, a computer was defined as a human who computed numbers using mathematical formulae, a definition which had existed since 1613 when it appeared in Richard Braithwaite's book, *The Yong Mans Gleanings*. In modern parlance, a computer is a programmable calculating machine powered by electronics, which excludes the mechanical Antikythera mechanism and Babbage's difference engine.

Even serial numbers lie! This is not the 220,003rd
Altair 8800 ever made – it's the third

Image courtesy of The Centre for Computing History, Cambridge

But must a computer be programmable? If so, the motor-driven Zuse Z1 (1936–37, hand-built by Konrad Zuse in his parents' home) was first off the blocks, since the oft-quoted Atanasoff–Berry Computer (1942) allowed you to reprogram the data, but not the code. If electronics are a prerequisite for such an honour, then the ENIAC, built in the US in 1945, can lay claim to being the world's first programmable electronic computer. (Pro tip: to be first in any field, simply describe your achievement with a more targeted focus!)

The problem of 'which came first' doesn't ease in the 1970s. The Altair 8800, released by MITS, is often considered to be the first microcomputer after its appearance on the cover of *Popular Electronics* in January 1975, but it was predated by Intel's 1973 Intellec-8 microcomputer. However, the Intellec-8 was only available to professional developers working on their i4004 and i4040 chips – and so, not to the general public. Does that count?

Even if we limit the scope by considering the first prebuilt home computer to be sold onto the mass market, then we might consider the Commodore PET (announced January 1977, but not shipped until September that year) or the Apple II (which had been shipping since June 1977, preceding even the TRS-80).

Again, the same answer of 'it depends' applies to the question of the first computer game. Both *Pong* (1972) and *Spacewar!* (1962) can be bested by William Higinbotham's *Tennis for Two* (1958), and even the latter echoes several predecessors: *Bouncing Ball* (1949), *Nimrod* (1951), *Tic Tac Toe* (1952), *Draughts* (1952), 'Sheep and Gates' (1952) and *OXO* (1952). Then there's the question of the first movie tie-in. That's probably the arcade game *Death Race* by Exidy (1976), which predates both *ET* and *Tron*, although Exidy have claimed it an unintentional tie-in – perhaps to avoid its lack of license.

```
GOTO 0 : REM First!
GOTO 1 : REM I'd buy that for a dollar
GOTO 1 : REM REM Captain Blood Kill 5 Duplicate Planet Find?
GOTO 1 : REM True
GOTO 2 : REM First!
GOTO 1000000 : REM Sales
GOTO 2455992 : REM The Cathode Ray Tube
```

1 : REM Captain Blood Kill 5 Duplicate Planet Find?

Line 1 began *most* BASIC programs, although some implementations would start from 0. And some would hold the printable version of the line number separately from its internal representation, meaning you could POKE the appropriate memory location to make it appear different on-screen, but still hold the same numeric value when running the program. (Consequently, this act had no purpose other than to amuse the programmer's own curiosity.)

Line 1 would usually be a REM statement indicating the name of the game and its author. In this case it's a reference to the 1988 game *Captain Blood*, from Exxos (ERE/Infogrames).

For those trying to parse the sentence, you need to know that the aim of the game is to find and destroy Captain Blood's five remaining clones, known as 'Duplicates'. The 'planet' refers to one of four inhabited planets, whose aliens you have to interrogate by learning their language through the UPCOM interface. (Those familiar with the line 'Darmok and Jalad at Tanagra', from the fifth season episode of *Star Trek: The Next Generation* in which the alien species speaks only in allegories, will understand the ideas involved.)

The game can be described as both engaging and irritating, not least because the interface would change according to player health. Whereas *Doom* would simply alter the player graphic to a more bloodied head as health decreased, *Captain Blood* would shake the mouse cursor, making control physically more difficult.

But compared to the 'Corrupt Data' sanity effect in *Eternal Darkness: Sanity's Requiem*, this might be considered rather tame.

Entry title suggested by Paul aka hardwareharry.

```
GOTO 1 : REM I'd buy that for a dollar
GOTO 1 : REM First!
GOTO 1 : REM True
```

1 : True

Every location in a computer's memory holds a number, usually in the range of 0 to 255. If, instead, we need it to reference a binary quantity – i.e., a boolean, which can be either true or false – or convert a number into a boolean, then it is usual to split this range into two parts, where a zero represents false and every other value is considered true. However, when determining the truth of an expression, like IF LIVES = 0, then the boolean result of the LIVES = 0 part would need to be converted back into a number so it can be stored in memory. False becomes 0, and true becomes 1.

Or -1, depending on the system! This might appear contradictory to the common notion of computers being binary, and binary digits being 1 and 0. On and off. But this case exists because in 2's complement (the number system by which numbers are usually stored internally) the number -1 is represented as 11111111 and is the complement of zero (00000000) – the complement operation being where every 0 is flipped to a 1 or vice-versa. Since the native machine code of the CPU doesn't understand about boolean values, only numbers, this determination of -1 or 1 is made by the high-level language. In our example this is BASIC. And most languages choose -1 because of the ease of switching between 00000000 and 11111111.

But it doesn't matter if that value is -1 or 1, as any non-zero value is treated as true when converting from numbers to booleans.

Most of the time.

The implementation of BASIC in two of the most pivotal machines of the era, the Sinclair ZX81 and ZX Spectrum, had elected instead to use 1 when converting from booleans to numbers. Furthermore, because of the limited memory (especially in the former), it was not uncommon to see code compacted to read:

```
LET X = X + (INKEY$ = "8") - (INKEY$ = "5")
```

Here the instruction INKEY$ reads the keyboard, without waiting for confirmation in the form of the ENTER or RETURN key. Importantly, the pseudo-variable INKEY$ is not updated while this statement is being interpreted. Therefore, INKEY$ can be either '5', '8', or neither. Never both.

So, if the '8' key was pressed (a right arrow on the early Sinclair machines) then INKEY$ = "8" would evaluate to true, get converted to 1, while INKEY$ = "5" would evaluate to false, get converted to 0 and make the whole line the equivalent of:

```
LET X = X + 1 - 0
```

In essence, X would be incremented, moving the character to the right.

Conversely, if '5' (in this context, it's unsurprisingly the left arrow) was pressed, then only the second expression would be evaluated to 1, and X would be decremented.

But if the BASIC interpreter had determined that the true should be -1, then the code would be equivalent to:

```
LET X = X + -1 - 0
```

Consequently, the character would move in reverse! So, if your machine was so poorly served by the magazines of the day that you were forced to port games from another computer, you would have to convert the key presses to something to match your keyboard and then reverse the logic.

Amusingly, the Sinclair ZX80 was Sinclair's first and only home computer to use -1 for true, making the upgrade path slightly trickier for the first generation of developers. (But if you had the perseverance to handle computers at this time, you probably had enough ability to realise the change quite quickly.) The reason for this was that the ZX80 had only integer BASIC, so flipping all the bits from 00000000 to 11111111 was a natural and fast operation. When floating point numbers were introduced there needed to be specific code. Most other machines adopted -1.

PS: Any developers who came to the hobby later than 1986 might be confused that a single equals sign is used for equality *and* assignment. That was common for BASIC implementations of the time.

```
GOTO 0 : REM False
GOTO 1 : REM I'd buy that for a dollar
GOTO 1 : REM First!
GOTO 1 : REM REM Captain Blood Kill 5 Duplicate Planet Find?
GOTO 2 : REM 2's complement
GOTO 8 : REM Type-in listings
GOTO 10 : REM BASIC
```

1.3591409 :
The square root of 0.25

According to the first revision of the ZX81 BASIC (known as the 550 ROM) 1.3591409 was the square root of 0.25, instead of the mathematically accepted answer of 0.5. Strangely, the square root of ¼ was reported correctly. So why did this come about, and how was it fixed?

The easiest way of answering this question is to examine the ROM of the original and revised versions of the Z80 assembly code. It is in a short section of addition code called ADDEND-0, used in one special case of a shifting routine that is called when the exponent of the two numbers differs by more than 32 – a rare occurrence. Furthermore, this shifting routine is called only twice as part of the larger addition code. The original version of the ADDEND-0 routine was:

Address	Machine code hex	Assembly instruction mnemonic
1732H	D9	exx
1733H	7C	ld A,H
1734H	95	sub L
1735H	67	ld H,A
1736H	AF	xor A
1737H	2E 00	ld L,0

Compare with the fixed version:

Address	Machine code hex	Assembly instruction mnemonic
1736H	D9	exx
1737H	AF	xor A
1738H	2E 00	ld L,0

Unusually for a code fix, instructions were removed instead of added. (Other code had changed between ROMs, thus the slightly different addresses.) Specifically:

Address	Machine code hex	Assembly instruction mnemonic
1733H	7C	ld A,H
1734H	95	sub L
1735H	67	ld H,A

These are the three instructions which attempt to handle the carry, generated by the addition routine. All three instructions combine to subtract the value of L from the value in H. As you've probably guessed, the bug is that this didn't need to happen, and so errors were introduced into *some* calculations. The square root is the most famous example, but in the *Sinclair User Annual* of 1983 it is also mentioned that squaring the number 0.25 using the code

```
PRINT 0.25 ** 2
```

computes as 3.1423844 instead of 0.0625.

The problem could have been fixed by withdrawing the machines from sale, issuing a recall notice, and installing a new ROM into each of them. But that was expensive, and Sinclair had a reputation for clever and cheap, not expensive. So, until corrected machines entered the sales chain, an interim workaround was found that used hardware to fix the problem already in software.

Understanding the problem

Of the three bogus instructions, the fatal flaw is at address 1735, ld H,A, which changes the H register in a problematic way because the carry value in the subtraction was changed according to some other logic. The logic itself is unimportant. So, only the ld H,A needs to be removed, because if it is then the other two instructions are inert, and the bug goes away.

The first key to understanding the solution lies in the address of the erroneous instruction, 1735. This is in hex and can be represented in binary as 0001 0111 0011 0101. (Appendix 256, Numbers, provides a handy conversion table for those that need it.) If we can detect the program counter being on that address, we can do *something* to avoid the error. One possibility is to increment that counter so the instruction is never executed, but that would require access to the internals of the CPU itself.

The second key is that the instruction ld H,A, when written as machine code, has the hex value 67 (or binary of 0110 0111.) So, if we can detect the address of 1735 and change a single bit in the data being read, then the instruction known as 67 will be something else, something that doesn't cause the error. But are there any Z80 instructions which are only one binary digit away from the number 0110 0111 that could be executed instead, and have no effect on the H register? There are: 0010 0111, or 27, has only one change in bit 6 and is an instruction called DAA. This stands for Decimal Adjust Accumulator and is used to change the value in register A (the accumulator) between traditional decimal and binary coded decimal. Since A is getting cleared by the XOR instruction immediately afterwards, it doesn't matter if we change A here.

In essence, the solution was to check for the program counter hitting 1735, and then tweak the instruction being fed into the CPU to be DAA.

The solution

How did they do it? By adding two 3-input NOR gates, contained in a new logic chip physically piggy-backed on top of the CPU, to look for this program counter, and force bit 6 of the data bus to 0, so that the CPU read the instruction as DAA instead. Simples!

As for the origin of the bug, it's a simple matter of a rush job. The ZX printer hardware from Sinclair (the one that printed onto shiny toilet roll) was late in arriving at the developers, Nine Tiles, and so much work was needed to reorganise the software to make space for the new printer code. This part (a subroutine of a shifting routine, called occasionally by the addition code) was simply overlooked.

GOTO 9 : REM Nine Tiles

$1^7/_8$: IPS

The cassette tapes used by most computers in the 1980s were formally known as compact audio cassettes and ran at a speed of 1⅞ inches per second. This meant a C60, with 30 minutes per side, would be about 281¼ feet long, or 85.73 metres. However, this doesn't give an exact measure for the number of bytes which could be stored on the tape, since every computer used a different system for saving to tape. Worse, some formats would need more tape if the data comprised 1s, rather than 0s.

```
GOTO 15 : REM Saving to tape
GOTO 15 : REM C15, C60, C90
GOTO 50 : REM Compilations
GOTO 300 : REM Kansas City
GOTO 451 : REM Fahrenheit 451
GOTO 65495 : REM Going faster
```

2 : Alignment

When you have an 8-bit processor, accessing a single byte is an obvious and straightforward operation. When you upgrade to 16-bits, it is more efficient to load two bytes, i.e., all 16 bits, at once. Sometimes the processor forces this upon you, so that accessing memory at an odd address results in an error. This error might be called an 'exception' or 'trap'. While a programmer is expected to understand this limitation, the end user should not be. Consequently, on the prototype Apple Macintosh, the copy and paste functionality would crash. Half of the time. This happened because the software needed to perform some clever logic: the clipboard data was copied around memory as the program with the original copy exited and the new program opened. If the size of the data in the clipboard was odd (which, statistically, would happen half the time) then one of these operations would accidentally reference an odd memory address. And crash.

```
GOTO 2 : REM 2's complement
GOTO 2 : REM First!
GOTO 2 : REM Last!
```

2 : BBC Micro

Some companies build a cheaper computer.

Some companies build a better computer.

Acorn were in the latter camp. If Vikings had existed in the 1980s, they would have sung glorious battle songs of the wars between Atari ST and Commodore Amiga, or between ZX Spectrum and BBC Micro, but it was usually a fight of ethos. The 1981 Acorn BBC Micro had everything you could need. Ever. If you wanted to add a serial printer, it had a port. Parallel printer? A different port! A laser disc, it had a port. More floppy disc drives, an underside port. A hard disk? Slap in a new ADFS ROM chip and hook it into the 1 MHz bus! An extra processor even? A port! This machine could be transformed into a game station, business machine, desktop publishing unit, education platform, or anything in between.

For those outside the UK, BBC stands for British Broadcasting Corporation and, as well as the state broadcaster for TV and radio, was the licensor of the name to the Acorn Proton, as the prototype computer was then called. By selling a machine with its BBC label, and then producing the BBC Computer Literacy Project, the broadcaster gave the 1980s generation its first exposure to computing, when casually demonstrating the machine on TV. In doing so they circumvented the rule preventing the BBC from advertising. (See the portrayal of Clive Sinclair in the film drama *Micro Men* – originally called 'Syntax Era'.)

Still, it also had a good quantity of games like *Repton*, *Chuckie Egg* and the immortal *Elite*.

The section number 2 relates to the Rifa X2, a capacitor in the power supply, which were generally the only components of the BBC Micro to ever malfunction and emit their magic smoke.

Mark Thompson considers this to be their favourite machine.

GOTO 250 : REM Acorn Archimedes

2 : 2's complement

This is how the individual bits of a byte are transformed to represent a decimal number. It was designed as an improvement over 1's complement because of the latter's hidden complexities. Consider this: for us humans to read the binary number 1100011, it is simplest to imagine that each 1 and 0 is represented in a grid, adding any necessary 0s to the left to fill all eight spaces.

128	64	32	16	8	4	2	1
0	1	1	0	0	0	1	1

We then sum all the numbers at the top of the columns holding a 1. So, 1100011 = 64 + 32 + 2 + 1 = 99.

This works fine for all possible 8-bit numbers between 0 and 255, inclusive, but doesn't represent negative numbers. For that we need an alternate set of numbers along the top by switching the most significant bit (i.e. the one with the largest value, on the left hand side) from 128 to -128.

–128	64	32	16	8	4	2	1
1	1	1	0	0	0	1	1

On the surface this looks like our primary school maths class, where we make 99 negative by simply flipping the sign at the start. But by repeating the sum, we have 11100011 = -128 + 64 + 32 + 2 + 1 = -29, which bears no resemblance to the original 99 or our anticipated -99. That is because creating a negative number in 2's complement isn't as simple as flipping the most significant bit (MSB) from 0 to 1. (That's the method for 1's complement!) Instead, me must flip *all* the bits. And then add 1.

So 01100011 is flipped to 10011100, and 1 is added to make 10011101. Checking this on the grid we see:

–128	64	32	16	8	4	2	1
1	0	0	1	1	1	0	1

-128 + 16 + 8 + 4 + 1 = -99

All machines in this book use 2's complement, instead of the 1's complement used in the Apollo Guidance Computer in the moon landings of the late 1960s and early 1970s. Although the latter is a fine system, it is something more suited to machine-led calculations than human ones, because it is so different to what we're used to. Furthermore, 1's complement has two ways of representing 0 (00000000 and 11111111) which makes for further complications.

For us humans, these negative numbers generally exist only with us. Processors carry out the arithmetic given, pausing only to mark the result as negative if the MSB is set to 1. They don't know if the value is *meant* to represent something which might have a minus sign or not. Determining this is a job for the programmer by indicating that a value is signed or unsigned. In doing so the programmer, not the processor, introduces a fixed limit on the range of numbers that a variable or memory location can hold. The total number of values is identical, but their position on the number lines moves.

Here, then, are some typical ranges for a given number of bits that you will probably meet in this book.

Number of bits	Number	Signed minimum	Signed maximum	Unsigned maximum
1	21	−1*	0	1
2	22	−2	1	3
4	24	−8	7	15
8	28	−128	127	255
9	29	−256	255	511
10	210	−512	511	1023
11	211	−1024	1023	2047
12	212	−2048	2047	4095
16	216	−32768	32767	65535
20	220	−524288	524287	1048575
32	232	−2147483648	2147483647	4294967295

by convention we rarely consider a single bit to be signed

Consequently, there are many limits, and bugs caused by those limits, since incrementing an unsigned number of 255 goes to 0 (not 256) and adding 1 to a signed number of 127 generates -128. The Nintendo game *The Legend of Zelda*, the first in its franchise, had a maximum of 255 rupees for this reason (although the 'Ghandi dropping nukes' bug in the MicroProse game *Civilization* where the leader's aggression of 1 went down by 2 with -1 wrapping around to 255, is a hoax according to Sid Meier's autobiography). Even for quantities that can never be negative, programmers often prefer to use signed numbers since they are easier to work with. For example, if you have 10 coins and try to buy an item costing 20, then the result is -10 and the code is obviously:

```
IF COINS_I_HAVE - ITEM_COST < 0 THEN
    PRINT "You can't afford this"
```

But calculating 10 − 20 with *un*signed numbers gives a result of 246, 65526, or 4294967286 depending on the number of bits available. All numbers are positive, which implies you'll have coins left over and are therefore able to buy the item.

```
GOTO 0 : REM NOP
GOTO 1 : REM True
GOTO 2 : REM Alignment
```

```
GOTO 2 : REM First!
GOTO 2 : REM Last!
GOTO 8 : REM Bits in a byte
GOTO 127 : REM 127 or 255?
```

2 : First!

Stone Raider II (1986) was a *Boulder Dash* clone for the Dragon 32. There was no 'Stone Raider I'.

In fact, it is a smart move to start counting from 2, since it gives the consumer the belief that there was a first version, good enough to deserve a sequel. With software, specifically games, a sequel is usually better than the original – almost unique in the field of creative arts. Compare with films; it is rare for a sequel to surpass its original predecessor, so much so that any sequel that surpasses its original goes onto a (short) list of notable exceptions, suitable for any late night pub discussion

Occasionally, the reason is more sobering. The first, and only, computer that Soundic/Hanimex released was called the Pencil II. Not Pencil I. Similarly, Acorn's second extension for the Electron was the Plus 3. In both cases, this was because the original hardware never made it to market and so, for internal continuity, they kept the original numbering system.

(In ancient Greece, when numbers were used for counting, the first number to have an actual name was 2, since you can't count 0 of something, and 1 is a 'thing' rather than a collection of things which needed counting.)

```
GOTO 0 : REM First!
GOTO 1 : REM First!
GOTO 2 : REM Alignment
GOTO 2 : REM 2's complement
GOTO 2 : REM Last!
```

2 : Last!

It is very easy to make your second product your last. Simply adopt 'The Osborne Effect' and all your efforts might result in you shipping a follow-up product – such as the Osborne Executive – that no one wants to buy, or that will be internally shelved or cancelled and disappear like the vapour of the Imagine 'megagame', 'Bandersnatch'!

'The Osborne Effect' is named after the Osborne Computer Corporation whose founder, Adam Osborne, announced the next generation of hardware before it was ready and, fatally, while the previous generation (the first successful laptop, the Osborne 1) was still selling. Cue cancellations from customers anticipating an improved product within weeks which, naturally, never arrived.

Such approaches are not always fatal. The follow-up to the 1982 Automata game *Pimania*, the snappily titled *My Name is Uncle Groucho... You Win a Fat Cigar*, like its predecessor, offered a real-world prize. It was released before *Pimania* had been won, but seemed to have little effect on the sales of either.

Conversely, another publisher, Ultimate, took no such chances. When they finally got all their bits in a row and completed the Sinclair Spectrum game *Knight Lore*, they held back its release as the current title, *Sabre Wulf*, was still on shelves. The (much superior) *Knight Lore* – and the half-finished 'Alien 8' – would almost certainly have dramatically affected the sales of *Sabre Wulf*.

```
GOTO 2 : REM Alignment
GOTO 2 : REM 2's complement
GOTO 2 : REM First!
GOTO 31900 : REM With prizes
```

2 : Psion Series 3

Although sold as a personal organiser, this device – the first to productise flash memory in computing – also included OPL (Organiser Programming Language) alongside its database, word processor and spreadsheet functionality. OPL first appeared in 1984, seven years before the Series 3, and featured on the original Psion Organiser. Its structured language had echoes of BBC BASIC; both eschewed line numbers, used VAR% for integer variables, and incorporated machine-specific instructions. In the case of the BBC it was commands like VDU, whereas with the Psion it was DIALOG and CALL. The language is now called opl-dev, and is open source.

As for the hardware, the 240x80 monochrome LCD, audio buzzer, and 128 KiB base memory were fine for productivity at the time, but the screen made it less suited to action games. Still, the Series 3 did lead to the 3a. One small letter for Psion, one giant leap for the consumer, as the CPU speed doubled (to 7.68 MHz), the memory doubled, the screen resolution doubled to 480x160 (and introduced its third colour, 'grey'!), the software in ROM grew from 384 KiB to 1 MiB, and it gained two proper audio channels.

Luckily, the price didn't increase by a factor of 2, with the base 3a unit starting at £269 compared to the previous £179.

Robin Harrison considers this to be their favourite machine.

GOTO 19 : REM Musicians with computers

2 : Epson QX-16

In 1984, the classic playground rivalry was between two companies, Sinclair and Commodore – specifically, their then flagship models, the ZX Spectrum and the Commodore 64. Around the office water-cooler, it was between CP/M and DOS. Epsom, unable to decide which team to support (or maybe realising that their CP/M-only machine, the QX-10, needed a boost), included both a Z80 and an 8088 chip in their QX-16. And a CGA card. This meant the case needed to be larger, which in turn meant Epson could add an internal hard drive for the first time.

But hardware means nothing without software. The QX range had Valdocs – which was slow and buggy, and which received such bad press it might have pushed users away from the machine entirely. A shame since, in the time before Windows existed to copy and paste content from one application to another, having your spreadsheet and word processor in a single package to share data was the height of modern technology.

Brian Johnson considers this hybrid to be their favourite machine.

GOTO 301 : REM Video Genie EG3003

2.04 : Commodore Amiga A500+

Unlike the Spectrum+, the Amiga 500+ had to work to earn its plus sign!

This 1991 Amiga contained the second generation of hardware, known as the Enhanced Chipset (ECS). But the greater 'chip' memory used by the graphics systems required a better integrated circuit (IC) to handle it. This IC was called Agnus, short for Address Generator Chip. In fact, it was fourth in a line of Agnus chips, each of them sporting spicy nicknames: 'Thin', 'Fat', 'Fatter' and 'Super'. The 500+ was indeed super!

Along with improvements in hardware came better firmware, Kickstart 2.04. This was the bootstrap ROM which provided the initialisation routines for the hardware, before booting the Workbench software (containing the Amiga's UI and main OS) or whatever else was in the internal 880 K disc drive.

But with improvements comes incompatibility, and it was the Kickstart ROM – rather than the machine itself – which caused problems. Consequently, Commodore, and additional third-party developers, provided solutions for the 500+ to use a downgraded Kickstart 1.2 or 1.3 ROM and thus restore compatibility with certain games.

Ian Ardley considers the Amiga A500+ (and the updated Plus specifically, not just the original A500!) to be their favourite machine.

GOTO 205.5 : REM How to draw a maze in one line

3 : There are three kinds of people in the world...

… those who can count and those who can't.

GOTO 7 : REM Seven jokes

3 : Optimising for size

Question: How long is a piece of string?

Well, the flippant answer is to say, 'Twice the distance from the middle to either end!'

But how long is a number? That is to say: if you have to store the number 3 in memory, how many bytes does it take? What about the number 30? Or 3,000,000?

This second question is a bit more difficult to answer, since any number lower than infinity can be increased in length by simply appending zero to the end. So does each new zero require an extra byte of memory? If so, what stops a computer from running out of memory if the program does nothing except repeated multiplications by 10?

In short, notation. To ensure a variable can fit into a fixed (and constant) amount of memory, every number, regardless of size, is formatted into a known pattern. Naturally, if this pattern has a fixed number of bytes it can't represent *every* possible value, so sometimes an addition or multiplication instruction will cause the result to be inaccurate. This is either because the value flows over the available space or because the new result is so close to the old value that it cannot differentiate between them in the space available, and so the number appears unchanged.

Most current machines use a notation referred to by the cryptic name IEEE 754, which uses four bytes to hold a number. Our beloved Sinclair ZX81 needed five. So the instruction

GOTO 10

would use seven bytes: one for the GOTO keyword token (all keywords on early

21

Sinclair machines were stored using a single character for the entire word, to save space), five for the number, and one to indicate the value was a number rather than a variable. Therefore, this one neat trick saves four bytes of memory, which is worthy of a clickbait headline!

```
GOTO SGN PI
```

This statement includes three tokenised symbols, occupying one byte each. When the program is run, the GOTO instruction tells the computer to jump to the new instruction located at the line numbered SGN PI and process it. But what is SGN PI? Well, as you might have guessed, PI is 3.1415926 and SGN is short for sign. The latter is a function, and like any function it takes an input, processes it in some way, and returns a result as output. In this case, 'sign' has the logic whereby any positive number answers with +1, any negative number gives -1, and zero returns 0.

Bonus points if you spotted that SGN PI is 1! Similarly, to round a number down to the nearest integer you could use the INT keyword, which would reduce PI to 3.

```
PRINT INT PI
```

Many such shortcuts are possible, with PI-PI, NOT PI, and SIN PI all representing zero. I leave other examples as an exercise for the reader!

Improving initialisation

These weren't the only memory-saving techniques being developed. In its default configuration, the Sinclair ZX81 had only 1 KiB and so needed to save every byte. Even initialising a set of variables was very costly.

```
10 LET A = 10
20 LET B = 12
30 LET C = 20
40 LET D = 30
```

This block of code requires a total of 64 bytes, 16 for each line, because this machine uses:

- 2 bytes for each line number
- 2 bytes for the length of the whole statement

- The statement itself, one byte per character, 5 in this case (LET counts as one tokenised character, remember)
- 1 byte for the newline delimiter
- 6 extra bytes for each number in the instruction (1 to indicate there is a number, and 5 for the number itself, like our GOTO 10 example above)

The last point is peculiar to early, low-power machines since the BASIC line editor would store numbers twice – once in a literal form, one byte per digit – so that it could be quickly displayed on-screen as a LISTing. And the second way it was stored was in a form where all digits were held in an internal format so it could be quickly processed when the program was run.

But it gets worse! This doesn't consider the memory required to store the value of the *variable* while the program is running. (In this case we need extra memory for the one byte of the variable name and five more for the number.) This solution is equivalent to the previous example.

```
 5 N$ = "10122030"
10 A = VAL N$(1 TO 2)
20 B = VAL N$(3 TO 4)
30 C = VAL N$(5 TO 6)
40 D = VAL N$(7 TO 8)
```

This first trick relies on the text string of N$ being stored in a total of 10 bytes (two quotes, and eight characters), instead of each of the original four numbers requiring 6 bytes *each*. However, there is still work to do, since the numbers in N$(1 TO 2) will require their own space. This can be further improved not by using variables called A, B, C, and D, but by using an array.

```
 5 N$ = "10122030"
10 DIM V(4)
20 FOR N = 1 TO 4
30 LET V(N) = VAL N$(N * 2 - 1 TO N * 2)
40 NEXT N
```

Line 30 moves a portion of the text in N$ from a given start position to a specific end position (inclusive) and then eVALuates the text as if it were a number. Javascript programmers know this as parseInt, and C programmers use atoi, with most languages having their own equivalent.

This could be further improved by replacing the literals, like 1, 2 and 4, with variables called O, T and F respectively, using the techniques on the previous page.

```
 6 LET O = SGN PI
 7 LET T = O + O
 8 LET F = INT PI + O
```

Making our main loop a much shorter (and confusing):

```
20 FOR N = O TO F
30 LET V(N) = VAL N$(N * T - O TO N * T)
40 NEXT N
```

On average, if you could replace a numeral in its literal form (e.g. 1, 2, 3) with a variable, you would save memory after using it four times.

The icing on the proverbial cake is to then remove the memory used by the run-time variable N$ so it could be used for other purposes.

```
45 N$= " "
```

With this knowledge of strings, you might wish to review the 17 bytes of memory used by:

```
10 LET X = 128
```

Compare with the 16 used in:

```
10 LET X = VAL("128")
```

Every character you type on the keyboard has its own character code (remembering that the ZX81 didn't use ASCII). So, if you needed a number which matched one of these codes, you could type the character and use the keyword CODE to convert it into a number:

```
10 LET X = CODE("■")
```

This produces the same result in just 14 bytes.

The CODE and VAL tricks are almost exclusive to the ZX80 and ZX81, since they were two of the few machines that did not support a DATA statement to hold arbitrary numbers or strings.

Condensing code

Such small programs rarely had instructions for the user, but those that did could optimise for space by using short words and adopting tokenised instructions. That is to say, since the Sinclair machines had keywords called INPUT, STOP, and TO, your 23-byte instruction to 'PRESS Q TO END THE GAME' could be changed to the terser 'INPUT Q TO STOP' which only uses 5 bytes, since each keyword takes only one byte, and includes its own space.

Such techniques weren't the special reserve of small, cheese wedge-shaped computers. Even the larger machines would use similar techniques to save memory. Indeed, they would often remove the spaces between BASIC keywords or omit the second number in a statement like N$ (3 TO). If variables could be saved along with the program, then you didn't need to include the statement to set the variable in the first place since the memory being used for the initialisation code would be duplicated in the variable data. So you would assign the variables directly in the BASIC interpreter since, by not using a line number,

```
LET A$ = "This is a long text string with all the
    instructions..."
```

would store the text in the variable. You could then save the program, and the variables were included automatically.

The one caveat of this approach is that after loading you just had to remember to *not* type RUN since that would invariably clear the memory of all variables. (Another reason why digital archaeologists need to read the loading instructions!)

Minimising machine code

So far, we've only seen BASIC examples – so to speak – since they are easier to explain. But saving memory in machine code is also necessary, especially in ROM code where the cost difference between a 4 KiB and 8 KiB chip was significant. (The code *had* to be optimised since manufacturers didn't make a 5 KiB ROM; this is a genuine example since the original ZX80 ROM code, before optimisation, was 5 KiB.) Sometimes the processor would have special, shortened instructions to help reduce the memory footprint. The Zilog Z80, for example, had a restart (RST) instruction which would jump to a new memory location. Unlike the traditional 3-byte jump (JP) instruction, RST occupied only 1 byte, but it could only target eight specific addresses, namely $0000, $0008, $0010, $0018, $0020, $0028, $0030 and $0038. So, naturally, you placed your most frequently used routines at those addresses, such as printing a character, reading a character, and displaying an error.

Even simple instructions can be improved. Conventional wisdom suggests we should simply write the value of zero into A with:

```
Machine code hex      Assembly instruction mnemonic
3E 00                 ld A,0
```

But we can improve upon this by misusing existing instructions! One common technique was to use 'exclusive OR', often seen as XOR or EOR, to set registers to zero.

Exclusive OR takes two numbers as input and produces one output. (The origin of these numbers, or where they're stored, doesn't matter at this stage.) As XOR is a bitwise operation, every bit in the first number is processed against its equivalent bit in the second, producing its result. This is identical to other bitwise operations like AND, or OR. The result of 1001 AND 1100 is 1000, since only the first bit is set to 1 in the first *and* second numbers. Similarly, 1001 OR 1100 is 1101. But what of XOR? Its truth table is somewhat strange.

A	B	Result
0	0	0
0	1	1
1	0	1
1	1	0

The first three rows look like the logic for a traditional OR operation, with a result of 1 when either A *or* B is 1. But the final row adds a twist. That is, if both A AND B are true, then the XOR result *isn't*. This has two amusing quirks.

Firstly, any XOR operation can be reversed by applying the result a second time. To see this, cover up the A input column with your finger so you can see only the B input and the result. Now, calculate a new XOR result based on the two numbers you see. Starting from the top this would be:

```
0 XOR 0 = 0
1 XOR 1 = 0
0 XOR 1 = 1
1 XOR 0 = 1
```

It is no coincidence that these numbers (0, 0, 1 and 1) exactly match those in column A. It's as if the result is a secret code, and you have the key (in the form of B) and can work backwards to find the secret message! This ability to reverse the operation was also prevalent in computer graphics, since drawing the graphic in XOR mode would cause it to appear on screen (lest any colour clashes), and drawing it again (also in XOR mode) would remove it, thus needing no extra memory to restore the background visuals which would otherwise have gotten destroyed.

Secondly, if the two inputs are identical (as either 0 or 1), then the result is always false. Cover up the middle two rows with another finger, and you'll see that 0 XOR 0 = 0, and 1 XOR 1 = 0. So, if both inputs contain the same number, then the answer would always be zero. No matter what the number, or how large it is, every bit of that number would become zero.

It is this second point which directs us towards the Z80 assembly instruction

```
AF      xor A
```

which does an exclusive OR operation using the accumulator and register A. Since the accumulator *is* register A, it is performing XOR on itself, meaning A will become zero. Always. Making this instruction one byte shorter and one cycle quicker than our original:

```
3E 00   ld A,0
```

(There is also the subtlety that the XOR version also sets the condition code flags which, depending on your use case, can be a benefit or a curse.)

Instead of using instructions in ways that weren't intended, other tricks were used to combat chips which simply didn't have the instructions desired.

The ROM inside the Apple 1 was just 256 bytes in size and was a basic memory monitor and could do only three things: read bytes from memory, write bytes to memory, and execute code. One section of the 6502 assembly code was thus:

```
29 07   and #$07
10 C8   bpl NXTPRINT
```

The and instruction is part of a previous modulus calculation, and it isolates the least significant three bits, clearing all others. This means the most significant bit, used to indicate negative numbers, is always zero. And zero always indicates positive.

The bpl instruction means 'branch if positive'. But since the previous instruction ensures the number is never negative, this branch will always change the program counter to the NXTPRINT location. The 6502 used bpl instead of

JMP because it uses only two bytes, rather than three. (The 6502, unlike other processors, lacked a 'branch always' instruction so this trick was often used.)

Diminishing data

Data could also be optimised. The Jupiter Ace was a 1982 machine by two ex-Spectrum designers who adopted Forth as its main language instead of BASIC in an audacious example of 'dumbing up'. The machine stored its 8x8 character set in ROM using just 641 bytes, instead of the 1024 that 128 characters would normally require. When the machine boots it creates the full character set by writing to a specific set of addresses in RAM, which will then be used to generate the screen display. The first memory saving technique was to not store the graphical characters, and instead build them programmatically. There are eight of these, repeated four times.

The Jupiter Ace graphic characters

For the remaining 95 characters, two other optimisations are made. Firstly, all these characters are stored without data for the top row because every top row is blank, because you need a small gap between rows of text, so they take seven bytes. Secondly, characters without descenders, such as upper case letters and the punctuation characters ? @ [ ] \ ^ , can have their bottom row auto-filled with zero, so these are stored in just six bytes. Ultimately, these savings were applied to so many characters in the font that the only symbol which required all eight bytes to be copied from ROM to RAM was the copyright symbol!

```
GOTO 0 : REM Abbreviations
GOTO 3 : REM Randomness
GOTO 10 : REM BASIC
GOTO 15 : REM REM SNAKESNAKESNAKE
GOTO 49 : REM Optimising for speed
GOTO 246 : REM The Indiana Pi Bill
GOTO 672 : REM 1K Chess
GOTO 754 : REM IEEE 754
GOTO 31900 : REM With prizes
GOSUB 128 : REM Bytes
```

3 : The stages of an oxbow lake

First, erosion caused by the moving water causes any bend in a river to become more pronounced.

Then, the meandering bend continues to such an extent that it forms a horseshoe shape, with the central neck of land eventually eroding.

Finally, with the river now having a fast-moving direct path, deposits build up between the new route and the original bend, causing the two to be separate.

And that, my dear geography teacher, is the only time in 30 years I've used that information!

And if you, my dear reader, get distracted from all the retro goodness in this book in order to want to read about oxbow lakes then I suggest you put this book down and read *National Geographic* for a while!

Your quest ends here!

3 : Randomness

A review of BASIC code written in the 1980s shows that there are three primary ways of generating a random number.

Although all three stem from the RND keyword, the manner in which it's used varies slightly. The Sinclair ZX81 uses it alone and produces a number that is greater or equal to 0 and less than 1.

```
N = INT(RND * 10) + 1
```

Since numbers between 0 and 0.99999 aren't always that useful, the rest of the code changes that range. First the multiplication upscales it to 0–9.99999, then by truncation to an integer 0–9, and finally to the more useful value of 1–10.

Given that a whole integer number is usually what you want, it is interesting to note that you had to do that conversion yourself. The machines from Commodore, Acorn, Apple, and Oric all used the variant:

```
N = INT(RND(1) * 10) + 1
```

Given that the random number generator produces a (floating point) random value with an upper bound of 1, the use of RND(1) does make some sense.

The Acorn BBC Micro went two steps further, however. It provided a random integer between 0 and N if you supplied N to the RND function as RND(N). Plus, it would return the previous random number generated if you used RND(0). This latter example was useful when your game went haywire and you suspected the AI of doing something silly because of the random number then you could simply use it to recall the last number without needing to store it in a local variable.

(Not that game AI was the only thing to use random numbers – *Elite* famously used it to generate whole worlds, along with their names.)

The final version, from the Dragon and Tandy TRS-80, thought that the random number generator should be supplied with the lower bound. That is: zero.

```
N = INT(RND(0) * 10) + 1
```

The coding books from publishers like Usborne had one program listing capable of being entered into multiple machines… if specific lines were changed to a variation shown in the key. These changes were usually to fix the variants of RND and CLS.

Of course, everything here about randomness is technically a lie. There is no such thing as randomness in old computers, only pseudo-randomness. That is because a purely deterministic machine, like a computer, cannot produce something unpredictable. Computer science refers to these as PRNGs, or pseudo-random number generators, since the numbers provided occur in a fixed sequence which is the same every time the program is run. The RND keyword simply returns the next number in that sequence.

If a computer game were to use a PRNG to modify its game play, then the game would not be random – every play-through would be identical. (Michael Larson won a lot on money on quiz show *Press Your Luck* by realising the lights were flashing in a non-random order.) This is useful for algorithmically generated data, such as in Carol Shaw's Activision game *River Raid* for the Atari 2600 or the 1988 game *Exile* for the BBC Micro, since the level data can be generated on the fly and doesn't need to be stored.

However, when programmers needed seemingly random numbers they would employ a trick where the PRNG is *seeded* with a number which starts the generator at a different position in its fixed sequence. But how can you seed the generator with a suitably random number, without first needing a random number? Naturally, it can't be anything hard coded into the program, so instead, the program will look at the time, date, or the number of milliseconds it took the player to start the game and use that number as a seed. Provided the seed is large enough, the start of the sequence cannot be easily predicted. (Something both Netscape and Chrome failed to ensure more recently when choosing a seed for their web encryption system!)

However, it *is* possible to generate truly random numbers via the use of external hardware which measures radioactive decay, electrons passing through neon gas, or even lava lamps.

```
GOTO 3 : REM Optimising for size
GOTO 8 : REM CHIP-8
GOTO 10 : REM BASIC
GOTO 205.5 : REM How to draw a maze in one line
GOTO 720 : REM Copy protection
GOTO 49152 : REM Commodore PET
```

3 : Tandy TRS 80 Model III

This 1981 machine, which went on to feature in the very first episode of *The A-Team*, was probably Tandy's best yet. It used the byword of *expandable*, and built on the business-oriented Model II by making a home machine that felt solid and professional. You would start with a choice between Level I or Level II BASIC, optional dual disk drives, and enough external access for parallel printers, serial ports and buses to add even more disk drives.

Graphically, it was of its time: a monochrome 64x16 character grid where each character supported standard upper/lower case alphanumerics and a series of pre-determined graphical elements. In this case, there were 64 of them, arranged in a 2x3 pattern giving a 128x48 resolution. Technically, the system would look at bit 7 (the most significant bit, represented by the number 128) and if it was 1 then the lowest seven bits would be passed to a graphic generator. Otherwise, it was a standard alphanumeric character. From a programmer's point of view, however, you could simply consider characters 128–191 as graphic characters in the standard font.

Like many old machines, there is still a community supporting the machine, with interfaces for USB keyboards, compact flash, and even WiFi.

Richard Lyne considers this to be their favourite machine.

```
GOTO 65495 : REM Going faster
```

4 : The first computer bug

The very first program was written in 1842–43 by Ada Lovelace, and computed Bernoulli numbers. As part of her translation of Luigi Menabrea's original book, *Notions sur la machine analytique de M. Charles Babbage*, Ada added a series of

Note G – Diagram for the computation of
Bernoulli numbers – Public Domain

notes which gave a real-world demonstration of how the Analytical Engine could be programmed, and how that might appear.

The very first bug appears on line 4 since the 'Statement of Results' does not match the operations given. In modern parlance this is a case of the comments not matching the code, with the former being in error. (However, this doesn't exclude the problem between lines 23 and 24 – you cannot simply repeat the operations as suggested without some extra magic.)

It is often argued that Ada was not the first programmer, and nor was this the first program. Determining the 'first' of anything is difficult because the definition of that 'thing' changes over time. For my money, Ada and her work represent what we today consider a programmer and programming. Otherwise, consider this: if this work had been done by a man, would *he* have been considered the first programmer?

RETURN

4 : 1292 Advanced Programmable Video System

If you had a TV game system in the mid-to-late 1970s, such as the Acetronic, Grandstand, or Hanimex, there was a good chance you were sitting too close to the TV and the game system was based on the 1292 Advanced Programmable Video System (APVS) technology, licensed by Radofin. Although the software was compatible between the machines, the physical cartridge port was not.

The technology consisted of two Signetics chips, a 2650AI for processing and a 2636N for audiovisuals. Despite this seemingly extravagant specification for the time, it could only render a background, one score line with four digits, and a total of four sprites. In the case of the latter, the system would generate an interrupt after a sprite had been drawn allowing a conscientious developer to reprogram the sprite for a reappearance further down the screen. But there was only 43 bytes of memory, so unless the games publisher would commit to placing extra RAM in the cartridge, you probably wouldn't have many more sprites, anyway.

Radofin were also responsible for the Aquarius.

Chris Dymond considers the APVS (but particularly the Voltmace Database) to be their favourite machine.

GOTO 4 : REM Mattel Aquarius

4 : Mattel Aquarius

Known internally by the codename 'Checkers', the Aquarius was the first home computer to be released by Mattel, who had had previous success in the console market with the Intellivision and 1970s LED handheld games like *Football*, *Hockey* and *Baseball*. The Aquarius was released in 1983, although none were on sale in the shops until the following year. On the one hand, it was everything you'd expect for a traditional micro: Microsoft BASIC running on a Z80 processor, with printer, modem, cassette interface and cartridge slot. On the other, it was a 'system for the seventies' as Mattel's Bob Del Principe once quipped.

Its first limitation was the 4 KiB RAM, when its competitors were already looking at 64 KiB as standard. Next was the graphics display – or rather, its lack of one. Reminiscent of the Sinclair ZX80 and its kin, the Aquarius incorporated a series of fixed graphical characters into its font. These characters included planes, robots, and explosions. There was also a set of 64 'bloxels'. Each bloxel was split into a 2x3 grid whereby any of the individual elements could be 'on' or 'off'. This increased its 40x25 text mode to mimic an 80x75 graphics display.

Unfortunately, the demise of Mattel Electronics took the Aquarius with it, having been on sale for just four months. The rights were then sold back to its manufacturer, Radofin, allowing them to sell existing stock and prepare their follow-up machine: the Aquarius II, or 'Chess'. It came with 20 KiB of RAM and Extended BASIC but was essentially an identical machine. Only 25 of them are known to exist.

John Southern considers the original Aquarius to be their favourite machine.

```
GOTO 14 : REM Chips
GOSUB 25 : REM Aquarius I and II
GOSUB 376 : REM Aquarius MX
```

4 : Amstrad numeric notation

There is a logic to the numbering of Amstrad's CPC (Colour Personal Computer) series, such as the 464, 664 (codenamed IDIOT, for Includes/Insert Disk Instead Of Tape), and 6128. The first digit indicates the product family, 4 indicated a cassette-based home computer, 6 featured a disc, with prefixes of 1, 2, 3 and 5 all representing printers. The other digits indicated the memory.

With their introduction of standalone word processors in the PCW range, the prefixes of 8 (dot matrix) and 9 (daisywheel) were added, and an initial digit of 1 (as seen in the PCW 10 and PcW16, replete with inconsistent capitalisation) was reclaimed from printers, and used instead for machines that attempted to break into the market for personal computers (lower case 'pc'). This ran contrary to accepted logic at the time that a Personal Computer (upper case 'PC') needed compatibility with IBM.

```
GOTO 4 : REM Bugs in Jet Set Willy
GOTO 4 : REM Peripherals for processing
GOTO 464 : REM Amstrad CPC 464
```

4 : Geneve 9640

The name of this machine may be unfamiliar, but the underlying origins are probably not. The Myarc Geneve is a clone of the Texas Instruments TI-99/4A from 1987. At that point in time Myarc was known as a vendor supplying expansion cards to be used with the Peripheral Expansion System (also known as the Peripheral Expansion Box, PEB) from Texas Instruments. The PEB was an add-on for the TI-99/4A which allowed the machine to address eight expansion cards. One held a 5.25" floppy disk drive, one held the interface with the TI-99/4A, and the other six were up to the user.

Myarc supplied many of these cards, such as memory, serial ports, and, er, entire computers! The Geneve was designed as a 'computer on a card' and provided backwards compatibility to its host machine. Given the release of the 4A in 1981 you'd expect some improvements for waiting six years, as it had been hibernating like a *Blue Peter* tortoise! What you got were an improved processor (TMS9995 @ 12 MHz, upgraded from TMS9900 @ 3 MHz), high resolution graphics including an 80-column text mode, an MS-DOS-like system called MDOS, and memory improvements all round.

Given the 2.8 million sales of the original TI-99/4A, you might have expected a good number of them to upgrade. Alas, the six-year wait and incomplete software meant that most users had moved on, or moved up. But those who waited until 1993 would get another upgrade! A group of Geneve owners managed to crowdfund a campaign to buy the rights to MDOS, Geneve's Advanced BASIC, and other source code from its creator. Consequently the software has been improved to add support for SCSI, IDE, and (as is compulsory, these days) a Raspberry Pi!

Jeffrey Kuhlmann considers this to be their favourite machine.

```
GOTO 4 : REM MSX
```

4 : Bugs in Jet Set Willy

The 1984 Sinclair Spectrum game *Jet Set Willy*, by retro célèbre Matthew Smith, was notorious for many things, not least because of the 'Attic bug' which made the game impossible to complete. Consequently, the publisher, Software Projects, released a set of official POKEs to fix it.

```
POKE 60231,  0 : REM Removes enemy from Conservatory Roof so
    the bottle to its right can be collected
POKE 42183, 11 : REM Moves an inaccessible (and invisible) item
    to a room where it can be reached
POKE 59901, 82 : REM Fixes the arrow position in The Attic
POKE 56876,  4 : REM Replaces a wall with a floor so you can
    navigate the rooms
```

These 10-second fixes are in stark contrast to modern games which require you to spend five hours downloading a 4 GB patch file… on the day of release!

Of these four POKEs, the third is the most important, since this corrects the misplaced arrow. By not being at an even number, the arrow flies away from the screen data and into memory locations that hold game data, thereby corrupting the game.

Luckily for them, making these changes was not rocket surgery (their technical simplicity is shown above) so anyone could make them. Had the copy protection, or loading scheme, been different they would have had to reproduce all the tapes and send out replacements. A much more costly endeavour.

```
GOTO 4 : REM Amstrad numeric notation
GOTO 4 : REM Peripherals for processing
GOTO 13 : REM Level 13
GOTO 14 : REM Canary traps
GOTO 70 : REM Bugs
GOTO 135 : REM Easter eggs
GOTO 147 : REM CLS
GOTO 256 : REM The Pac-Man kill screen
GOTO 256 : REM The $2.56 reward program
GOTO 35899 : REM PEEK and POKE
```

4 : MSX

It's possible to claim that MSX has probably sold more units than any other computer. This is because of a clever use of weasel words! MSX was a *standard* by which computers could be built, rather than any specific machine. Consequently, hundreds (if not thousands) of manufacturers could take the reference design, then enhance and build as appropriate, and ensure compatibility with all the existing MSX machines. Although perhaps seen as a way of lowering the barrier to entry for small manufacturers, the spec was created by the larger firms, with MSX computing debuts arriving from Panasonic, Canon, Casio and Sanyo.

The standard required that Microsoft MSX BASIC be used and the cartridge ports be identical. This ensured a much better guarantee of compatibility than other 'write once/run anywhere' promises the IT industry has made in its lifetime!

In total, four MSX specifications were created: the MSX and MSX2 for world-wide use, and the MSX2+ and MSX Turbo R intended for the Japanese market. At each iteration the requirements changed, such as increasing the ROM from 32 to 48, then 64, and finally 96 KiB; updating the version of MSX BASIC; or adding new video modes. (The audio requirements changed just once, moving from the AY-3-8910 in MSX to Yamaha YM2149 thereafter. Although from MSX2+ you could optionally include other chips, too.)

As such it was one of the few machines never to be cloned, since such a thing cannot exist with an available standard. Furthermore, contrary to belief, the Spectravideo SV-328 is not a clone. It was made *before* the MSX, and was the machine which inspired the specification. But, since it used mostly the same chips and design, porting software to it was not overly difficult.

Amador Navarro Lucas considers this to be their favourite machine.

```
GOTO 80 : REM RC2014
GOTO 1200 : REM BASICODE
```

4 : Peripherals for processing

Thinking of the processor as the heart of a computer makes it difficult to believe it could be replaced or enhanced. But it has been done, both as peripherals which both let you stop the computer's existing CPU from running, and let you add an additional CPU to the mix!

Years before game cheats were using aimbots or wallhacking, or NES players were buying Game Genie cartridges, or Commodore users were keeping up with their Datel Action Replay devices, Romantic Robot were selling the Multiface.

(Given the word 'robot' originates from a Slavic root, it is culturally appropriate that two Czech-born engineers created the company, which has now become a record label.) This was a peripheral which could stop the current software from running, allowing you to view the memory, change it, save it to tape or microdrive, and then start it running again.

Although sold as a 'utility' tool for backing up software, it could take memory snapshots (like emulators do) to restart games at non-standard save points (if such a feature even existed), and reverse engineer games to find cheat POKEs and understand how they worked.

This magic worked by means of a single control line on the expansion port called /NMI (numbered 17) which would disable the ROM when the voltage applied to this part of the circuit was pulled low to 0 volts. At this point the Multiface ROM would essentially take control of the machine, using its own ROM code in the first 16 KiB of memory to make screenshots or edit memory.

It was also an early example of the Streisand Effect in action, where an attempt to hide information inadvertently causes wider-spread dissemination – although in this case it was almost certainly intentional. To help consumers understand what this device did, and that it could help them illegally pirate games, the makers ensured that no one would (mis-)understand their intentions by writing a clear message on its adverts:

PIRACY IS ILLEGAL!
MULTIFACE 1 is NOT designed to encourage PIRACY!

Instead of manipulating their existing machine, those folk looking to increase the power of their computer usually just bought a more powerful computer. But those lucky enough to own an Acorn BBC Micro could introduce a second processor via the mystical TUBE.

The TUBE was considered an interface and consisted of a custom chip and a set of protocols. It was treated like any other device in that you had to initiate a connection to it (known as 'claiming' it), send and receive messages via four FIFO (First In, First Out) buffers, and release it when done. Since all interactions with the main CPU – now relegated to basic input/output functions with the keyboard and screen – had to be through these buffers, software could not always be ported straight across to the co-processor if it attempted to access memory directly. Instead, it would have to be written 'correctly' by using the officially supported message passing interface, provided by the TUBE.

The co-processor chip itself (referred to in Acorn's own documents as the 'para-site') could be from any denomination, although Z80 and 6502 were the most common; the latter was useful for running BBC software faster since the work could be done on the parasite while all the IO and screen handling would be handled (as normal) by the main CPU. Since the parasite had its own memory bus, it could be used to provide more memory to the system, as was necessary with the Robocom BitStik CAD system.

A historical note here is that the very first ARM chips, present in almost every mobile phone and IoT (Internet of Things) device, were first tested by connecting it to the TUBE of a BBC Micro. (The ARM micro-architecture was also modelled on a BBC Micro.) Reportedly, it was so power efficient that when the chip was running, the ammeter, which was testing the power consumption of the chip, read 0! Due to some quirks of design, there was power leaking through protection diodes which connected the pins on the data and address buses to the +5v rail. This +5v rail was in turn connected to the rest of the chip internals. So, provided that a few bits of the program were a 1, their respected pins would be at +5v, and there would be enough current leaking back to power everything else! Ultimately the consumption was measured at sub 1/10 watt. (All chips in 1986 were designed to work with less than one watt, since that was the thermal limit of chips encased in plastic, and to encase them in ceramic would increase the cost significantly.)

The designers of the Commodore Amiga had the intuition to revisit the co-processor idea in 1987, by building a separate bridgeboard that included a basic PC clone with either an 8088 CPU (the A2088XT) or an A2286 (with a 'modern' 8 MHz 80286.) It worked in a similar fashion to the TUBE; there was software on both sides, with the Amiga providing data about the keyboard and mouse to the PC half of the equation, while the PC returned the favour by returning the screen data that the Amiga could then display. Ultimately, it was not a success since the cost was comparable to buying a standalone PC and it could be difficult to configure. At least the 'big box' Amigas, like the A2000, had vacant slots with which you could gain performance by adding special accelerator boards (like the GVP 030).

The number 4 represents the number of buffers used to communicate with the co-processor and, coincidentally, the number of the 'Support Group Application Note' which Acorn wrote to explain the workings of the TUBE.

```
GOTO 4 : REM Amstrad numeric notation
GOTO 4 : REM Bugs in Jet Set Willy
GOTO 28 : REM Peripherals for output
GOTO 30 : REM Storage
GOTO 31 : REM Peripherals for input
GOTO 100 : REM The extent of computer upgrades
```

GOTO 666 : REM In-jokes
GOTO 720 : REM Copy protection

4 : Reverse Polish Notation

Modern school mathematics uses a notation called *infix*, where a simple expression might appear as:

$$X = (3 + Y) * (2 + Z^2)$$

This is so named since the operators (multiplication, addition, and power) are in between the values to be operated on. But with Reverse Polish Notation (RPN) each operator is only added to the expression after the numbers it is expected to operate on. So, the above calculation could be presented, reading left to right, as:

$$3 \ Y + 2 \ Z \ 2 \ \char`\^ \ + \ *$$

The typical explanation is to imagine stacking each element, from left to right, with each one falling on top of the previous.

+
Y
3

When an operator is placed on the top of this stack, such as +, it removes two items, evaluates the addition, and places that result (in this case $3 + Y$) back onto the stack.

3 + Y
–
–

This happens again with 2, Z, 2, and so on. You can try the above on paper, to see that both expressions are identical. But what this really shows is that RPN needs only nine symbols to match the equivalent infix version of 13. There is also no explicit requirement for additional memory, as all RPN calculations occur within the existing memory allocated to the data structure, called a stack. With the infix version, the computer would need to make a mental note of the $3 + Y$ and the $2 + Z^2$ results to later multiply them together. (And by extension, store the 2 and Z^2 partial results in other memory.)

The stack is a natural feature of CPU instructions sets, so there is a natural fit for using reverse notation. When compute power is at a premium you can improve performance significantly by being a human that thinks like a machine, rather than trying to program a machine to think like a human.

Although most home computers used BASIC and infix notation as their language of choice, one notable pair of computer designers decided that RPN was an improvement. This machine was the Jupiter Ace, from a company called Jupiter Cantab, formed by two ex-Sinclair employees, Richard Altwasser and Steven Vickers who, as the anthropomorphised machine on the advert said, were dumb enough to sell it for £89.95! But dumb they weren't; Steven's father, Tom Vickers, worked on the Pilot ACE designed by Alan Turing, and their machine was '10 times faster and 4 times more compact than BASIC'. Both claims were true, but a language that used RPN was too steep a learning curve for the home computer minds of the era.

If it wasn't for the output, you'd probably never guess that this sleek box hid a Jupiter Ace!

From the personal collection of Andrew Nightingale

The name of that language? Forth!

RETURN

5 : Atari 800XL

When the Atari 400 was expanded with a proper keyboard and 48 KiB of RAM it became a proper machine for secretaries and called 'Colleen'... sorry... the

Atari 800, then the 800 was expanded to the 800XL in 1983. The 800XL, the third edition in the Atari 8-bit range, comprised a 64 KiB machine, built-in BASIC, and a parallel bus interface (PBI) that would connect to an expansion box containing five slots for add-on cards.

The 800XL was an interesting one from a business perspective, being caught in the crossfire of the Commodore–Texas Instruments price wars of 1983. While both Commodore and TI were involved in a race to the bottom, selling machines as cheaply as they could, Atari too were forced to lower their prices in an attempt to remain visible. Had Atari realised the video game crash was going to decimate their home video consoles too, perhaps they wouldn't have competed in such a reckless price drop.

Steven Hamilton considers this to be their favourite machine.

GOTO 6 : REM Nintendo Game Boy

5 : Keys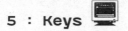

Detecting multiple different keys is up to five times faster than checking for a single specific key because of how they are wired up in a matrix.

To detect a keypress with the ZX Spectrum, for example, you would read from a specific port (such as 0xFE) and look at the data you got back. This data would contain five useful bits, indicating the state of five specific keys. Port 0xFE represents the first row, containing the keys Z, X, C, V, and caps shift.

	16	8	4	2	1
Keys on port FE	V	C	X	Z	Caps shift

Most hardware manufacturers decided that negative logic would be used, so a pressed key would turn one of the bits in 255 (0xFF) to zero, instead of the other way around. So, if the data was 255 (0xFF) then none of those five keys was pressed. If it was any other value, a second check would determine which bit was zero, and therefore which key was down.

Caps shift, for example, would have a zero in the least significant bit of the result, making it 11111110, or 254. A 'Z' would be 11111101, or 253, and so on.

By way of example, here's the complete matrix.

Result in binary	11101111	11110111	11111011	11111101	11111110
Port FE	V	C	X	Z	Caps shift
Port FD	G	F	D	S	A
Port FB	T	R	E	W	Q
Port F7	5	4	3	2	I
Port EF	6	7	8	9	0
Port DF	Y	U	I	0	P
Port BF	H	J	K	L	enter
Port 7F	B	N	M	Symbol shift	space

Reading the rows horizontally shows how the keyboard layout was mapped in a very direct way, and how adjacent keys could be programmed to act identically.

For a final worked example, the case to check for the letter 'G' requires us to read the port (0xFD) and check that the result is 11101111 (or 0xEF), which is simply done by looking for a 0 in bit 5. (You don't check for the result equalling 11101111 since more than one key might be down at a time.)

Coincidentally, most Spectrum keys also had 5 different operations on them: G, }, ABS, THEN, and GO TO.

When you pressed a key, the machine would determine which mode you were in (as determined by the cursor), check whether any shifts had been pressed, and use this information to output the appropriate operation.

Cursor	Cursor Mode	Key text colour	Shifts required	Result
K	Keyword	White	-	GO TO
L	Letter	White	-	g
L	Letter	White	CAPS	G
L	Letter	Red	SYMBOL	THEN
E	Extended	Green	-	ABS
E	Extended	Green	SYMBOL	}
C	Capital	White	-	G
G	Graphic	White	-	The graphics characters, on digits 1–8 only

The cursor transitioned automatically from K to L after entering a keyword, and from L to E when CAPS SHIFT and SYMBOL SHIFT were pressed. It would also change magically back to a K after an instruction that required a follow-up keyword, such as THEN.

GOTO 40 : REM Keyboards
GOTO 201 : REM Cursor keys

5 : SCRUMPI

What's in a name? If the letters SC and MP appear in it, then there's a reasonable chance it's a machine from the 1970s using the National Semiconductor Simple Cost-effective Micro Processor (SC/MP) chip, known affectionately as 'SCAMP'.

The SCRUMPI was probably the first single board machine from the UK, released in 1976 from Bywood Electronics. It was similar to the Sinclair MK-14 (also a SC/MP design, issued in 1978), a microcomputer kit that consisted of a CPU, 256 bytes of RAM, and some support chips. SCRUMPI's IO was more primitive, however, as all input was given through 16 switches (although a keypad add-on later surfaced) with output comprising just 24 LEDs. Like the Altair 8800 from 1974, its use was limited to the study of assembly instructions and basic CPU operation and so slotted nicely into the niche filled by electronics enthusiasts and their (decidedly non-mainstream) magazines.

Knowing what Sinclair achieved after their explorations with the MK-14, it is possible that honour could have instead gone to SCRUMPI. But since its creator, John Miller-Kirkpatrick, died in 1978 at the age of just 32, we can but speculate.

As for the number 5? There are four common word stems in which the letters SC and MP appear – scamp, scampi, scrimp, and scrumptious. SCRUMPI is fifth.

Tim Gilberts considers this to be their favourite machine, and so is someone that would definitely agree with the adverts which read, 'Oi loikes SCRUMPI.'

GOTO 50 : REM Signetics Instructor 50

```
5 MODE 7
```

6 : Oric Atmos

After their moderate success with the Oric 1, Tangerine Computer Systems, based in St Ives just outside Cambridge, created the Atmos. The original model had thin-slit calculator keys, comparatively low resolution graphics (at 240x200), and reliability problems with the tape loading routines. In 1984, the subsequent Oric Atmos improved upon this by upgrading the keyboard – but not much else! Sure, the implementation of BASIC got a version bump to 1.1, and the developers had time to add a few more bugs into the ROM (while neglecting to fix the tape loading issues), but the spec was otherwise unchanged.

The biggest benefit of buying an Oric Atmos at the time was that all the peripherals, originally promised for the Oric 1, were becoming available. This meant that disk drives could be used for safe storage, Prestel modems for communication, and colour plotters for output. All were available via the in-built ports. (The delays weren't entirely Tangerine's fault, as their factory burned down.)

It was very popular in France, where the updated Oric Telestrat was sold until 1988 by Eureka. Yugoslavia had a yen for the machine too, and licensed the Atmos as the Nova 64, while Bulgaria cloned it as the Pravetz 8D. (The use of 64, by the way, is an interesting claim. While both it and the Atmos had eight 8 KiB chips inside it, the ROM masked out 16 KiB of that memory, allowing only 48 for BASIC programs.)

Famously, the Sinclair Spectrum exhibited colour clash on pixels within each 8x8 tile. The Oric Atmos had the same problem, but was limited to only six pixels in a 6x1 area.

Xander Mol considers this to be their favourite machine.

GOTO 15 : REM Saving to tape

6 : Nintendo Game Boy

For a company whose heritage involves selling playing cards, taxi services, and hotel rooms by the hour, Nintendo in the 1980s found themselves becoming the kings of the hand-held consoles. First in 1980 came the Game & Watch. Then, in 1989, came the Game Boy.

To many, the Game Boy is touted as using a Zilog Z80 processor, but it actually used a design by Sharp called the LR35902 which was based on (some might say copied) the Intel 8080 (the chip on which the Z80 was based). However, whereas the Z80 was designed to be backwards compatible with the 8080 so that *binary* code could run unaltered, the LR35902 changed enough that it required you to re-assemble the *source* code, and rewrite the code when missing opcodes were found.

Considering its impact and range of games it seems incredible that it started with just six launch titles: *Alleyway*, *Baseball*, *Super Mario Land*, *Tennis*, *Tetris* and *Yakuman*.

Linda Kirby considers this to be their favourite machine.

GOTO 1000 : REM Sega Master System

6 : King's Parade

In 1977, Sinclair Radionics, occupying a space above a travel agent named Lunn Poly at 6 King's Parade, Cambridge, changed its name to Science of Cambridge. The following year, it released its MK14 computer. It later became Sinclair Research Ltd, at which point both its name and address became synonymous with the launch of the UK computer industry, with the Sinclair ZX80, ZX81 and Sinclair Spectrum.

At this time Sinclair's rival, Acorn, were based at 110 Fulbourn Road. Concidentally, the binary for 6 is 110.

Coincidentally, Stephen Hawking's first Cambridge house with his wife, Jane, was also numbered 6. It's just round the corner, on Little St. Mary's Lane.

GOTO 6 : REM The ZX Spectrum Screen Display
GOTO 25 : REM Willis Road, Cambridge, UK
GOTO 80 : REM Sinclair ZX80
GOTO 110 : REM Fulbourn Road

6 : The ZX Spectrum
Screen Display

The ZX Spectrum's screen display typifies the machine: ingenious cost-cutting that results in something idiosyncratically Sinclair. The specification quotes a 256x192 pixel resolution with 15 colours, which would require 196,608 bits, or 24 KiB. This would be excessive on the 48 KB model, and impossible on the 16 KB version. Somehow the Spectrum performs a Jedi mind trick to use 6912 bytes. So, although the specification is true, it is only true from a certain point of view.

The screen layout consists of two parts: a high-resolution black-and-white bitmap where each of the 256x192 pixels can be individually addressed, and a low-resolution colour attribute screen where the same area is divided into 32x24 blocks (of 8x8 pixels each). Each block is one byte and contains a foreground colour (the ink) and a background colour (the paper), and attributes to flash the area or switch the colours into 'bright' mode. (Here we note that 'bright black' is simply 'black', and can argue whether 'bright red' and 'red' really constitute two colours, a doubling technique also present on the Amiga with Extra Half-Brite (EHB) mode.) Consequently, if a red character moves into a block with a green tree, because there's only one attribute to serve both items, either the character turns green, or the tree becomes red. This is the infamous colour attribute clash.

Developers learned to compensate by designing their games in ways that minimised this clash, such as only moving the characters within a fixed number of blocks, not attempting pixel-level scrolling, and drawing the moving graphics in monochrome.

The other point of note is that the black-and-white bitmap is not contiguous. If you watch a loading screen appear you will note the lines do so in a strange order. First row 1, then row 8, then 16, and continuing in steps of 8 until 64 when it starts back on row 2, then 9, and so on. On completing the first third of the screen, it moves to the next third in the same fashion, before loading the last third. If you see a game which concentrates (read: restricts) its action to specific thirds of the screen, then this is the reason.

If you consider a position on the screen X,Y in binary then the memory address can be calculated knowing this:

15	14	13	12	11	10	9	8	7	6	5	4	3	2	1	0
0	1	0	Y7	Y6	Y2	Y1	Y0	Y5	Y4	Y3	X7	X6	X5	X4	X3

Given the work needed, programmers would often pre-compute a table which mapped Y positions to screen addresses, so they could use a saner numbering scheme.

The attribute bytes, however, are contiguous. Just to be different! (There is a logic as to *why* it is built this way, but it involves knowledge of DRAM and ULA, which these parentheses are too small to contain!)

It is also worth remembering the ZX Spectrum's white border, resembling a Polaroid photograph: since you only need memory for the pixels you store, these could be generated programmatically from a single border colour.

This original method for generating a screen can be found in a document entitled simply, 'Display for a computer', and was covered in patents GB19820011723, EP0107687 and WO8303916.

```
GOTO 6 : REM King's Parade
GOTO 82 : REM Sinclair ZX Spectrum+
GOTO 16777216 : REM Colour
```

7 : Commodore 128

Take off your glasses and the C128 looks like a Commodore Amiga... kinda... But in 1985 the overlap of the 8-bit C128 and the 16-bit Amiga *is* blurred. Of the three operating modes available within the C128 machine, the backward compatible C64 mode makes the machine look like its standard 8-bit predecessor, albeit with BASIC 7.0 installed.

For those moving away from games, the C128 had a second processor, the Z80, that allowed the machine to run CP/M 3.0 for serious applications and users that wanted a cheaper PC.

Finally, C128 mode was its native configuration and allowed both processors to work together, along with the custom video chip (the VDC) for an 80-column display and colour graphics. But without the hardware sprites of the C64, game developers would need to do extra work to make use of the C128's power.

Despite being mostly seen on the periphery it was far from a waste of silicon, selling nearly 6 million units during its four-year lifespan. One of those sales was to Laurence Gonsalves, who considers this to be their favourite machine.

```
GOTO 500 : REM Commodore Amiga
```

7 : Seven jokes

There are 7 jokes in this 'joke ring'. These entries are not connected to any other in the book. Which means if you're reading this, you're not following the GOTO statements properly! So stop cheating and GOTO section 0. Or...

GOTO 10 : REM There are 10 kinds of people in this world...

8 : Bits in a byte

But not always! It was not uncommon for there to be 6 bits in a byte, particularly when that would cover all the basic ASCII symbols from 0 to 63. Nowadays it is accepted to mean 8 bits, although some prefer to use 'octet' to remove any potential ambiguity.

Some older machines would have a non-'power of 2' data bus for integrity reasons – that is, the hardware was so flaky that, for example, 4 data bits would require an additional 3 error-checking bits that could be used to correct the data through techniques such as Hamming codes, which are able to detect data errors automatically through parity checks.

```
GOTO 2 : REM 2's complement
GOTO 8 : REM CHIP-8
GOTO 8 : REM Type-in listings
GOTO 127 : REM 127 or 255?
GOTO 1000 : REM A kilobyte
```

8 : CHIP-8

A review of available emulators might lead one to believe that the CHIP-8 was the most popular computer ever created. In fact, there may be more emulators for the platform than there are pieces of original software. (Much like there are more spin-offs in the Star Wars franchise than there are original films.) However, this machine never existed. CHIP-8 is an interpreted language containing 35 opcodes which *looked* like the assembly of a mid-70s CPU. A single maze could be generated with code such as:

```
Address     Machine code hex     Assembly instruction mnemonic
0200        a2 1e                ld I, 21eH
0202        c2 01                rnd v2, 01H
0204        32 01                skipeq v2, 01H
0206        a2 1a                ld I, 21aH
0208        d0 1                 drw @r, v1, 4H
020a        70 04                add v0, 04H
020c        30 40                skipeq v0, 40H
020e        12 00                jp 200H
```

```
0210      60 00          store v0, 00H
0212      71 04          add v1, 04H
0214      31 20          skipeq v1, 20H
0216      12 00          jp 200H
0218      12 18          jp 218H
```

The machine code bytes would then be interpreted by another processor so the program could run. The interpreter code for the RCA 1802 chip (from the Radio Corporation of America) was only 512 bytes, but was compact enough to run basic TV games like *Breakout*, and achieved something quite impressive for 1976. Indeed, it was present in the (otherwise unknown) Telmac 1800 and COSMAC VIP machines. The CHIP-8 designers ensured that every instruction was two bytes long with the most significant four bits (i.e. first nibble) representing the opcode. (In the case of the first instruction above, a2 1e, the a is the opcode.) The other 12 bits contained the opcode-specific data but were formatted precisely to be read quickly by the machine, with no attempt to make a human programmer's life easier!

The arithmetic operations, for example, start with an opcode nibble of 8 in bits 15–12, and always work on two 4-bit registers which would follow immediately after the 8. Then, once they were safely stored, the final four bits (3–0) could determine what to do with the values in the registers – a direct assignment (0), a bitwise OR (1), or subtraction (5).

15–12	11–8	7–4	3–0
8	First register	Second register	Operation

Shades of Java (and the JVM), RISC, and Reverse Polish Notation.

The clues that indicate CHIP-8 is not a 'real' CPU are found in high-level instructions that look more like library functions than assembly commands. They include instructions that handle timers, generate random numbers, draw to the screen (and return any graphical collisions), read key presses, and play sound. But providing these instructions at a high level meant that the implementation in RCA 1802 could do so more efficiently than any purely interpreted version could hope to.

```
GOTO 3 : REM Randomness
GOTO 8 : REM Bits in a byte
GOTO 8 : REM Type-in listings
GOTO 205.5 : REM How to draw a maze in one line
GOTO 1200 : REM BASICODE
```

GOTO 2000 : REM The future
GOSUB 4 : REM Reverse Polish Notation

8 : Type-in listings

Nowadays, we find most new software online. Previously, you would install it using a DVD or CD-ROM. Going further back there were floppy discs (of various sizes) and cassette tapes. Some companies could even afford to include discs or tapes on the covers of their magazines, or in transparent pockets in the back of books.

In the early days, when the duplication and distribution of magnetic media was more expensive, many publishers would print entire programs in a magazine. To accommodate the widest magazine readership, listings would be in all shapes and sizes. The authors were both amateur and professional programmers looking for a little extra cash. Sinclair Programs offered £25 for a program (regardless of language, size or complexity), or £10 for a beginner's routine (often very small), but some magazines would allow the developers to earn as much as £50 for a single program (around £160 in today's money). They sent a cassette tape of their software, along with a printed listing, to the magazine for consideration by the editorial team who would then try the program to make some form of value judgment on it, ensuring that each issue of the magazine contained a mix of games and educational and business software.

While the magazine-buying public might be happy to spend an hour typing in a listing from a magazine, the editor at the magazine wouldn't, so the cassette was a necessary evil.

However, many magazines did not always print the listing from what they loaded from the tape; they printed the listing submitted to them by the author. Consequently, the visual quality of the text would vary so much that some programs would not work! There were many reasons for this. Sometimes the listings would be simply wrong, as the author might have printed out the program to paper, only to discover a problem and, not wanting to waste more paper, simply sent an update only on cassette. But sometimes it was as simple as the 8 looking too much like a B! Most of the time it was possible for an average programmer to determine the correct symbol from the context in which it was used. But the people typing in these listings weren't necessarily as skilled as those submitting them, and frustration ensued as the program refused to work.

For the novice user there was often confusion in listings such as this:

```
1 PRINT CHR$ (RND*CODE"{GRAPHICS}{SHIFT}E{SHIFT OFF}{GRAPHICS
  OFF}");
```

It might be obvious that the words {GRAPHICS} and {SHIFT} are not meant to be written literally, letter for letter, into the program, but it wasn't obvious to everyone!

However, since these meta-instructions were considered part of a programmer's genetic memory, magazines often didn't waste valuable column inches explaining the same instructions every month.

When a magazine listing did print graphic characters, other difficulties arose if you couldn't determine where one character ended and the next one began:

When computers supported higher resolution graphics, with more than nine variations, it was almost impossible to distinguish between them on the printed page since they were small and in black and white. Naturally, some programmers developed a shorthand to help distinguish between them, often with an underlined capital letter. A would be the first graphic. B would be the second. And so on. But not everyone adopted it, and so the problem was only ever half solved.

On the Sinclair Spectrum this problem was made more complex by the fact that you would program the graphics directly into the code. When you first typed the graphic characters they would appear in the listing as A, B, C, etc.

```
10 PRINT "A"
20 FOR f=0 TO 7
30 READ a: POKE USR "A"+f,a
40 NEXT f
50>DATA 24,60,195,255,195,211,
195,255

K
```

Before

But after you had run your program, which redefined the graphic characters, they would appear in the listing as those graphical characters. (And it was nigh on impossible to change them back!)

After

While a BASIC program is fairly easy to understand because of the contextual information present, anything written in machine code was less so. Due to reasons of space and money, machine code programs were usually given as a long list of numbers, rather than the full assembly code. (Plus, not everyone owned a compatible assembler.)

```
10 LET C$ = "00C3BE76C98F020040DD228740FD228940C9CD9840C9FD
   2A8940DD2A8740C9FD2A8940C9CB7FC8ED"
20 LET M = 16514
30 FOR I = 0 TO LEN(C$) - 1 STEP 2
40 POKE M + I, 16 * CODE C$(I) + CODE C$(I + 1) - 476
50 NEXT I
```

The magic in line 40 would convert each pair of hexadecimal digits in the C$ variable by manipulating the character code of each hex digit. (The -476 was to offset the value back to the 0–255 range since 0 was character code 28, with A starting immediately afterwards, and 476 = 16 * 28 + 28.)

This represented the machine code of:

```
4082 : 00 c3 be 76 c9 8f 02 00
408A : 40 dd 22 87 40 fd 22 89
4092 : 40 c9 cd 98 40 c9 fd 2a
409A : 89 40 dd 2a 87 40 c9 fd
40a2 : 2a 89 40 c9 cb 7f c8 ed
```

With BASIC programs, it was generally assumed that you knew how to type the listing into your computer, but machine code programs came only with a rudimentary hex loader program with none of the clever safety checks performed by the BASIC interpreter – so a mistyped program could crash the computer and you'd have to type it in again.

Over time, people added checksums to this type of listing, so it looked like this:

```
4082 : 00 c3 be 76 c9 8f 02 00 40 dd 22 87 40 fd 22 89 = 1791
4092 : 40 c9 cd 98 40 c9 fd 2a 89 40 dd 2a 87 40 c9 fd = 2299
```

Here, each of the 16 characters on a line is added up and the computer checks that it totals the number shown after the equals sign. Of course, if there's a mistake it doesn't tell you *where* the error is, or *how* to fix it, but it does let you know that the program is very unlikely to work.

(The checksum was used throughout computing. The French company Victor, developers of the 1983 machine Hector 2HR, obviously didn't get the memo as their tape system elected to not use them. Nor did Quantel, makers of the professional video and graphics system, Paintbox.)

```
GOTO 1 : REM True
GOTO 8 : REM Bits in a byte
GOTO 8 : REM CHIP-8
GOTO 10 : REM BASIC
GOTO 30 : REM Storage
GOTO 30 : REM Monmouth Street
GOTO 33⅓ : REM Revolutions per minute
GOTO 672 : REM 1K Chess
GOTO 1200 : REM BASICODE
```

8 : DEC PDP-8

Any machine that sold 50,000 units in the 1980s would probably be branded a failure – or, at best, an also-ran. But in 1965, before the world ever heard the terms Z80, Intel, or probably even the word 'computer', this was thought a massive number, and deservedly so.

(This is in spite of, or maybe because of, the fact the DEC PDP-8 was available until 1990!)

Digital Equipment Corporation (DEC) built the PDP-8 minicomputer to be cheaper and smaller than its competitors. It had 4 KiB of memory, 12-bit words, and instructions which would, in today's parlance, probably be considered RISC. For the first generation of programmers this meant writing a lot of basic mechanical boilerplate code yourself (such as implementing a stack), since compilers weren't available upon release. For example, you need six instructions for one 'does X = Y?' comparison, and subtraction was performed by turning one number into a negative and adding them.

Arthur Schiller considers this to be their favourite machine.

GOTO 754 : REM IEEE 754

9 : Nine Tiles

This is the company founded and run by John and Kate Grant, based in Waterbeach, Cambridgeshire, which designed and built the internal ROM software for Sinclair in the early 1980s. Their first project together was the Sinclair ZX80. The 4 KiB implementation of BASIC was rather, er, basic, with one instruction per line, and no support for floating point numbers.

The follow-up, the ZX81, provided a floating-point library (coded by Steven Vickers, who also wrote the manual), some fixes, a new character set, but not a lot else. The hardware in the ZX81 was a significant improvement, most noticeably in that the screen didn't blink every time you pressed a key. But it was still a black and white mute. Even so, it used all but one byte of the 8 KiB ROM.

With the ZX Spectrum, the BASIC had a major overhaul with a 16 KiB ROM supporting the colour and sound functionality of the hardware, along with multi-instruction lines, functions, and so on. This is the only ROM created by Nine Tiles that was transferred to Amstrad as part of the £5 million Sinclair deal in 1986. This was not an intentionally smart move by Nine Tiles, but an accidental one.

The ROM code was, in each case, written as 'work for hire'. There was no royalties involved, or any intricate licensing deal – just a simple case of Sinclair paying an amount of money to Nine Tiles (either as a 'per hour fee' or 'fixed price for the work') and getting the code in return. These were simple times, and such deals were common and lacking in modern rigour. So when Amstrad started their due diligence it was discovered that Sinclair didn't own the rights since they had not explicitly bought them, and Nine Tiles hadn't thought to offer them. Although Amstrad were buying Sinclair, what they were really buying was the Spectrum. The ZX80 and ZX81 were already relegated to history. It fell to Jim Westwood, chief engineer at Sinclair, to drive his car from Milton in North Cambridge and ensure that the Spectrum rights were transferred correctly. Unfortunately, the deal was happening over an Easter weekend and John Grant was holidaying on the Grand Union Canal. Although he knew where John was – roughly – Jim was unable to find him. Due to the rush and panic, when John returned from holiday to finalise the sale of Sinclair to Amstrad, only the copyright of the Spectrum ROM was reassigned because it was the only deal-breaking element left in the contract.

Compare this to the version Alan Sugar (or, more probably, his ghostwriter) covers in *What You See Is What You Get*. According to Sugar, he needed someone to take a cab from London to the river Ouse near Ely, with a bankers draft, to get the Sinclair IP rights signed over to Amstrad on the river bank. (I count at least five mistakes there!)

The one ZX Spectrum item that Nine Tiles did get to keep was their prototype. It is currently a museum exhibit at the Centre for Computing History in Cambridge.

The prototype Sinclair ZX Spectrum
Image courtesy of The Centre for Computing History, Cambridge

```
GOTO 1 : REM I'd buy that for a dollar
GOTO 1.3591409 : REM The square root of 0.25
GOTO 10 : REM New pence
GOTO 80 : REM Sinclair ZX80
GOTO 81 : REM Sinclair ZX81
GOTO 256 : REM The $2.56 reward program
```

10 : BASIC

Most programmers of a certain age (i.e. over 40) began developing software for fun in the syntax era of the 1980s with a language called BASIC. BASIC stands for Beginner's All-purpose Symbolic Instruction Code and was invented in 1963 by John G Kemeney and Thomas E Kurtz at Dartmouth College in the US, and launched the following year. Over the years the language has been changed and adapted for use on many computers, and throughout the 1980s it was the first core language for most developers. This was because it was supplied, for free, with the machine and was ready to use as soon as the computer booted up. Younger readers might be surprised to learn that a microcomputer of the era would generally boot up, and be ready to use, in a fraction of a second! The first thing such a computer would normally display was a command prompt allowing you to type commands for the BASIC interpreter to process. This allowed people to easily write games and software on their own computer, without learning a lot of technical jargon. It also allowed them to load programs from either cassette tape or disc.

BASIC became popular because it was easy to understand, and hard to do anything in it that would physically damage your computer. (Unlike with machine code!) It used common-sense words to describe the actions the machine would take, like PRINT to display messages on the screen, for example.

```
PRINT "This is in BASIC...";
```

Compare that with the equivalent version for the Dragon 32, written in its native language – 6809e assembly, a version of machine code:

```
        clrb
        ldx #1192
        ldy #txt_message
nxt
        lda b,y
        ora #64
```

```
        sta ,x+
        incb
        cmpb #25
        beq nxtln
        bra nxt
nxtln
        ; the rest of the code goes here
txt_message
        fcc "This is in machine code..."
```

The code above must:

- Know where on the screen to write the text (determined by `ldx #1192`)
- Know how many letters to print (25, from the `cmpb #25`)
- Ensure the letter is a printable character (`ora #64`)

Although BASIC was easier than writing in the computer's own machine code language, this simplicity made it a lot slower, because the BASIC interpreter had to work in the most general case. For example, it always updated the cursor position, even if you didn't need it to. It always checked the screen position was valid. It always had to handle text that extended beyond the right-hand edge and continue it on the next line. And so on. These might not seem like time-consuming tasks, but to do them constantly, and several times a second – on a machine a million times slower than your phone – meant there was a very definite and noticeable slow-down.

One major advantage of BASIC, however, was its portability: one program written in one version of BASIC could, with very little effort and alteration, work on another version of BASIC. Consequently, books were published with a generic BASIC listing and indications of specific lines that needed changing for each micro. The front of the book would contain a key, such as:

```
% Commodore 64 and VIC 20

* BBC and Electron

+ Spectrum

O Apple

X TRS-80
```

58

You'd then look for those symbols at the start of each line:

```
O%   20 CLS
```

Then consult the replacement 'Conversion lines' at the bottom of the listings.

```
O Line 20 Replace CLS with HOME
% Line 20 Replace CLS with PRINT CHR$(147)
```

As a language, BASIC is considered quite a poor choice, as it forces the developer into making sub-optimal decisions that are considered bad habits in more 'grown-up' languages. For example, it relies on the GOTO statement which formed the basis of a famous 1968 paper by Edgar Dijkstra called 'Go To Statement Considered Harmful'. It also lacked a good way to handle errors. Some versions supplied the programmer with an ON ERROR instruction which enacted a single command (such as GOTO 10000) and affected any error, at any point in the program. Some variants of the language had only global variables: if you set the value of X in one part of the program, any other part of the program could see that value, and potentially change it without permission from the first part.

So while the quality of software written this way wasn't the highest, it did introduce the topic to a whole generation of new enthusiasts, many of whom have become the digital pioneers of today.

```
GOTO 1 : REM True
GOTO 3 : REM Optimising for size
GOTO 3 : REM Randomness
GOTO 8 : REM Type-in listings
GOTO 10 : REM Disabling the break key
GOTO 10 : REM PRINT "Always get someone to cheque your work. ";
GOTO 10 : REM Tales of Chuckie Egg
GOTO 10 : REM Toshiba HX-10
GOTO 10 : REM New pence
GOTO 10 : REM Seconds
GOTO 15 : REM REM SNAKESNAKESNAKE
GOTO 49 : REM Optimising for speed
GOTO 1200 : REM BASICODE
```

10 : Disabling the break key

When a program is written in BASIC you start it by typing RUN at the command prompt. This tells the computer to invoke a specific part of the BASIC interpreter whereby it takes each line of the program in turn, works out what it is meant to do, and then presents appropriate instructions to the CPU in a form which the computer understands directly, so it can be processed. (It is much like a human interpreter translating between a French and English speaker.) However, after each line of BASIC has been interpreted the computer checks the keyboard to see if the break, or escape, key has been pressed. If it has, then the program stops, and the user can view or edit the program before trying again.

When developing software this is a very useful feature. Unfortunately, this also makes it easy for people to see your program (which you might not want), or to change it (making the game easier, perhaps), or even to illegally copy it.

Consequently, one of the pieces of hallowed knowledge for BASIC programmers was often 'how to disable the break key'.

The Acorn BBC Micro had two keys to stop programs. The first was the ESCAPE key, which would stop the current BASIC program at any point, but this could easily be disabled with:

```
*fx 230,0
```

The second key, BREAK (or F10), would delete the program from memory and reset the whole interpreter. However, BBC BASIC also had an OLD instruction which would recover the previous (older) program from memory after a reset. Consequently, BASIC programmers wanting to keep their program secret would invoke another magical command to reprogram the F10 key.

```
*key10 OLD||M RUN||M
```

Some computers, like the Dragon 32, had a physical reset button on the side of the machine, as well as a break key. In this case, the reset button was attached directly to the hardware, meaning there was no way to stop it. But the Dragon, like many machines, had a set of 'vectors' in RAM. These were memory locations containing data, or pointers to program code, that would be executed by the OS ROM upon certain events. By placing these vectors in RAM a piece of software could take control of specific events that would normally be handled exclusively by the ROM. In this case, address 113 (0x71) was the restart flag in RAM, and rewriting it to zero with

```
POKE 113,0
```

would cause the reset button to trigger a destructive cold start routine at the memory location 0xB3Ba, instead of the usual warm start one at 0xB44F.

The use of vectors also helped ZX Spectrum BASIC programmers. Whenever the break was pressed, an error was generated. And whenever an error was generated, the ROM checked the data in memory locations 23613 and 23614. Those values referenced the memory address to jump to whenever an error appeared. So, if you pointed locations 23613 and 23614 to somewhere that referenced address 0 (the cold start routine), the break key would restart the machine.

```
10 REM Change the error vector to point to address 23298 (= 91
   * 256 + 2)
20 POKE 23613,2
30 POKE 23614,91
40 REM Set the address to 0
50 POKE 23298,0
60 POKE 23299,0
70 REM Rest of program goes here
```

Of course, all these techniques can be subverted by removing these protections before you RUN it!

```
GOTO 10 : REM BASIC
GOTO 10 : REM Tales of Chuckie Egg
GOTO 10 : REM Toshiba HX-10
GOTO 10 : REM New pence
GOTO 10 : REM PRINT "Always get someone to cheque your work. ";
GOTO 10 : REM Seconds
GOTO 99 : REM Press to continue
```

10 : Tales of *Chuckie Egg*

At my school there were *Chuckie Egg* competitions every breaktime to see who could score the most points on this colourful, and rather charming, A&F game. Although many versions existed, it was the version for the Acorn BBC Micro which became best known since it was the computer deemed 'educational' enough to be allowed into schools. (Including fictional schools, such as on BBC TV's *Grange Hill*.) This was because the UK government, via the Department for Transport and

Industry, wanted to encourage computing in schools by paying half the cost of any micro in an approved list. It was a short list: just the BBC Micro, the RM 380Z, and the Sinclair ZX Spectrum. Schools almost universally preferred the Acorn since it had a powerful specification created by the BBC (the UK's British Broadcasting Corporation), and used in their Computer Literacy Project. The BBC was incredibly powerful for the time and even the kids that never utilised its full power (i.e. almost all of them!) discovered a feature in BBC Basic which meant that

```
*run chuckie
```

could be shortened to:

```
*chuckie
```

Then they discovered they could change the file name to simply the letter 'e', and so only needed to type

```
*e
```

to start the game. Not typing those 10 characters gave advanced players an extra few seconds in the game, which was often the difference between first and second place.

(Similarly, some Commodore 64 fans would type LOAD "*",8,8 as the double '8' was quicker to type than the conventional LOAD "*",8,1.)

```
GOTO 10 : REM BASIC
GOTO 10 : REM Disabling the break key
GOTO 10 : REM Toshiba HX-10
GOTO 10 : REM New pence
GOTO 10 : REM PRINT "Always get someone to cheque your work. ";
GOTO 10 : REM Seconds
GOTO 103 : REM Research Machines 380Z
```

10 : There are 10 kinds of people in this world...

...those who understand binary, and those who don't!

GOTO 31 : REM Why do computer scientists get Halloween and
    Christmas mixed up?

10 : Jupiter Ace

Whenever anyone mentions the Jupiter Ace, the first two comments are always:

1. I want one, but they're too expensive
2. It uses Forth, you know

The Jupiter Ace came from Richard Altwasser and Dr. Steven Vickers, the same people that designed and built the Sinclair Spectrum. Indeed, the keyboard is processed using near-identical code, and circuitry, to the ZX81. Only the bottom line of the keyboard is different due to the introduction of symbol shift at row 0/ mask 0x02 causing the letters to 'shuffle along'.

Jupiter Ace
Image courtesy of The Centre for Computing History, Cambridge

But despite its ZX81 heritage this 1982 machine is more akin to a black-and-white Spectrum, with its 32x24 tile map of 8x8 user-defined graphic characters, single channel beeper, and some interesting visual artifacts caused by the way the display and CPU have to vie for the attention of parts of memory.

63

Oh, and it uses Forth, you know!
Martyn Davies considers this to be their favourite machine.

```
GOTO 31 : REM Canon Cat
GOSUB 4 : REM Reverse Polish Notation
```

10 : Toshiba HX-10

'Hello Tosh, gotta Toshiba?', as the HX-10 advertising campaign went during the 1980s. It's part of the biggest family in all computing – MSX. Created by Kay Nishi at Microsoft Japan in 1982, MSX embodied the idea that home computers should have a standard, like VHS tapes provided for consumer video recording. It was thought that if each manufacturer built hardware and software to a fixed specification, using Microsoft eXtended BASIC, then everything would 'just work'.

The concept was valid, and thousands of different machines were made, mostly in Japan. Some were enhanced for music production, some had extra graphics capabilities, although all could load and run the same software. But it never succeeded in the way that the IBM PC did. Indeed, the Commodore VIC-20 sold more units in its first year than all the MSX machines combined. Such are statistics, often used – much like a drunk uses a lamppost – more for support than illumination!

At least the HX-10 lives on in memory for being colourful: a white alphanumeric keyboard, black function and selection buttons, along with blue cursor keys, a red STOP button, and a special green GRAPH key.

```
GOTO 4 : REM MSX
GOTO 10 : REM BASIC
GOTO 10 : REM Disabling the break key
GOTO 10 : REM Tales of Chuckie Egg
GOTO 10 : REM New pence
GOTO 10 : REM PRINT "Always get someone to cheque your work. ";
GOTO 10 : REM Seconds
GOTO 1200 : REM BASICODE
GOTO 5150 : REM The first personal computer
```

10 : New pence

The full title for the UK sterling 10p coin. This was used in coin-operated arcade cabinets for years as the default unit of payment. It is also the incremental monetary unit, as bigger more expensive games required 20p to play. And then

50p. Naturally, it wasn't long before game design incorporated this, allowing you to purchase extra lives if another 10p was inserted before the 'Continue Play?' countdown hit zero.

It is the equivalent of the US quarter, or the Japanese 100 Yen which, according to legend, supposedly became unavailable because of the excessive popularity of *Space Invaders*. That is, of course, highly improbable since any money spent on the game would have been taken to the bank by the owner and thus returned to circulation.

Just as line 10 introduced programmers to BASIC, 10p introduced gamers to the arcades, so it would truly be wonderful to start a new legend that this is not a *coin*-cidence!

```
GOTO 1 : REM I'd buy that for a dollar
GOTO 9 : REM Nine Tiles
GOTO 10 : REM BASIC
GOTO 10 : REM Disabling the break key
GOTO 10 : REM Tales of Chuckie Egg
GOTO 10 : REM Toshiba HX-10
GOTO 10 : REM PRINT "Always get someone to cheque your work. ";
GOTO 10 : REM Seconds
GOTO 256 : REM The $2.56 reward program
```

10 : PRINT "Always get someone to cheque your work. ";

When home computer sales moved from adverts in hobbyist electronics maga-zines to the high street stores, their visibility and importance increased in the eyes of the public. And mischievous teenagers. The same demographic that saw value in typing 5318008 into upside down calculators would find an in-store display computer and type:

```
10 PRINT "THOMAS IS AN IDIOT ";
20 GOTO 10
```

They would then leave it running, as the screen was filled with the idiocy of Thomas's antics to the bemusement and frustrations of the Saturday staff.

From this code, the two streams of technologists diverged. For one category, this would be the first and last code they would ever write. They had learned to use a space, or full stop, after the text so that the end of the last word wouldn't run into the start of the first. They had also learned that the semicolon would ensure each repeat of the text followed immediately after the previous one, and didn't begin again on the next line. Some had even learned to count the number of letters in the message to ensure it wasn't a multiple of the screen width.

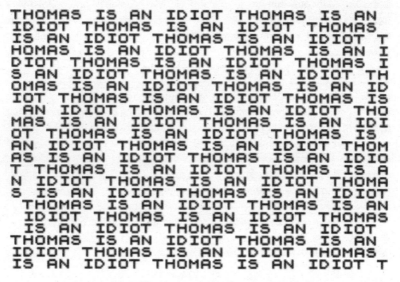

As seen in all good newsagents. And WH Smith.

The second stream of technologists looked beyond this simplicity, wondering how the machines worked behind the scenes. They went on to invent the world. (Once such developer is Matthew Adams, responsible for the title of this section.) But this book isn't about them, so we'll leave them here!

The range of messages was usually limited to profanity and stupidity, with occasional glimpses of ingenuity such as:

```
10 PRINT "15 PEN";
```

These messages would appear on the screen forever until someone pulled the plug (literally, as not many machines had a reset button in the early years), or until the computer printed 'Scroll?' (as the Spectrum did, unless you knew about POKE 23692,255), or until the break/escape key was pressed. Of course, some enterprising folks found a way to disable that key…

```
GOTO 10 : REM BASIC
GOTO 10 : REM Disabling the break key
GOTO 10 : REM Tales of Chuckie Egg
GOTO 10 : REM Toshiba HX-10
GOTO 10 : REM New pence
GOTO 10 : REM Seconds
GOTO 135 : REM Easter eggs
```

10 : Seconds

In August 1983, Apple CEO Steve Jobs delivered a motivational speech to the Mac developers. He asked them to 'shave 10 seconds off of the boot time. Multiply that by five million users and that's 50 million seconds, every single day. Over a year, that's probably dozens of lifetimes. So if you make it boot 10 seconds faster, you've saved a dozen lives. That's really worth it, don't you think?'

(One second, by the way, is formally defined as 'the unperturbed ground-state hyperfine transition frequency of the Caesium 133 atom', where the transition is 9,192,631,770 Hz. But I guess you knew that!)

```
GOTO 10 : REM BASIC
GOTO 10 : REM Disabling the break key
GOTO 10 : REM Tales of Chuckie Egg
GOTO 10 : REM Toshiba HX-10
GOTO 10 : REM New pence
GOTO 10 : REM PRINT "Always get someone to cheque your work. ";
GOTO 49 : REM Optimising for speed
GOTO 2147483647 : REM Seconds
```

```
10 PRINT TAB(12,2) CHR$(131);CHR$(141); "CRITTA
   CATCHA"
```

11 : Luxor ABC80

While much of the computing scene was dominated by the UK and US it is always a pleasure to shine a light elsewhere. In this case, Sweden, where a small company in Motala called Luxor created the Advanced BASIC Computer 80 in 1978. It provided personal computing to homes, schools and offices, while simultaneously providing a platform for industrial automation through its expansion bus. (Albeit a proprietary one called the 'ABC' bus.)

As the name suggests, it was a Z80-based machine and, in keeping with the times, had its own implementation of BASIC residing in ROM. One of its notable features was that it was 'semi-compiled' (similar to modern just-in time (JIT) compilers), making it faster than its competitors at the time, the Commodore PET and Apple II.

For ABC users, the number 11 evokes two memories. One is ERR 11 which the ABC80 used as shorthand for a syntax error. (To look up the error code with a textual description one simply removed the plastic tray under the keyboard.) The second memory is of the machine code routine stored at address 11 which outputs text to the screen – but if executed from BASIC, without first setting up the necessary registers, it writes pages of garbage text to the screen. A fun, if mean, way to introduce new users to their ABC80.

Both Thomas Kristiansen and Thomas Michanek consider this to be their favourite machine.

GOTO 10 : REM Jupiter Ace

12 : Celebrity

Some are born with celebrity, some achieve celebrity, and some have celebrity thrust upon them. The first machines were so anonymous they had to be sold, often in kit form, to hobbyists from electronics magazines since there was no computing press – nor any computer stores.

So when computers wanted to be *home* computers they needed star power, imported from those already in people's homes, via the TV – from *Star Trek*'s William Shatner promoting the Commodore VIC-20, to the incumbent lead actors of *Doctor Who*, Tom Baker and Lalla Ward, extolling the virtues of Prime computers.

But machines and engineers were still anonymous. Only the CEOs had the clout to become recognised, often by appearing at trade shows, or being interviewed in the business or technology sections of the current affairs shows. Jack Tramiel (Commodore and Atari), Steve Jobs (Apple) and Bill Gates (Microsoft) all realised the value of image.

Perhaps Clive Sinclair was earlier than most, with his face appearing as early as February 1980 in *Electrical and Radio Trading*, promoting the Sinclair ZX80. He also benefited from being in the UK, where the press at the time was very confined, and so he became a celebrity in his own right, appearing in an infamous TV commercial for his QL computer and earning column inches for his non-company exploits that survived long after his C5 electric car had run out of juice.

```
GOTO 13  :  REM Points
GOTO 19  :  REM Musicians with computers
GOTO 400 :  REM Atari 400
```

13 : Level 13

After completing level 13 on *Mine Storm* for the GCE Vectrex, the game crashes thanks to a bug. Since none of the development team at Western Technologies could get that far it was never discovered. (At least GCE provided a patch, by manufacturing and shipping a new cartridge.)

This is just one of many 'kill screens' in gaming history. The 1981 space shooter *Galaga* crashes on level 256, whereas maze game *Dig Dug* ends on 256 since the enemy character, Pooka, starts at the same position as the player, instantly killing them. Sometimes the kill is metaphorical, as the game becomes unplayable. Level 100 of light gun shooter game *Duck Hunt* (shown on screen as level 0 due to another bug) has the ducks moving so fast they can't be shot, and the first version of *Tetris* for the NES could not be completed after level 28 since the pieces fell too fast to move them into the corners.

```
GOTO 4   :  REM Bugs in Jet Set Willy
GOTO 13  :  REM Points
GOTO 13  :  REM ROT
GOTO 14  :  REM Canary traps
GOTO 70  :  REM Bugs
GOTO 135 :  REM Easter eggs
GOTO 147 :  REM CLS
GOTO 256 :  REM The Pac-Man kill screen
GOTO 256 :  REM The $2.56 reward program
```

13 : Points

This was the score achieved by Sir Clive Sinclair when he appeared on the BBC TV quiz show *Celebrity Mastermind*, broadcast on 3 January 2011. Disappointingly, he took final place, being beaten by Robert Webb with 21 points, Helen Skelton, and winner Stephen Mangan who scored a total of 29, including 15 on his specialist subject, *The Hitchhiker's Guide to the Galaxy*. Clive's (perhaps overly broad) specialist subject was 'British Inventions Since 1940'.

```
GOTO 12  :  REM Celebrity
```

```
GOTO 13 : REM Level 13
GOTO 13 : REM ROT
```

13 : ROT

In the days before the web, discussion forums on the Internet were largely a text-only medium. Usenet, a distributed discussion forum, began in 1980 and used a hierarchal system of groups to allow content to be discovered. Information about computers would be under the general 'comp' name, with information about the Acorn systems being in 'comp.sys.acorn' and games for the Acorn going one layer deeper with 'comp.sys.acorn.games'. Unlike email, where a single message is stored by each recipient, here every message was held on a comparatively small number of news servers that anyone (without needing an account) could read. Being text-only meant spoilers could not be hidden behind a button or selectively ignored. Instead, ROT13 was used.

ROT13 is short for 'rotate 13', and is a simple encoding method whereby each letter (and only the letters) is moved 13 places in the alphabet. Given that the (English) alphabet is 26 letters long, you could move the letters forward *or* backwards and get the same result, and the same process could be used for encoding and decoding the information. So the phrase

```
Ur vf yhxr'f sngure!
```

would read as

```
He is Luke's father!
```

when processed as ROT13. This provided a good, simple way to hide spoilers, punchlines, offensive comments, and other information in plain sight. (Obviously it's only a basic cipher, and not very good for secrets.)

```
GOTO 13 : REM Level 13
GOTO 13 : REM Points
```

14 : Canary traps

Canary traps are pieces of code that are never intended to be found, and included so that copyright infractions can be uncovered simply. This might be through the inclusion of data which is never used, or very specific code that triggers something so obviously unique that no one could accidentally write it. Sometimes called mountweazels, such traps were common with cartographers who amended their maps with non-existent streets (such as Lie Close), or misspelled names. But they have found their place in many fields of endeavour.

Famously Chris Haney and Scott Abbott, the makers of board game Trivial Pursuit, were taken to court in 1984 for including a question about the first name of TV detective, Columbo, played by Peter Falk. As it happens, his first name is never given in the show. But during the 1970s Fred Worth had written a series of trivia books. In one such book he had given Columbo the first name of Philip, so that if anyone copied this piece of information into a book, or game, it could be traced back to his original book. Unfortunately, for Worth (and authors the world over), the court ruled that facts could not be copyrighted. And, from a certain point of view, the court were correct in their verdict; quizzes like Trivial Pursuit are nothing more than facts (the answers) which can be determined from a secondary fact (the questions).

A similar argument was used by the company Franklin Computer Corporation when they were taken to court for their machine, the Franklin Ace 100. It was, in very real terms, a clone of the Apple II with identical chips, architecture, documentation, and the 14 pieces of software which constituted the OS. Subtlety was never their strong suit, since even their adverts proclaimed their machine was 'sweeter than an Apple'.

There was also a mention of 'Apple' in the manual where a, er, manual search-and-replace had not changed it to 'Ace'.

Franklin argued that to make a fully compatible machine, they needed a fully compatible OS. Consequently, the OS was a work of utility and not creativity, and therefore not subject to copyright. Case 82-1582 of the United States Court of Appeals, Third Circuit, uses the phrase, 'they are utilitarian objects or machine parts'. Franklin admitted copying, even arguing that it was necessary because there were too many entry points into the code to make a compatible version. However, the work on reverse-engineering the PC BIOS, and VTech's effort to create a clean room implementation of the Apple in their Laser 128 machine, shows this was a solvable problem, and by 1986 Franklin had succeeded in becoming a footnote in their own story.

(A similar tale of IP-blindness is told by Rod Cousens, formally at Activision et al, who saw his games pirated in a store and mentioned it to the owner. The owner had made the *physical* copies of the tapes on display and, therefore, believed it was him who owned the games.)

Even though Apple had won the case, this episode convinced Steve Jobs that something needed to be added to the code in future ROM software, in case the law was not as kind next time – perhaps other developers would be smart enough to obfuscate the copied code so that it couldn't be tracked. The result was the 'Stolen from Apple' trap, which appears in the 128 KiB and 512 KiB versions of the original Apple Macintosh. The trap was a simple piece of code, at address 0x4188A4, which could be invoked by the system debugger to decompress a 32x32 icon to fill the screen, containing prison bars and the words 'Stolen!! © Apple'.

Unfortunately we can't include it here. For copyright reasons.

```
GOTO 4   : REM Bugs in Jet Set Willy
GOTO 13  : REM Level 13
GOTO 14  : REM Chips
GOTO 14  : REM Computer kits
GOTO 70  : REM Bugs
GOTO 135 : REM Easter eggs
GOTO 147 : REM CLS
GOTO 256 : REM The Pac-Man kill screen
GOTO 256 : REM The $2.56 reward program
```

14 : Chips

When Sinclair Research was still known as Science of Cambridge, they sold a small microprocessor system called the MK-14 (also a postcode in Milton Keynes) based around the INS8060 CPU (aka SC/MP) from National Semiconductor. In fact, they based the whole board around their reference designs and components, which ultimately used 14 chips. Thus the name. Had Sinclair continued this legacy we would have had the ZX21, followed by the ZX4, ZX26 Spectrum, and the QL45. (Technically speaking, some ZX81s had five chips – two 2114 RAM chips instead of a single 4118, but who's counting? Oh yeah… us!)

If developers believe naming is hard, then perhaps Simon Jones turned the problem on its head. Simon designed the Quantel IMAGE card (Image Manipulation And Graphic Effects) which provided an upgrade for the video workhorse machine whose graphics were seen in action on almost every 1990s TV show. He used the Altera EPF8282 FGPA to handle the operations required by the main Inmos T805 Transputer. And he used a lot of them. Towards the end of the design phase he realised there were 80 (or 81) of these 8282s in use. So, when designing the last bit of the circuitry (and having several ways of doing so) he chose the option that would result in 82 of the chips being used. 'Just for the hell of it.'

14 : Computer kits

Innovation begins with makers. If you wanted a computer when no such thing existed, you had to build it. The Homebrew Computer Club in Menlo Park, California, typified this thinking. They would share components, circuits and ideas. But for every hardware tinkerer, there would be 100 potential tinkerers who could be sold completed machines, or even kits. The first Apple machine, the Apple 1, was sold in this way, as were the first machines from Acorn and Sinclair with the System 1 and MK-14 respectively, both early incarnations of the current 'system on chip'.

MK 14, rear of circuit board showing the soldering
a hobbyist was expected to manage

Image courtesy of The Centre for Computing History, Cambridge

Even when the machines were focused towards home use, kits were available to those eager to build (or save money). Unfortunately, builders sometimes over-estimated their ability. One purchaser of Acorn's kit, the Atom, contacted support for help with their machine. They claimed to have built it according to the instructions, and read the notice that care must be taken when soldering chips, because over-heating could destroy them. They had solved this problem by fixing them in place, instead, with glue!

Acorn, wanting to build a PROfessional Atom, called their next machine Proton. (Another atomic reference, which continued with their subsequent BBC-lite machine, the Electron.) Consequently, the Atom was their final machine available in kit form.

```
GOTO 4  : REM Geneve 9640
GOTO 14 : REM Canary traps
GOTO 14 : REM Chips
GOTO 1802 : REM Netronics ELF II
```

15 : C15, C60, C90

The C15 was the most common length of compact cassette tapes produced in the 1980s for computer use (with a smattering of C10s from the likes of the Altai Computape, which was produced without a leader). The number represented the duration in minutes (rather than the physical length, which was used in professional environs) and 'C' meant simply 'cassette'. The C60 and C90 were more suited for 'killing music' via home taping!

While there was no intended difference between them, other than their duration, the longer tapes were often thinner and more prone to breaking since, with more tape on each spool, there was more opportunity for it to stretch to a point where the wow and flutter turned the incomprehensible computer screeching into something that even a machine didn't understand! So hobbyists, forced into using cassettes because of the high price of disk drives, would generally avoid anything over C15. (Unless they were pirating many games onto a single C90.)

In general, the quality of these tapes was also lower than the chrome or metal variants intended for music. (A VHS compared to much superior Betamax, say.) However, this was a benefit. The sounds of computer data on a tape fit within a very tight frequency range, and the load procedure was prone to failure: many computers would often get confused by very high ringing sounds that could appear due to the medium. So, if the computer couldn't hear the much higher frequencies that high fidelity would reproduce, you would have more chance of a successful load.

A small selection of the many cassette brands
catering to the nascent computer market

It was also advantageous for these cassette players to be mono since there could be phase shift between the left and right channels on stereo recordings, which could also introduce problems.

However, the tapes being thin and error-prone didn't stop professional publishers releasing compilations on them – sometimes without checking that there was enough tape on the spool to fit all the games!

```
GOTO 1⅝ : REM IPS
GOTO 15 : REM REM SNAKESNAKESNAKE
GOTO 15 : REM Saving to tape
GOTO 50 : REM Compilations
GOTO 300 : REM Kansas City
GOTO 451 : REM Fahrenheit 451
GOTO 65495 : REM Going faster
```

15 : REM SNAKESNAKESNAKE

Most BASIC programs would, traditionally, start on line 10 with each subsequent line number going up in increments of 10. This would allow the programmer to add line numbers in between, such as 15, in case they forgot something. Even with the best planning in the world, it is highly unlikely that any BASIC program would start at line 10 and continue in uniform increments throughout the code. This was especially true of BASIC variants which didn't support multiple instructions on a single line.

(The code on our line 15 has been suggested by Kevin Frei, who might similarly start their Snake program on line 5!)

In contrast to modern languages, which do not have line numbers, this facility meant that the developers could implement some neat tricks, often seen in adventure games.

```
GOSUB 1000 + ROOM * 10
...
1000 PRINT "You are in room 1, a dusty corridor" : RETURN
1010 PRINT "You are in room 2, the pantry" : RETURN
1020 PRINT "You are in room 3, a staircase" : RETURN
```

(Remember, computers count from 0 while humans count from 1. So the computer refers to the first room in it's memory as 0, but it is displayed for the benefit of its wetware cousins as 'room 1' when printed.) This approach used less memory than the more structured approach of

```
READ D$(1), D$(2), D$(3)
PRINT D$(ROOM)
...
DATA "Room 1 description", "Room 2 description", "Room 3
     description"
```

since the latter held the room descriptions in both program memory and variable memory.

The natural disadvantage of the former method was that you had to manage the total number of rooms carefully, and not use code at line 3000 if you were likely to have 20 rooms in your game. You also had to be sure that the ROOM variable could never fall outside the range, lest it jumped to some random part of the game code.

Furthermore, some BASIC interpreters had a RENUM command to make each line a nice round multiple of 10 again, to help the programmer find more space on their program's number line. However, the nice set of instructions at lines 1000, 1010, 1020 etc. were changed to something else, while the GOSUB 1000 + ROOM * 10 code remained untouched, and the program broke completely.

The solution to both problems was solved, inadvertently, by a computer that most have never heard of – the Camputers Lynx. This machine, made in

Cambridge, used floating point numbers for its line numbers. So you could have instructions at 10, 10.1 and 10.05 if you so wished.

```
GOTO 3 : REM Optimising for size
GOTO 10 : REM BASIC
GOTO 15 : REM C15, C60, C90
GOTO 15 : REM Saving to tape
```

15 : Saving to tape

In the 1980s, cassette tape was a cheap and readily available medium, but it was notoriously bad for storing software because the cassette was designed to hold music, which is analogue, while a computer program is digital. Consequently, every computer needed a method of converting the digital data of a program into something that resembled music. Of course, computers of that era couldn't produce proper music, so the result was a series of beeps at specific frequencies. For example, 'zero' might be a short burst of sound at 1201.9 Hz, and a 'one' would be a slightly longer burst at 2403.8 Hz.

At this point we would hit our first problem: what if the tape player wasn't that perfect and the frequency was 1200 Hz upon playback, instead of 1201.9? Well, luckily, the computer designers realised this problem early on and determined a range of frequencies that would be acceptable as 'zero' and 'one'. Over time though, as the tape or the player became worn, both the pitch and duration of the signals became less obvious and fell outside of the range specified by the original programmers – and so the tape would fail to load.

(As some hobbyists used portable tape players powered by batteries it was not uncommon for the recording speed to vary as the batteries wore out! Consequently, a program could be saved one day and load perfectly well the next, since both halves of the process used the same *slower* tape speed. But when the batteries were replaced, and the tape reverted to its original speed, it became impossible to load those older programs.)

Some machines would load the data in blocks, so the tape could be retried in sections, instead of as a whole. Even so, tape loading was so temperamental it was not unusual to write the volume and tone settings of the cassette player onto the tape inlay whenever a successful combination was found.

Another trick utilised the tape counter. The counter reset button was held down until the program started to load, and then released. This meant the program would start on 000 so, if it failed to load, one could rewind to zero and try again. (Sometimes this would be to retry the whole program or just the last block, depending on the machine.) Given a program might take eight minutes to load, it was usual to go away and do something else, during which time you might forget an arbitrary counter, so 000 was easier to remember. Also, some tape players would auto-stop the rewind process when zero was reached, making this an obvious choice.

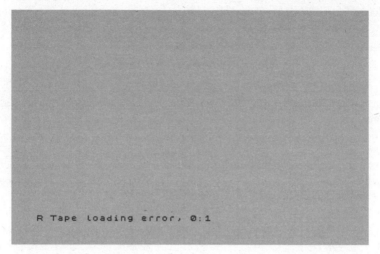

R Tape loading error, 0:1

The Sinclair ZX Spectrum failing to load a program. Again.

When cassette tapes included several different programs, it was also customary to write the tape counter numbers for each program onto the label. This was a symptom of slow loading times since most computers allowed you to type:

```
LOAD "PROGRAM NAME"
```

and the computer would trundle through the entire cassette looking for the program you'd asked for, and then load it. (Unless you had a Sinclair ZX80 that didn't support file names.) Since cassettes could often be half an hour in length, or more, this was a frustratingly long time to wait for the program to start loading, especially if you needed several attempts to get the volume and tone controls correct. So the counter was used to quickly find the right place on the tape. This enabled the user to directly 'load the next program on the tape' with a command like:

```
LOAD ""
```

This instruction was also less prone to missing files caused by spelling errors in the filenames (by both the user and publisher) and so became the norm, regardless of the specific syntax of the machine. Remembering, of course, that there were variations named

```
CLOAD ""
```

as used on the Dragon, with

```
CLOADM ""
```

reserved for machine code programs. A similar distinction existed on the BBC Micro, with

```
CHAIN ""
```

which was a literal chain of the commands LOAD and RUN for BASIC programs and

```
*RUN GAME
```

for machine code.

The Commodore 64 required both a filename pattern against which to match, and a suffix for the device number:

```
LOAD "*", 8

GOTO 1% : REM IPS
GOTO 15 : REM C15, C60, C90
GOTO 15 : REM REM SNAKESNAKESNAKE
GOTO 50 : REM Compilations
GOTO 300 : REM Kansas City
GOTO 451 : REM Fahrenheit 451
GOTO 65495 : REM Going faster
```

16 : RAM Pack

To reduce costs, many computers would come with the bare minimum of hardware. The easiest element to limit is the RAM. There were memory expansion cartridges to upgrade the Mattel Aquarius (4 KiB), the Commodore VIC-20 (3 KiB),

Jupiter Ace (3 KiB), and both Sinclair ZX80 and ZX81 (1 KiB each). In each case, the internal buses of the machine were made available for additional memory circuit board(s) to be connected.

But on the ZX81, there was a problem.

There was a difference between the angle of the machine and the 16 K RAM pack – 16 degrees of difference, in fact. So if your machine was not on a stable surface then the RAM pack could wobble, causing the machine to crash. Sometimes after a minute. Sometimes after an hour. But invariably just before you decided to save your work!

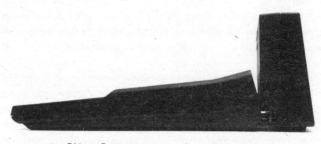

Profile of the ZX81 and its 16 K RAM pack

It could be argued that more crashes were caused by overheating due to small heat-sinks and poor airflow, rather than wobble. Many solutions were conceived for the problem; most commonly the RAM pack would be held in place with Blu-Tack filling the gap. Some people would remove the circuit boards from both the machine and the memory expansion and mount them securely to a new board, solder the two components together, or strap the components to a piece of wood with aluminium brackets. Others fixed the problem with money, either by buying a non-Sinclair RAM pack (like those from Memotech), or simply upgrading to a ZX Spectrum.

(Acorn Electron users, for all the taunts of being a 'cheaper BBC Micro', would have the last laugh since their Plus 1 expansion unit came with screws to hold it securely to the machine.)

GOTO 81 : REM Sinclair ZX81

18 : Certificate 18

In 2003, PEGI (Pan European Game Information) was formed to provide guidance on the suitability of a particular game for a given age range. The current set of age ratings are 3, 7, 12, 16 and 18, although not all countries which have adopted the rating legally require or enforce it. It is still very much a self-regulated system, but the line between regulation, censorship and freedoms has always been blurred.

Games sold by mail order from the classified ad pages at the back of a magazines were often the work of hobbyists and small companies, unable to afford full-page adverts and publicity departments. Without screenshots to entice an audience, they'd rely on titles like 'Violent Zombie Killer' to (over?)sell them. But there was no way of knowing that the Mr A. N. Other who sent the postal order was over 18 or not. And while it was fairly obvious that any game with the title 'Strip Poker' should probably not be sold to youngsters, they no doubt were. Indeed, the producers of such work might have been banking on that fact. Although anyone who expected some titillation by ordering *Softporn Adventure* would have been disappointed to discover it was a text-only adventure game. (Yes, it's a real product!)

Another technique used to age-limit games was found in the *Leisure Suit Larry* franchise, started by Sierra in 1987. It began with five trivia questions (picked from 160 possibles) that only someone growing up in the 1970s and/or in America would know. It was thought that a minor would not actually make it past such questions to the risqué gameplay within – although it soon became known that you could press Alt+X to bypass these questions.

```
GOTO 720 : REM Copy protection
GOTO 31900 : REM With prizes
```

18 : Elliott 903

In the Venn diagram of computers featured in this book that use transistors and have 18-bit words, there is just one – the Elliott 903.

Designed and built by the Elliott Brothers in 1965, this was the civilian (i.e. non-military) version of their 900 series for use in research, data processing and scientific applications. The machine would process each bit of the 18-bit word on one of 18 identical circuit boards. Building the machine in this way made it easy to repair, as the faulty board could be replaced wholesale. Detecting the fault was similarly easy, as one only had to swap circuit boards around to see how the error moved from bit to bit.

As a computer it was very capable, but it was just that – a computer. It had no input, unless you bought a separate paper tape reader. (Even with a paper tape, you still manually entered a bootstrap program on the front panel switches to initiate the loading process.) There was no output, unless you could read the LEDs on its front panel, or could understand the squeak of the processor, or bought a teletype printing machine. Monitors were a later addition, and although it never received any official audio add-ons (machines of this era rarely needed them), it was possible to attach a speaker to part of the circuit and rapidly change its voltage, producing a squeaking tune.

Elliott 903

Image courtesy of The Centre for Computing History, Cambridge

Programming was by paper tape. If you weren't using an assembler, you'd first load in the programming language (usually Algol or Fortran) followed by the code itself, ensuring both could fit into memory. If the 8192-word magnetic core memory wasn't enough, then it was possible – by buying a separate unit – to write the assembled code to paper tape.

Philip Searle considers this to be their favourite machine.

GOTO 8 : REM DEC PDP-8

19 : Musicians with computers

Almost all modern music uses a computer at some point in the production process, even if it is only used to act like a glorified tape recorder. In the 1980s the Acorn BBC Micro, which probably had the best sound capabilities of any home micro, would be used to control other machines to make the sounds. When the Commodore Amiga arrived, 8-bit samples meant the computer could be used as an instrument in its own right, with trackers (a form of music sequencing software) like Ultimate Soundtracker, Soundtracker, and OctaMED, along with copious discs of samples.

But musicians weren't only interested in the computer for its musical qualities. In 1984 the Thompson Twins released an adventure game to promote their single 'Doctor, Doctor' on a cover-mounted flexible record, rock band Journey worked with Data Age to create *Journey Escape* for the Atari 2600, and Shakin' Stevens included a *Head On* clone called *The Shaky Game* on the cassette version of his album, *The Bop Won't Stop*.

At the less salubrious end of the spectrum (pun intended), the Sinclair ZX81 was used to create a pop video. In 1983 the late Chris Sievey, creator of comedy character Frank Sidebottom, released a 7" vinyl single called 'Camouflage'. On the B-side were three computer programs for the ZX81. There were 1 K and 16 K versions of the game *Flying Train* and a music video. The latter was a karaoke-style lyrics display, with synchronised words and occasional graphics. This is noteworthy not only because he created the software himself, but also because the ZX81 had no sound or colour and, since the ZX81 hi-res graphics trick hadn't been properly exploited yet, only a 64x48 display area.

The same idea was used later in 1983 on *XL-1*, the second solo album by Pete Shelley, which contained a lyrics video for the Sinclair ZX Spectrum. With more memory available, each song had a slightly different set of algorithmically generated patterns. Instead of being hidden in the grooves of the 33⅓ record, or tucked away neatly on its own side, this program was listed as side two, track six. Fortunately, there was a locking groove after side two, track five so, had you forgotten to lift the arm, you wouldn't have been presented with the piercing square wave of the Spectrum's sync tone of 2496 Hz!

Exploring computer-based music outside of 'home' computers, you need only look to the Fairlight CMI (Computer Musical Instrument), an early 1980s synthesiser and sampler which cost as much as a house. It was used by musicians such as Duran Duran, Stevie Wonder and Kate Bush, but ultimately found fame providing the machine gun vocals for Paul Hardcastle's single, '19'.

```
GOTO 12 : REM Celebrity
GOTO 33⅓ : REM Revolutions per minute
GOTO 1500 : REM Computer sounds in music
GOTO 6581 : REM Sound generation
GOTO 31250 : REM MIDI
```

20 : GOTO 10

Scarfolk Council recommends that for more information you read this again.

```
GOTO 10 : REM PRINT "Always get someone to cheque your work. ";
```

20 : What is retro?

Everyone has their own opinion on what they consider retro. Maybe it's the machines they grew up with. Or anything older than 20 years. Or anything before 1990. If we wanted to be scientific and put a number on this, then we have several pre-existing etymologies to consider.

We often discuss life in terms of generations. The previous generation did this. The next generation will have to deal with that. An anthropologist might consider that the average person is born to a 34-year-old man, and a 29-year-old woman, giving an average generational gap of 31.5 years. But age isn't culture, and technology moves too fast to be measured on such time scales.

In hardware we often categorise the generations thus:

Gen	Years	Technology
1	1946–1959	Vacuum tubes
2	1959–1965	Transistors
3	1965–1971	Integrated circuits
4	1971–1980	Very-large-scale integration (VLSI)
5	1980–	Ultra-large-scale integration (ULSI)

But given our retro machines fall solely within the VLSI and ULSI areas, we need another parameter to differentiate them. One measure is the number of data bits a machine could process: the 8-bit era of the Commodore 64 and ZX Spectrum, followed by the 16-bit era of the Amiga and Atari ST, and finally the 32-bit realm of the Sega Saturn. But this definition has limitations. It assumes there is only one bus in the machine, connecting all the component parts together. It also assumes that a CPU, which processes 8 bits at a time, sends them. The Motorola 68008, present in the Sinclair QL, is often termed an 8/32 bit processor, because it has an 8-bit data bus for communication with the memory, but performs all calculations internally at 32 bits.

Attempts at providing a succinct generational split for game consoles have similar issues. Whether you try and group them by technology, storage medium or year, there is always overlap (and therefore argument). Only in recent years, with the console market becoming a two-horse race between Sony PlayStation and

Microsoft Xbox, and the phrase 'next gen' being used to launch any new machine, have distinctions been made, albeit in a purely marketing sense.

In modern times we have three main classes of people:

1. Users that consume content
2. Those that create content
3. Developers that make content tools

Until recently everyone needed to be a developer (or at least learn enough BASIC to type LOAD) so perhaps, in the computer world, we might try and craft these distinctions according to the work of their audience:

Gen	Years	Audience
1	1946–1973	Distracted university folk
2	1974–1979	Electronics tinkerers, building their own hardware
3	1980–1990	Software hackers, with diverse 8-bit home computers
4	1991–1996	Creative developers, the rise of 16-bit and multimedia
5	1997–	General audience, with the acceptance of homogeneous PCs

Retro could therefore be described as the generation in which you discovered computers. Or the one before. Either way, the only correct definition of retro is whatever you want it to be. The current technology scene has given us a perpetual invasion of privacy, regular data leaks and an always-connected culture – so anything that takes us away from that has to be fun, and therefore retro.

GOTO 20 : REM A friendly number

20 : A friendly number

According to Michael Tomczyk, assistant to Commodore president Jack Tramiel, this number was chosen for the VIC-20 because it simply sounded friendly, and was not connected to the near miss of it having 22 characters across the screen.

When released in Japan in 1980, its maiden voyage, the machine was named VIC-1001 because of the popularity of the movie *2001: A Space Odyssey* and the colloquial unfriendliness of the number 20. (Its other original name, 'The Commodore Spirit' was rejected because 'spirit' in Japan means something akin to 'ghoul from hell'. Cue thoughts of Boglins!)

GOTO 20 : REM What is retro?
GOTO 1000000 : REM Sales

```
20 PRINT TAB(12,3) CHR$(131);CHR$(141); "CRITTA
   CATCHA"
```

25 : Willis Road, Cambridge, UK

The HQ for Sinclair Research, from 1982, was previously a bottling factory for distilled water. It was later sold to the local council and now forms part of the Anglia Ruskin University. It was included as part of a 2012 conference and tour to commemorate the 30th Anniversary of the Sinclair ZX Spectrum.

The original sign on Willis Road. Photo by the author.

GOTO 6 : REM King's Parade

25 : Aquarius I and II

A fairly rare Aquarius, and a frightfully rare Aquarius II
From the personal collection of Roy Templeman

RETURN

28 : Peripherals for output

The most common improvement to a computer's output was via sound – and the machines most lacking in quality sound were, unsurprisingly, made by Sinclair.

To improve upon audio, peripherals such as the Zon Z-81, ZX-AY and DK'Tronics 3 channel sound synthesiser were brought to market. (The Zon Z-81 was notable for using a short 23-row connector, instead of the usual 28, making it also compatible with the humble ZX81.) They were usually based on the AY-3-8910 and AY-3-8912 chips, found in later Spectrums and the Atari ST, and provided three channels of sound, across eight octaves, without impinging significantly on the processor.

Unfortunately, not all software could make use of this new audio hardware since it needed to be programmed specifically for each physical device. Furthermore, some pieces of hardware could not be used in conjunction with other hardware since microcomputers generally had only one expansion port. So, if neither your joystick adapter nor sound unit had a 'through' port, you couldn't use both. Worse, some software and hardware would fail to work in particular combinations, with neither manufacturer being aware of it. Luckily, because of the physical structure of the computer, one could simply unplug the offending unit(s) and reboot.

However, when it comes to audio, it is Currah and Cheetah that are best remembered. Currah provided us with improved sound, speech synthesis via its μSpeech, and sometimes a combination of both with 'Speech and Sound'. Whereas Cheetah had a sound amplifier (which made the existing single 1-bit beep louder, rather than adding additional voices), a 'Sweet Talker' speech add-on, and a drum machine.

Yes. A drum machine.

The amusingly named and easy to mishear 'SpecDrum' contained little more than a digital-to-analogue (DAC) converter chip (an 8-bit ZN428E DAC) and an amplifier. For £29.95 you could buy the small black plastic add-on and some custom software which would combine (up to) three drum samples, loaded from cassette, into a single 8-bit value which it then wrote to the DAC, with the resultant voltage being sent to the amplifier and then speaker. Given that the CPU was responsible for providing this data to the hardware, each value was supplied in exactly 173 units of time, known as 'T states'.

It was a rudimentary machine, but it worked. The same hardware could have been used for more elaborate sample playback, but apparently wasn't. Instead, it was limited to the supplied LinnDrum samples, and those on the additional cassettes containing Afro, Latin, and Electro sounds.

A version for the Amstrad, called AmDrum, was also released.

```
GOTO 4   : REM Peripherals for processing
GOTO 30  : REM Storage
GOTO 31  : REM Peripherals for input
GOTO 100 : REM The extent of computer upgrades
```

30 : Monmouth Street

Many of us will know this as an address in Bath, UK. It is etched into most minds as being the place where Future Publishing were based for most of their exist-ence, having moved there in January 1990 from their previous location at 4 Queen Street. They produced so many magazines that there was probably one for every computer on the market. (And quite a few of the consoles.)

Essentially, if the title had 'Format' in it, it was probably Future. Plus, they bought out some of the 8-bit magazines, making them responsible for the latter-day editions of *Your Sinclair* and *Your Commodore*. Also, as we moved into the 32-bit era, they produced the *Official UK PlayStation Magazine* which garnered a new generation of fans. Literally, a new generation.

```
GOTO 8   : REM Type-in listings
GOTO 30  : REM Storage
```

30 : Storage

Cassettes were never destined to be the medium of the future, so others were chosen. The Rotronics Wafadrive and Sinclair Microdrive were both storage systems that used cartridges containing a tape loop, onto which a digital signal was written. Neither was particularly effective, though, as the speeds meant the tape stretched, shortening their life, highlighting Sinclair's desire for miniatur-isation to a fault. Quite literally, in the case of the Microdrive, as its compressed form factor caused it to malfunction! The CD, advocated as the future of music by TV's *Tomorrow's World*, was also adopted, briefly, on the Spectrum with the Codemasters *CD Games Pack* which loaded games via the joystick port.

The games pack's accompanying cable took the analogue audio signal from a CD (since this was recorded like any normal music CD, rather than a CD-ROM) and converted the analogue volume into a digital signal which pressed the (virtual) fire button on the joystick port. Since CD audio was a lot cleaner, and less liable to speed fluctuations, the loading routines did not need any delay loops to handle the inconsistencies of a cassette signal. (As a bonus, the loading process was silent.)

To bootstrap this process, a cassette held the loader program, which was a variation on the one in ROM. But once the first game had been loaded from CD (taking around 30 seconds, instead of five minutes) you could press the letters Q, U, I and T to re-trigger the loader which had been built into each of the 30 games.

At the opposite extreme, you could make program loading more frustrating by trying to do so via the radio (as happened with BASICODE, broadcast by the Chip Shop on 200 KHz long-wave in the UK), or TV, since some stations would broadcast the audio of a program over the air – which predated WiFi. To avoid the inevitable complaints of screeching computer signals, there were even attempts to distribute software by light, as on the 1985 UK TV show *4 Computer Buffs* which showed a flashing white disc in the bottom right corner of the screen and which, with the aid of a simple electronic circuit, would be converted into code. For the keen reader, this circuit can be found on page 184 of the March 1985 issue of *Personal Computer World* and needs a photo-transistor and suction cup.

```
GOTO 4 : REM Peripherals for processing
GOTO 8 : REM Type-in listings
GOTO 28 : REM Peripherals for output
GOTO 30 : REM Monmouth Street
GOTO 31 : REM Peripherals for input
GOTO 100 : REM The extent of computer upgrades
GOTO 1200 : REM BASICODE
```

```
30 PRINT TAB(9,6) "CATCH AS MANY CRITTAS"
```

31 : Canon Cat

The designer of 1987's Canon Cat was Jef Raskin, employee number 31 at Apple and initiator of the Apple Macintosh project. Unlike the Mac, the Cat combined the keyboard with the main processor and monitor to form a single unit, complete with carrying handle. It was aimed at those undertaking basic admin work, given that it was only capable of processing text.

Being text only, and without a mouse, Jef added various interface ideas like the 'Leap' buttons which allowed simple navigation throughout the document. There was an inbuilt MODEM for sending portions of text to another Cat or remote system. It could act as a messaging centre for email-like communications, could process maths in the text, had a spell-checker, and the entire memory could be saved to disk with two buttons. But much of this functionality went unnoticed.

It was a full-scale computer, with a proprietary OS written in tForth, relegated to one single task. But the 'just a word processor' market wanted more from their machine in 1987, and so the Cat was withdrawn from sale after just six months.

Andrew McVeigh considers this to be their favourite machine.

GOTO 80 : REM Sharp MZ-80A

31 : Peripherals for input

Once the ZX Spectrum had become the de facto games machine, a joystick interface was the most commonly purchased item, with versions built by companies such as Kempston, Sinclair, Comcon, Protek, AGF, DK'tronics and Fuller. They worked in a couple of different ways. Some, like the programmable joystick interfaces from DK'Tronics and AGF, had pre-loader software that allowed you to assign each joystick position (and the singular fire button) to any key on the keyboard. Naturally, this had the advantage of working with any game, but it required explicit configuration each time you loaded a game.

For a more seamless experience, the games themselves would need to be purposefully programmed to read the appropriate port and interpret the data accordingly. For a single joystick interface, like Kempston, it meant that code only needed to read a single port, in this case 0x1F or 31. To support a double joystick, as provided by the official Sinclair Interface 2, multiple ports were necessary as the directions mapped onto two sets of keys: 1 (left), 2 (right), 3 (down), 4 (up) and 5 (fire) for the first stick, and 6 (left), 7 (right), 8 (down), 9 (up) and 0 (fire) on the second. Curiously, though, these don't map to the cursor keys shown on the keyboard, 5 (left), 6 (down), 7 (up), 8 (right), which suggests that joysticks weren't considered in the original design.

If joysticks weren't your thing, there were also mice, light pens, trackballs, etc., each with their own hardware and necessary suite of custom software.

A few video input devices were made, such as the Data-Skip VIDEOFACE Digitiser for the Spectrum, which took input from a TV signal and converted it into a local format. Although impressive, its use was limited as the downscaling of images from TV resolution to that of a home computer rendered them unappealing, requiring significant artist time to fix. Those wanting to use it to capture full motion video would soon discover the 41 KiB of memory left in the ZX Spectrum was enough for roughly $3/10$ths of a second.

```
GOTO 4 : REM Peripherals for processing
GOTO 28 : REM Peripherals for output
GOTO 30 : REM Storage
GOTO 100 : REM The extent of computer upgrades
```

31 : Why do computer scientists get Halloween and Christmas mixed up?

Because Oct 31 = Dec 25

```
GOTO 50 : REM Alan Turing appears on the UK £50 note...
```

33¹/₃ : Revolutions per minute

A popular pub quiz question from the 1980s was 'What is the average number of grooves on an LP record?' The answer was two, one on each side, and was intended to catch out people that thought that a vinyl record was a series of concentric circles and that they needed to count them. However, the answer is not always two.

As far back as 1898 people had experimented with multiple interleaved grooves. Whichever track played would essentially be random: the needle could land in either groove and, once in the groove, stayed there until the end of the record. This was used to include different versions of the same song, often with an alternate ending, or completely different material. Its use was mainly novelty, rather than practical, as deftly demonstrated when TV comedy troupe Monty Python used the technique for their three-sided record, *Matching Tie and Hand-kerchief* (1973). Knowing that the physical format can be hacked into something unconventional provides an opportunity to seek out new tricks.

Prodigal, an obscure Christian rock band from 1984, used another facet of LP manufacture on their album *Electric Eye*, namely the run-out groove. Usually the run-out groove is a locked groove, an endless loop which plays silence until the arm is lifted. The Beatles probably popularized its existence on their album *Sgt. Pepper's Lonely Hearts Club Band* (1967), when they devised a variation by adding a sound collage at the end of side two which would loop indefinitely, as the needle sat contentedly in the run-out. In Prodigal's case, they kept the run-out groove silent, but added a second groove after it that hid a Commodore 64 program. By placing the needle in exactly the right place after the run-out, i.e. closer to the central label, you get 13 seconds of audio containing a short BASIC program giving quotes from Albert Einstein and Jesus.

Accessing the groove was intentionally tricky, since the screeching sound of software loading could be construed as somewhat demonic for the audience of a Christian rock band. Users with modern record players might find accessing this track even more difficult, since most now have an auto-return feature which stops the arm from being moved too close to the centre of the disc.

A ˉFloppy-ROMˉTM supplied with ˉInterface Ageˉ
Photo by Michael Holley

Software wasn't always *hidden* on records, as some were produced with *only* the computer data. However, in this case, the form factor was generally a flexi disc. This type of record was also made of vinyl, but was of sub-millimetre thickness (compared to 0.5–2mm for traditional discs) and only contained a single grooved side of between three and six minutes, depending on the revolutions per minute. In contrast to traditional vinyl, it was incredibly cheap to manufacture, and could be included in (or on) magazines to provide software that the end user could record onto cassette for later playback into their machine. If convincing a computer to load from audio tape was a problem, then flexi discs only made it worse. They were very light, and the needle was so heavy, that it would often stop the disc from spinning, or the arm would bend the disc just enough to distort the sound. Although computers have a better tolerance for slightly out-of-pitch tones than I have for slightly out-of-pitch singers, it would be enough to prevent loading. Therefore the flexi disc needed to be placed on top of a 'proper' record to increase the friction, and weighted with a coin stuck down with Blu-tack on top of it. (Without being stuck, the centrifugal force could cause the coin to spin off the disc.) It was then a matter of luck whether you managed to make a good recording of the disc before it wore out. One of the first such recordings, in *Interface Age* magazine, suggests between 10 and 20 attempts.

This disc, from May 1977, was described in the magazine's editorial as 'new and exciting' and destined to 'initiate a programming revolution'. They certainly believed it, as they had been working on the idea since August 1976, and ultimately dedicated nine pages to this process, describing the trials of sending tapes through the mail, cutting the disc by feeding the software directly from the output of a Southwest Technical Products 6800 computer, and loading it via MIKBUG, a program to interface with serial data. (For readers without MIKBUG, a hex dump for a binary loader program was also printed in the magazine for you to type in.)

There were two tracks on the disc, one with patterns to test the cassette alignment, and a second with the BASIC interpreter itself. The code could be loaded by the standard Kansas City Cassette interface into any 6800 machine with 6 KiB of memory, such as the MITS Altair 680.

Unavailable at Andy's Records, with or without record tokens
Photo by the author

Such discs would appear sporadically until the mid-1980s. Perhaps the most famous example appeared as a free cover disk with issue 36 of *Computer & Video Games* magazine in October 1984. The Thompson Twins, an electro-pop band comprising Tom Bailey, Alannah Currie and Joe Leeway, made a tie-in disc with their then-current album, *Into the Gap*. Alongside a special message from 'The

Twins', it contained the audio for an adventure game named after their *Doctor! Doctor!* single, developed by Quicksilva for the ZX Spectrum. (A Commodore 64 version came later for those who sent away for it, making it even rarer than the Spectrum version.) By solving the mystery of the potion within the game, you could win a trip to their concert and meet the band backstage. Despite the game itself being totally forgettable due to adopting many of the unfair game-play mechanics used in bad adventure games, it is still fondly remembered and helped pave the way for better subsequent cover-mounted products.

Finally, it is amusing to note the three playback speeds of vinyl records: 33⅓ for albums, 45 used by most 7" and 12" singles, and 78 for records produced prior to the 1960s (originally made from Shellac). Note that anyone born in 1933 was 45 years old in 1978.

(There were also a number of records made at 16 rpm, mostly for spoken word releases, but these are significantly lesser known.)

```
GOTO 8 : REM Type-in listings
GOTO 19 : REM Musicians with computers
GOTO 300 : REM Kansas City
GOTO 1500 : REM Computer sounds in music
GOTO 6581 : REM Sound generation
GOTO 31250 : REM MIDI
GOTO 31900 : REM With prizes
```

40 : Commodore 64

According to the *Guinness Book of World Records*, or as you might learn from Roy Castle and Norris McWhirter on Record Breakers, this machine is the highest-selling computer ever, so it's impossible to dispute that this machine is a classic, and difficult to find anything new to say about it!

So let me repeat this for the die-hard Sinclair fans at the back, with their fingers in their ears: this is the highest-selling computer ever! It had an SID (Sound Interface Device) chip which played music (not BEEPs). It had eight hardware sprites... per scanline. Scrolling. Mice, paddles, and joysticks using a *built-in* interface. And more!

For those with their (fore)sights on business smarts, Jack Tramiel, Commodore CEO, gave it 64 KiB of RAM knowing that prices would drop to affordable levels by the time the machine was ready to be built. Also, by owning the silicon fabricators, they subsumed development costs into the overheads of the existing company. (Had they still been around in 2022, they would have avoided the worldwide chip shortages.)

Plus, from a numerology perspective, its original name of VIC-40 has an identical number (in hex) to the final '64' designation in decimal.

Dunc, Robert Bernstein and Paul Fearns all consider this to be their favourite machine.

(I, personally, do not! See you in the playground!)

GOTO 7 : REM Commodore 128
GOTO 205.5 : REM How to draw a maze in one line

40 : Keyboards

Given computers of this era would boot directly into BASIC, it was expected that every user would type something into the machine, even if that something was simply LOAD. So computers, as opposed to consoles, needed a keyboard. How many keys that keyboard needed, however, was open for debate.

The accepted minimum seems to be 40 keys – 26 letters, 10 numbers, space, return, and two shift keys. (And nothing to do with the tenuous fact that 40 is the only number where the letters 'forty' appear in alphabetical order.) The two shift keys are necessary since there are 35 punctuation marks (at least, on my keyboard here) so, if you want upper and lower case letters, you need to either add more keys solely for punctuation or allow the letters to support both cases and a symbol.

MK14

Image courtesy of The Centre for Computing History, Cambridge

But this presumes the need to type text. If you're writing code, and can do so with hexadecimal numbers, then a simpler keypad is sufficient. Back in the 1970s, the MK14 from Science of Cambridge and the Acorn System 1 (the only machine in this book to be part of a spaceship's central console, in the TV series *Blake's 7*) had 20 and 25 keys respectively.

Acorn System 1
Image courtesy of The Centre for Computing History, Cambridge

The MITS Altair 8800 was programmed in binary, with 16 on/off switches (not keys!) to set either the address *or* the data, with eight additional switches to control which. (For the completists, it had an on/off switch which brings its total to 25.)

As computers with inbuilt keyboards evolved to separate keyboards – often with a curly wire, like Brian May's guitar lead – and then back to laptops with inbuilt keyboards, the layout has continued to change to this day. Perhaps there will never be a standard.

Incidentally, there is an oddity with nearly every keyboard; by default, every key initiates a lower case letter, despite having upper case printed on them.

```
GOTO 5 : REM Keys
GOTO 201 : REM Cursor keys
```

```
40 PRINT TAB(9,7) "AS YOU CAN IN 60 SECONDS"
```

42 : The meaning of life

This number is probably the most recognisable integer in all of geekdom, all thanks to Cantabrigian Douglas Adams and his 1978 radio series and subsequent book, *The Hitchhiker's Guide to the Galaxy*.

But 42, as well as being the answer to the meaning of 'life, the universe and everything' is also the ASCII for '*' – which, aptly, is used as the wildcard symbol meaning 'everything'.

(It's also 6x9 in base 13, XLII in roman numerals, and 101010 in binary, but all are less significant.)

GOTO 65 : REM Origins

49 : Optimising for speed

While a few speed optimisations were available to BASIC programmers, the language was already sufficiently slow to convince most would-be game developers to start learning assembly!

As an interpreted language, many of the optimisations you would make for size also applied to speed – such as removing the spaces from between words – since if the interpreter has fewer characters to process, then it will naturally be quicker. Similarly, moving onto the next program line took most interpreters *very* slightly longer than processing the next instruction on the current line. So code with lots of : would work slightly faster in most cases.

Less obvious optimisations came from using control statements like REPEAT and UNTIL. These statements were the lifeblood of structured BASIC programming, since they didn't need to indicate the next instruction with a line number. Unfortunately, most BASICs weren't structured and relied on GOSUB and GOTO. In these cases, it was always preferable to start your program with:

```
10 GOTO 1000
20 REM My most used subroutine
30 RETURN
40 REM My second most used subroutine
50 RETURN
```

This is because, with every GOSUB or GOTO, BASIC needs to look up the memory location of a given line number. It does this by starting at the beginning of the program and working through each statement until it finds the number in question.

Or it finds a line number larger than the one it was looking for, at which point it picks that instead (this case allows you to write GOTO 90 and let the program continue with line 91, 92, or whatever happens to be next). Naturally, the earlier the routine appears in the listing, the fewer skips the BASIC interpreter needs to make in order to find the appropriate line, since each line skipped can take a not insignificant amount of time.

The majority of speed improvements in BASIC came from machine-specific tricks, rather than general rules of thumb. Users of Acorn's BBC BASIC, for example, had a significant advantage by using special variables called A%, B%, and so on. This was, firstly, because these variables could only ever store integers. Given that floating point numbers needed to be emulated in software, this had a significant impact in all calculations involving them. The second reason is that these variables were identified by only a single letter, requiring slightly less parsing time. Finally, the third benefit came from the BASIC interpreter storing those variables in memory between the addresses 0x0400–0x046B, so it could access their values directly as they were at a fixed and known location. All other variables were stored on the heap. The heap is well named since finding anything stored on it requires the BASIC interpreter code to rummage around looking for the variable name in question before being able to return its value. Such a rummage could be slow.

Ironically, with interpreted BASIC, the slower the machine, the fewer opportunities it provided for speed improvements. On the Sinclair ZX81, for example, the 'true' part of a conditional IF statement could only contain one other instruction. It was therefore possible to write:

```
100 IF X = 31 THEN LET X = 0
```

But not:

```
100 IF X = 31 THEN LET X = 0 ELSE LET X = X + 1
```

Such a seemingly simple addition to the (already slow) machine would have helped so many pieces of software, as it was not uncommon to see code like this:

```
100 IF X = 31 THEN LET X = 0
110 IF X <> 31 THEN LET X = X + 1
```

This caused the machine to interpret two lines, and make one completely redundant comparison. Even support for multiple statements would have permitted a faster implementation with:

```
100 IF X = 31 THEN LET X = 0 : GOTO 120
110 LET X = X + 1
120 REM THE REST OF THE CODE...
```

For those that noticed the inefficiencies, and cared enough to fix them, the logic could be reworked:

```
100 LET X = X + 1
110 IF X = 32 THEN LET X = 0
```

```
GOTO 0 : REM Abbreviations
GOTO 3 : REM Optimising for size
GOTO 10 : REM BASIC
GOTO 10 : REM Seconds
GOSUB 1597463007 : REM Inverse Square Root
```

50 : Compilations

Compilations have generally been a good deal for the consumer – a curated selection of quality media packed into a single purchase. The music industry had realised this years ago, with the *Now That's What I Call Music!* series still going strong decades after the *Top of the Pops* and *The Hits Album* collections are but nostalgic footnotes. Even if you already owned five or six songs, you were getting another 20 that you *might* like for minimal outlay.

The software industry also adopted this approach with *They Sold a Million* and *Soft Aid* (both 1985). The former was a compilation of million-selling games (which itself sold a million) from an Ocean and US Gold collaboration called Hit Squad, while the latter was – like Band Aid and Live Aid – a charitable enterprise aimed at helping with famine relief in Ethiopia. But one compilation stands out from the crowd:

Cascade *Cassette 50*.

As its name suggests, it contained 50 different programs for your computer, literally your model, since versions of it were made for twelve of the most popular micros of 1983. With developers of each game earning around £10 for their efforts you should set low expectations, knowing they even failed to live up to that! All the programs fell into at least one of these categories:

1. written in BASIC
2. highly mediocre clone of a more popular game

3. frustrating to play
4. wrongly labelled (e.g. the ZX81 game *Jet Fighters* is on the label as 'Jet Flight')
5. not present on the tape

The latter was certainly the case on the Acorn Electron as the last two games were missing, like Spangles from a modern sweet shop. (No one checked if the games actually loaded after mastering!) Unlike the infamous note in the margin of Diophantus's *Arithmetica*, as owned by Pierre de Fermat, they did have a truly marvellous demonstration of bad software – which this cassette was too short to contain.

But with the whole tape costing just £9.95, what did you expect – a brand new Timex digital watch? Funnily enough, if Cascade didn't know that their claim to historical fame was to be a poor-quality compilation, then they cemented it by also providing every customer with a free watch that, at the time, cost about the same as the tape. With such titles as 'Startrek' (unlicensed, of course), 'Black Hole', and 'Smash the Windows' – plus that watch – it's easy to see why people wanted one... until the reviews came out...

```
GOTO 1⅞ : REM IPS
GOTO 15 : REM Saving to tape
GOTO 15 : REM C15, C60, C90
GOTO 300 : REM Kansas City
GOTO 451 : REM Fahrenheit 451
GOTO 65495 : REM Going faster
```

50 : Alan Turing appears on the UK £50 note...

Whoever made that decision was right on the money!

```
GOTO 1023 : REM Have you heard of that new band, '1023
   Megabytes'?
```

50 : Signetics Instructor 50

Before computers had full-sized keyboards and colour screens, they had switches, LEDs, and seven-segment displays. Other than memory, they generally lacked support chips as they were essentially playgrounds to explore the CPU.

In 1978, processor manufacturer Signetics took this approach literally with their Instructor 50 machine, promoting it as a tool to teach their Signetics 2650 CPU. As a processor it was not without merit – it sported seven registers, an ALU, binary coded decimal (BCD) arithmetic, and 75 instructions handling arithmetic as well as logical, branch, and program flow. Interestingly, it also had an eight-level return address stack in the chip itself – thereby ensuring all the memory was kept for the programmer, and eliminating the possibility of programs corrupting the stack.

Unlike other training machines, this came with a tape interface and an S-100 expansion bus, the standard at the time for connecting peripherals and I/O boards directly to the CPU. Its tech specs were roughly par for the course, with a 2 KiB ROM containing the monitor software, and 640 bytes of RAM (of which 512 were available to the programmer.)

Unfortunately, it became an 'also-ran' of the era by being the less famous cousin of the MK-14 and Acorn System 1. The latter has an interesting heritage – Steve Furber, co-creator of the BBC Micro, built his first computer at the Cambridge University Processor Group using a Signetics 2650.

Simon Anderson considers this, the first machine they owned, to be their favourite.

```
GOTO 4 : REM 1292 Advanced Programmable Video System
```

```
50 PRINT TAB(9,10) "KEYS:"
60 PRINT TAB(9,11) "A & S .... LEFT & RIGHT"
```

64 : Spanish import law

There are so many things connected with the number 64. The 64 K address space of 16 bits (0 to 65535). The numeral on machines such as the Dragon, Pecom and Oric Nova. And 1964 was the year in which BASIC was released.

But it's also the threshold in a slightly obscure piece of Spanish legislation from September 1985. The law was that any imported computer with memory of 64 K or less would be taxed at the rate of 15,000 pesetas per machine. Consequently Amstrad, who were wanting to sell their 64 K CPC 464 machine into the Spanish market, would see their 25,000-peseta price tag raised to 40,000, which would certainly have killed any chance of sales there. So they upgraded the RAM to 72 K, by adding an 8 K chip on a new daughterboard.

However, as we've seen, the address space of a 16-bit machine is only 64 K so extra circuitry would be required to make use of this memory. Other computers of the era would use bank switching technology, or something similar, allowing the programmer to choose which memory chip (in its entirety) would be used at any given time. Amstrad didn't, though; their solution was simply to not connect the chip! This meant they could print '72k' on the case, show over-zealous customs officers that there was 72 KiB worth of memory chips inside the machine, and import their machine into the market at a reasonable price.

The 8 KiB RAM chip on its daughterboard

It was called the CPC 472.

It is not known if these chips even worked. Maybe they were taken from the rejects bin at chip supplier, Orion. It is not even known if the Amstrad engineers in the UK added the board, or if the work was carried out by the Spanish distributor Indescomp. Rumours and theories abound, but the pictures prove the existence of this fabled machine.

Exposed view

What you can't see from the picture is how stiff the cabling is. It is almost impossible to turn the board over any more than it is in this picture. That, at least, would make it difficult-to-impossible for a casual tax inspector to notice that the pins were not connected.

```
GOTO 640 : REM Ought to be enough for anybody
GOTO 1701 : REM Licensed and unlicensed material
GOTO 38911 : REM Bytes
```

64 : Custom keyboard for the Commodore 64

An epic alternative keyboard design
From the personal collection of David Youd

```
RETURN
```

65 : ASCII stupid question...

...get a stupid ANSI!

```
GOTO 3 : REM There are three kinds of people in the world...
```

65 : Origins

Of all the originating standards, ASCII (American Standard Code for Information Interchange) is one of the oldest, first published in 1963, although its roots are in a much earlier teleprinter code. The first letter of the alphabet, 'A', is code 65.

Of all the 'my first programming language' posts you might see online, BASIC (as established, Beginners' All-purpose Symbolic Instruction Code) is often cited as the leader. Indeed, it's the reason every major UK high street newsagent and computer store had scrolls of silly messages, facilitated by BASIC and the GOTO 10 instruction. Although the original version of BASIC was known as Dartmouth BASIC, and launched in 1964 with just 15 instruction types, it didn't get the necessary character string abilities until the following year. So, from a certain point of view, most developers around today had their origins in a language created in 1965.

Of all the developers and retro enthusiasts in the world today, most would consider themselves part of Generation X, characterised (rightly or wrongly) as being cynical and disaffected. But the Gen X generation hit the sweet spot in being young and curious enough at the point when computers began moving into the home and took up residence under the family TV. While many institutions disagree on the final birth year of Gen Xers (the US Federal Reserve Board uses 1980, whereas the Brookings Institution suggests 1981) they both agree on the first birth year: that members of Generation X were first born in 1965.

Coincidence?

GOTO 151 : REM Pokémon

70 : Bugs

At a quarter to four on the afternoon of 9 September 1947, Admiral Grace Hopper discovered a bug. Literally. A moth had been found in one of the relays, causing the Mark II Aiken computer at Harvard University to malfunction.

Hopper's logbook reads simply:

15:45 Relay #70 Panel F (moth) in relay. First actual case of bug being found.

Although this might be considered the moth-er of all bugs, it was not the first time the term was used. Edison had used it in a figurative sense, to mean things that go wrong because a bug is crawling around inside a (mechanical) machine, looking to break it.

In this case the bug came off worse than the program; the repeated opening and closing of the relay contacts would have beaten it to death with the same certainty as a member of the USS Enterprise beaming down to an unknown planet while wearing a red shirt! But there were worse errors to come that affected computing.

9/9

0800 antan started
1000 " stopped - antan ✓ {1.2700 9.037 847 025
     13 °c (032) MP - MC {...} 9.037 846 795 conect
     (032) PRO 2 2.130476415) 4.615925059(-2)
         conect 2.130676415
     Relays 6-2 m 033 failed special speed test
     In tuboy " 11.000 test "
         Relays changed
1100 Started Cosine Tape (Sine check)
1525 Started Mult + Adder Test.

1545 Relay #70 Panel F
      (moth) in relay.

     First actual case of bug being found.
1630 antangent started.
1700 closed down.

Source: US Navy. NH 96566-KN

At one level there is the benign, but logically suspect, error message of:

Keyboard not found, press F1 to continue

This can occur as part of the PC boot up process known as the BIOS, or Basic Input Output System. There was a common error handling routine which would either allow you to continue (via F1), or to enter setup mode (with F2). Consequently, the text would have been dynamically generated, giving the programmers plausible deniability over the infamously stupid message.

Another example of an embarrassing bug, though less benign in this case, is the strange text in Generation I Pokémon games where the character MissingNo appears. The glitch happens as part of the Old Man's tutorial when the player's name is copied from the usual part of its memory to a temporary store (so that the player can be called 'Old Man' during the tutorial). Unfortunately, that temporary data store gets overwritten by wild Pokémon so when there's a wild battle on Cinnabar's east coast, the characters of the player's new name are used to determine the species of Pokémon you encounter.

Further up the chain are the totally infuriating bugs which stop the user being able to complete their task and might require the developer to send out updates.

One famous example of this is the Software Projects game *Jet Set Willy*, released in 1984, where bugs meant the game could not be completed. Annoying for the players who sank hours into the game before finding out from next month's magazine, and expensive for the publisher who had to remaster the cassettes with corrected versions. (The player's ire probably doubled knowing that there was a prize for the first person to complete the game, and this bug meant they'd just suffered a setback.)

Even further along the scale are those bugs with fatal, or potentially fatal, consequences. For example, in 1962 the Atlas Agena rocket carrying Mariner 1, America's first interplanetary spacecraft, was forced to self-destruct because it moved too far off-course and NASA didn't want it accidentally crashing into a populated area. Luckily, home and microcomputers are used in such low-risk environments that we should suffer nothing more painful than a frustrating game.

```
GOTO 4 : REM Bugs in Jet Set Willy
GOTO 13 : REM Level 13
GOTO 14 : REM Canary traps
GOTO 135 : REM Easter eggs
GOTO 147 : REM CLS
GOTO 256 : REM The Pac-Man kill screen
GOTO 256 : REM The $2.56 reward program
GOTO 65495 : REM Going faster
GOSUB 4 : REM The first computer bug
```

```
70 PRINT TAB(9,12) "K & M .... UP & DOWN"
```

80 : Columns

The mark of a high-end computer was the quality of its text output. The 22 columns of a VIC-20 were clearly a toy when compared to the 32 characters of the Spectrum or the 40 of the Commodore 64. Both, in turn, looked paltry compared to mode 0 on the BBC Micro, which had 80. For 80 characters is what you needed for quality word processing. It's a number which originates with the punched cards that IBM introduced in 1928 because 80 holes could be reliably punched (and read) on the size of cards that Herman Hollerith, the statistician and inventor, had previously used to collate the 1890 US Census results. Hollerith chose the size to be 3¼ x 7⅜ inches, to match the US currency of the time, so that they could be stored in drawers that already existed and were in use by banks.

The 80 column editors are still the standard and originate from here.

And it has more truth than the idea that the space shuttle was designed with the size of a horse's ass in mind!

RETURN

80 : Tangerine Microtan 65

Among the many computer kits available in 1979, the M65 was one that wanted to be more. Although the base unit was capacity-challenged, with a mere 1 KiB of RAM, 1 KiB of ROM, and a hexpad keyboard, the modular design, with its 80-pin connectors, allowed more memory, graphics resolution, disks, and serial ports to be connected, ultimately turning itself into a 3U rack unit machine, with a full keyboard and a multitude of programming language options.

It also connected to a TV, rather than use the eight seven-segment LEDs present in most kits. While many machines that used TV displays in this era faced the problem of flickering images, the M65 didn't. Knowing that the flicker occurs if both the display circuitry and the CPU access memory at the same time, the easy solution is to build circuitry that stops it from happening. The cheap solution is to realise that there is a point in the 6502 timeline when the CPU never tries to access memory, and so instead of adding hardware you simply ask the display circuits to only access the memory at these points in the timeline.

Masterful!

Richard Owens considers this to be their favourite machine.

GOTO 6 : REM Oric Atmos

80 : Sharp MZ-80A

If a Zilog Z80-based machine from 1981 makes you think of limitations, then you're probably thinking of the ZX81. But unlike its more famous Sinclair rival, the MZ-80A had upper and lower case characters, a proper keyboard, sound, a printer port, up to 48 KiB of RAM (32492 bytes usable) and a 40x25 character display. What they had in common, though, were creative users. ZX81 developers discovered that you could trick the computer into believing the character set was stored somewhere else in memory, achieving a pseudo-hires mode. Sharp users realised that with careful timing you could change which 'Sharpscii' character would appear *whilst it was being drawn*, achieving a similar pseudo-hires effect by combining the top half of one character with the lower half of another.

Physically, it was an all-in-one box, with both monitor and tape deck built-in with the keyboard. Contrastingly, in the firmware, where the ROM contained only the necessary OS components, the BASIC interpreter needed to be loaded. Every time.

At least you could load a different language, if you wished, without having to lose memory to a BASIC interpreter you'd never use.

Ben Sharpworks considers this to be their favourite machine.

GOTO 2 : REM Epson QX-16

80 : RC2014

Not all 8-bit retro machines were built in the 8-bit era. The RC2014 dates from 2013, and originated with the desire to build a replica Sinclair ZX80. In 1980, it was the norm for hobbyists to build their own machines. It was a double win: purchasers of the kit version would often save £20 on the £99.95 pre-built version, and advertisements could claim it as being 'under £80*' – that asterisk meant it was £79.95, and assumed your time building, debugging, rebuilding and re-debugging was all worth less than £20!

The RC2014 follows on from the Sinclair ZX80 and Altair 8800, adopting a backplane which does nothing except connect each module together: the CPU, ROM, RAM, serial I/O and clock. As history follows, it repeats. Just as in the 1980s, hobbyists are now taking the basic RC2014 and putting it in their own projects, such as with RCade, or creating modules to interface with an LED matrix, IDE hard drive or ZX Printer.

One nice feature for tinkerers is that the 64 KiB ROM is framed as eight banks of 8 KiB so you can store completely different OSes (or alternate versions of the same one) in different banks, and switch between them by simply moving the upper address lines of A13, A14, and A15 between 0 and 1.

Spencer Owen, unsurprisingly, considers this to be their favourite machine!

GOTO 14 : REM Computer kits

80 : Sinclair ZX80

The ZX80 was the first true microcomputer from Sinclair Research Ltd, who later went on to major success with the Sinclair ZX Spectrum. Named after the Z80 chip inside it (the 'X' standing for the secret extra ingredient, according to the Sinclair PR machine), it was the first UK machine to sell for under £100, fully built.

GOTO 81 : REM Sinclair ZX81

```
80 PRINT TAB(9,16) CHR$(130); "PRESS A KEY TO START"
```

81 : Sinclair ZX81

This was an evolution of Sinclair's previous machine, the ZX80. So much so that you could replace the ROM in the ZX80 with that of the ZX81 and get a very similar experience. Reports differ to whether the '81 was named as an increment from '80 or to match the year of release. If it is the latter, however, this may be the only computer to be named for its year of release! (The vast majority are named by their memory, with the ordinal number of their release coming a distant second.)

Its creator, Sir Clive Sinclair, died in 2021 at the age of 81.

GOTO 16 : REM RAM Pack
GOTO 82 : REM Sinclair ZX Spectrum+

82 : Sinclair ZX Spectrum+

If you were a true Sinclair fan on the 6th of April 1986, then you probably hated Amstrad on the 7th! Their purchase of the name and brand had suddenly illuminated the harsh economic truth of the hobbyist industry: love can be bought. Yet, the machine originally given the name ZX82 went on to last another six years, until 1992, under Amstrad's stewardship – compared to four with Sinclair. And they produced more variants of the machine than anyone else.

But not *everyone* else.

Outside of the officially licensed clones (all made by Timex, and destined for either Spain or India), there were many others, made mostly across Eastern Europe and South America. (At the time of writing, Wikipedia lists an amusingly coincidental 82 of them.) These locations are not a coincidence. During the 1980s Europe was still divided into 'East' and 'West' with modern electronics being too expensive – and often too illegal – to travel to the former, so copies were built from smuggled Western versions. The law also prevented imports into South America, so their clones, such as the Microdigital TK90X and TK95, became very popular.

The Spectrum+ was identical to the original 48 K design, meaning there were no compatibility issues; it had a proper keyboard – if less iconic – and provided a much needed reset button. This reset button could have been added by any first-year electronics student, as it comprised of a single switch that pulled pin 26 of the CPU to ground (0v). In fact, converting an original Spectrum into a + could be done with a DIY conversion kit.

Consequently, of the four official Sinclair Spectrums, the Spectrum+ was probably the best expression of the original intent, which might be why Mark Steele considers this to be their favourite machine.

GOTO 399 : REM Sinclair QL

84 : LCD displays

For many, the Nintendo Game Boy (1989) represented the first use of an LCD (Liquid Crystal Displays) in a gaming device. But for some of us, there is an example which predates this by nine years.

In 1980, Nintendo produced the Game & Watch, a small handheld device, inspired by a calculator, which could play games and display the time. Later versions improved upon this by providing an alarm, too. The images were fixed in place and could be on or off, so animation consisted of turning one LCD segment off and the next one on. Furthermore, each LCD section had to be distinct from the others, enforcing an aesthetic whereby any character limb intended for animation had to be completely separate from the body, like a ring pull from a 1980s can of cola. It also followed that segments could not cross over each other.

Squibs Arcade – a modern software remake

The Game & Watch port of *Donkey Kong*, introduced in 1982, gave us another innovation, the D-pad. Like the arcade version of *Space Invaders*, it would use the physicality of the device to overlay high quality colour artwork over the black-and-white electronic display to increase the visual appeal of the machine.

Despite the limitations of the device a total of 61 games were created, selling over 43.4 million units worldwide. Each of these games had two variations, 'Game

A' and 'Game B', although 'Game B' was usually only a faster and more difficult version of 'Game A'. After all, with a singular set of images, it was difficult to make any significant changes to the game play, although the games *Squish* and *Flagman* did attempt to do so.

The Game Boy in 1989 marked the next advancement of the LCD screen, with a 160x144 pixel screen with four colours – or rather, four shades of green! There was, however, a trick that developers discovered: because it takes a short but definite amount of time for the LCD to change state, they could create a transparent image by turning the LCD on and off on alternate frames.

As for the connection to the number 84, it is the number of LCD segments in the first Game & Watch game, *Ball*.

```
GOTO 205.5 : REM How to draw a maze in one line
GOTO 16509 : REM ZX81 1K Display
GOTO 2455992 : REM The Cathode Ray Tube
GOTO 16777216 : REM Colour
```

86 : BBC cassettes

The BBC Micro didn't just have problems with tapes loading incorrectly... it had problems when saving! The first version of the operating system (released in 1981 and called 0.1) would occasionally mis-save the first block (called block 0) of the program. By being unable to load the first block, all subsequent blocks would fail, and the program was lost. There was a program, *cat, which was intended to verify the recording, but it didn't actually test that the program was valid, only that there was *something* there on the tape.

Acorn BBC Micro, Model B
Image courtesy of The Centre for Computing History, Cambridge

The pain doesn't stop there! If you tried to verify the contents of the tape by re-loading the program it would erase the program currently in memory. Which was fine if the recording worked, but if it failed, you would have no program in memory to re-save, and no usable recording either.

So, what was an Acorn user to do? Ingeniously, the idea was to load the program back as a raw block of memory, which stopped the original program from being erased in case the load failed. Furthermore, if your program was large, there wouldn't be room for two copies in memory at once, so you'd load it into memory address 32768 (0x8000 in hex). This was in read-only memory, and the operating system was broken enough to not realise!

As a result, the loading routines would bring the program data in from the tape, verifying it as it went, and would attempt to write it into ROM. Since the loading routines didn't check that the data was written correctly into memory, it didn't stop with an error and would continue checking the file.

The command, in case you're curious, was:

```
*load "", 8000
```

Early users were pleased to know that this bug was fixed promptly in version 1.0 of the OS.

```
GOTO 6 : REM Oric Atmos
GOTO 1200 : REM Acorn BBC Micro baud rate
```

99 : Press to continue

Before joypads, joysticks, and wimpy graphical user interfaces – windows, icons, mice and pointers – you had to type your responses. There was no cancel button. So how would a retro game request input, but also give you the option to say 'thanks, but no thanks'?

Machine code programmers could intercept the break, or escape, key and simply move on to the next part of the code. If you did that with a BASIC program, however, the game would stop, and you would have to hope you could restart it again. Sometimes that was easily done with:

CONT

This CONTinued with the next instruction. Otherwise, it would re-run the same line again. But that led to complications on many machines which incorporated several instructions on a single line. You might be breaking out of instruction 5 of 8 on that line, but `GOTO 3020` would restart the game on instruction 1 of 8. At which point, anything could happen.

So BASIC programmers had two methods: `INKEY$` and `INPUT`.

`INKEY$` was the better option, since it checked the keyboard at that precise moment in time and didn't wait for the user to hit return. This was the only option for real-time BASIC games. It was also used to pause the game until the user hit 'any' key, or as part of a 'Play again?' prompt. In magazines you would often see code like:

```
200 PRINT "Play again?"
210 I$ = INKEY$
220 IF I$ = "Y" THEN GOTO 10
230 IF I$ <> "N" THEN GOTO 210
230 STOP
```

But this approach was tedious if you wanted more than one character to be entered. At that point it would be easier to use `INPUT`, which accepted an arbitrary number of characters from the user and continued onto the next line only after enter, or return, had been pressed.

```
200 PRINT "Play again?"
210 INPUT A$
220 IF A$ = "Y" OR A$ = "YES" OR A$ = "y" THEN GOTO 10
230 STOP
```

The only complication would then come if you wanted to offer the player the option of saying 'none of the above'. You needed to represent this with an alternate value. Say 0. Or -1. Or 99.

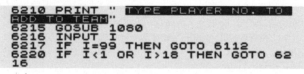

Football Manager - ZX81
Source code by Kevin Toms

Opinions differ on the best value to use. But this real-life BASIC example, taken from Kevin Toms' 1982 series of *Football Manager* games, uses 99 and features in both the Sinclair ZX81 and Spectrum versions. So, you had to select either the football player by their number or 99 to continue. This came from Toms' time working on mainframes where it was often used for menu selections, when all you had was a keyboard and needed a generic two-digit field, and so it trickled down in the Sinclair machines of the 1980s.

It's interesting to note that in BASIC

```
INPUT A
```

asks the user for a *number*, and only a number. Depending on the variant of BASIC, this input mechanism would sometimes allow you to write:

```
90 + 9
```

and INPUT would evaluate the expression to 99 before assigning it to the variable in question.

In contrast,

```
INPUT A$
```

would accept a text string, which could include letters and punctuation as well as numbers. Naturally the former could not support words like 'none', but either would permit 99 to be entered, so Toms used that convention throughout. So much so that when he recreated the game as *Football Star* Manager* on iOS and Android in 2016 people asked that he include '99 to Continue' as an option. Which he did.

(However, blindly accepting *any* number assigned through INPUT A could cause its own problems. In Firebird Software's *The Wild Bunch*, for example, it was possible to buy *half* a gun by writing 0.5 or 1/2 into the input field!)

Of course, he could have used A$ in all cases, but that would require additional code to convert the string into a number, and validation logic to check it really was a number. Both would require extra memory that the ZX81 version certainly couldn't afford.

```
GOTO 10 : REM Disabling the break key
GOTO 99 : REM Dots
```

99 : Dots

There are 99 dots in the Acorn logo, as seen on the BBC Micro.

GOTO 99 : REM Press to continue

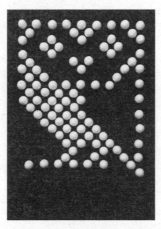

The Acorn owl made from polystyrene balls

100 : The extent of computer upgrades

In metaphysics there is a question that asks whether an object – let's call it the Ship of Theseus – is the same object after all of its original constitute parts have been changed for others. What about just one part? Or two? Is there a point when it can no longer be called the Ship of Theseus, and should instead be referred to as 'The Ship – version 2'?

(To simplify the question one could instead ask if a broom, with just a brush head and handle, is the same broom if we triggered changes in both items!)

A similar question exists for us with microcomputers since most of them could be upgraded throughout their lives. Sometimes this would be as simple, and necessary, as adding a tape deck or disc drive, or an improvement to the input devices with perhaps a joystick or light pen. Or even a plug-in speech synthesiser or video digitiser.

In the case of the MITS Altair 8800, available in 1975, upgrades were essential since the computer which the designer, Ed Roberts, wanted to make wasn't possible on a single board. Instead, he designed a *backplane* which did little more than connect together removable circuit boards, one of which would contain the CPU, another memory, and so on. These boards were connected using 100-pin edge connectors, and so became the S-100 bus. (This standard was also used by the 1978 machine, the Exidy Sorcerer.) Having the entire bus exposed to every device meant that literally anything was possible since each card could have full control of the machine – be it data, addresses, or power – without being limited by the protocols of a more focused connector, such as a serial or parallel port.

This idea continued into the 1980s, with most machines having an exposed connector for peripheral devices. The Apple II had multiple connectors mounted inside the case, while the Commodore 64 had just one visible, at the rear of the machine. Some manufacturers would build peripherals which extended the courtesy by providing a 'through' connector on their device, for further expansion. Some didn't. And some, like the Acorn Electron, needed a special add-on (the Plus 1) before *other* peripherals could be added!

The most exotic hardware peripherals usually belonged to the Sinclair family of machines, probably because the machines started off so limited! But this idea of modular computing allowed Sinclair to sell, and people to buy, a very cheap computer and upgrade only what they felt was lacking for their specific purpose. This launched a cottage industry, in both hardware and software, along with magazines, user groups, and Microfairs.

But a computer made in 1981, like the ZX81, doesn't need to stay in the past. For example, the ZXpand+ now provides extra RAM, a sound chip, and joystick port, along with an SD card interface and serial port. Or there's the Chroma 81 which provides colour to existing games, and hi-res graphics. But given this means a black-and-white, mute, 1 KiB computer from 1981 can now provide colour, Atari ST-quality sound, with 40 KiB of usable RAM – along with serial ports, joysticks, and SD memory – can this still be called a ZX81?

```
GOTO 4  : REM Peripherals for processing
GOTO 28 : REM Peripherals for output
GOTO 30 : REM Storage
GOTO 31 : REM Peripherals for input
```

103 : Research Machines 380Z

For a machine to survive in schools, it needs to be rugged. This certainly applies to version 1 wetware (i.e. pupils), version 2 wetware (i.e. teachers), and hardware. Apart from the Acorn BBC Micro and ZX Spectrum, only the RML 380Z made it onto the approved list for UK schools. Its 19-inch black metal case made it well-suited to the tough job, as well as it matching the colour of boys' National Health spectacles.

Internally, the 380Z was also a machine to be reckoned with. Despite a reclusive reign, between 1977 and 1985, it came with a kingly 64 KiB of RAM (of which 56 was user usable), CP/M, and fully upgradeable design courtesy of a passive backplane which held a number of cards. One could upgrade the machine with more RAM, graphics capabilities, or floppy disks, networks and serial interfaces.

The memory monitor was accessed by Ctrl+F, which allowed the usual functions for entering hex codes and jumping to specific memory locations. One such instruction, J103, would resume the current program via a warm restart, had anyone – usually another pupil – hit the reset button conveniently located on the front panel!

Phil Steer considers this to be their favourite machine.

```
GOTO 128 : REM Elan Enterprise 128
```

110 : Fulbourn Road

The address in Cambridge, England, which housed Sinclair's main rival, Acorn, and later ARM.

The decimal of 110 is 6.

```
GOTO 6 : REM King's Parade
GOTO 199 : REM Acorn Electron
```

```
110 ENVELOPE
    1,1,16,12,200,3,1,5,126,0,0,-126,126,126
120 VDU 23,241,66,60,126,219,255,102,189,129
```

127 : 127 or 255?

An 8-bit byte can store numbers as high as either 127 or 255, depending on whether you treat the value as signed or unsigned. While it might seem beneficial to want to use the whole 0 to 255 range on small 8-bit machines, this was rarely done as negative numbers are more than casually useful, since, without them, we could never jump backwards in a program.

Instead of using all the bits, there are many cases where the range is intentionally limited to 0 to 127, so the seventh (aka the most significant) bit could be used for other purposes. Many BASIC interpreters would use this as a termination bit, so the BASIC keyword 'POKE', for example, would not be stored by the ASCII values of 80, 79, 75 and 69, but as 80, 79, 75 and 197. In this way, the CPU could check for the last character in the string by looking only at the most significant bit to see if it was set. This saved memory by not requiring an extra byte to store only a terminating character, such as 0 (NUL).

The choice to use the most significant bit as a terminator helped in writing more compact implementations of BASIC. Since the most significant bit, 128, is also treated as -128, CPUs would have a 'negative flag' which would be set after arithmetic operations where the result had this bit set. Since this flag would be set automatically from the previous instruction, the termination logic happened for free.

Often the total range would be limited to 1–127, as this left zero free for internal use. This is why the number of supported printers in Windows 2.1 is 127.

```
GOTO 2 : REM 2's complement
GOTO 8 : REM Bits in a byte
GOTO 1000 : REM A kilobyte
GOSUB 128 : REM Bytes
```

128 : Bytes

To visualize just how little available RAM there is in the Atari 2600, consider that this sentence is the same size – 128 bytes!

```
RETURN
```

128 : Elan Enterprise 128

Delays are an accepted, although unacceptable, part of the technology industry. Sinclair famously took many months to deliver some of their products, only for them to be returned the following day for repair. Back in 1983 when, on average, two computers were released every month, the industry was moving so fast that Elan's announcement of a new machine – the Enterprise – capable of addressing 4 MiB of RAM, with custom chips for graphics (called 'Nick') and sound ('Dave'), felt like the next generation was about to arrive early.

The Enterprise landed in 1985. Late.

The industry had moved on a lot since the machine's inception, and the company was in too much financial trouble to support it properly, or provide software through its Entersoft business, so it faded from the geek consciousness of the time.

What remains is a deferred success with a small following in Hungary (of the EP128, not the EP64), and memories of the primary colours used on the buttons that might have inspired the Amstrad CPC464.

Paula Maddox considers this to be their favourite machine. (As does Spencer Shanson, who mentions it as their favourite 'obscure' one!)

GOTO 11 : REM Luxor ABC 80

```
130 VDU 23,240,24,60,255,110,239,110,239,189
```

135 : Easter eggs

There are many types of Easter egg, but the overall definition can be said to relate to any piece of code or data that can be discovered, without impacting on the software itself. It is a loose definition that might overlap with canary traps when the outcome is always benign.

In its simplest form, an Easter egg would be a piece of text that could only be discovered by looking in the right place. On the Acorn BBC Micro, for example, 768 bytes near the end of memory contain a 'Thanks' list to the various 'contributors to the development of the BBC Computer'. What makes this case interesting is the memory in question (inside the OS 1.2 ROM between memory addresses $FC00 and $FF00) overlaps with the IO system, so you can't easily retrieve the data.

But when the ROM code was visible in its entirely, programmers would often employ steganography to hide the text, lest a manager question why their development budget was being used on non-essential trivialities. On the Commodore PET the implementation of BASIC was supplied by Microsoft and, concerned their code might be used elsewhere, included a piece of code triggered by the BASIC command:

WAIT 6502,1

It would then process and print a series of bytes, hidden in amongst some hard-coded constants used in the sine function. Those clandestine bytes were:

A1 54 46 8F 13 8F 52 43 89 CD

A simple analysis of these numbers shows nothing untoward. Most are not even valid characters. So, let's rewrite them as binary.

```
10100001 01010100 01000110 10001111 00010011
10001111 01010010 01000011 10001001 11001101
```

Then replace the first two bits in each number with 00, as would happen with the simple instruction "AND 00111111", also known as masking off the bits.

```
00100001 00010100 00000110 00001111 00010011
00001111 00010010 00000011 00001001 00001101
```

Now, every number falls within the range of valid characters which, because this was the Commodore PET, is not ASCII but its own format, PETSCII. But as a piece of good luck waiting to happen, PETSCII character 1 is an A, character 2 is a B, etc, so we only need to look up the Nth letter of the alphabet:

00100001 (binary) => 21 (hex) => 33 (decimal) => !
00010100 (binary) => 14 (hex) => 20 (decimal) => T
00000110 (binary) => 06 (hex) => 6 (decimal) => F
And so on, until we have:

!TFOSORCIM

Looking backwards, the next step going forwards should be obvious!

The final kicker is that the text was written directly to screen memory, not via the usual text printing code, so any programmer who uncovered the message by accident could not simply look at the 'print to screen' routine to reverse-engineer the secret.

Microsoft introduced a different Easter egg, with even more obfuscation, in their BASIC ROM for the KIM-1. Repeating their modus operandi for backwards text, ending in an exclamation mark, hidden in mathematical constants, they included the bytes:

A6 D3 C1 C8 D4 C8 D5 C4 CE CA

This time, you could only uncover the message if you performed an XOR operation on every byte with the magic hex number 0x87 (or 135, in decimal).

The XOR truth table was

A	B	Result
0	0	0
0	1	1
1	0	1
1	1	0

So, writing those hidden bytes in binary, along with the number 0x87 (10000111), you can perform an XOR on each pair of binary digits to produce a set of numbers which map directly onto ASCII.

```
Data:    10100110 11010011 11000001 11001000 11010100
0x87:    10000111 10000111 10000111 10000111 10000111

Result:  00100001 01010100 01000110 01001111 01010011

Data:    11001000 11010101 11000100 11001110 11001010
0x87:    10000111 10000111 10000111 10000111 10000111

Result:  00100001 01010100 …
```

And now over to you, dear reader …

When text is no longer adequate, or you have unused space in the ROM, then graphics are the next logical step (and a lot more interesting than random junk that would otherwise be used). For example, if you were to hold down the CTRL and ALT keys of a Tandy Color Computer 3 (aka the CoCo 3) then you'd see an image of 'The Three Mugateers' – Mark Hawkins, Tim Harris and Todd Earles, who were the Microware employees that worked on the BASIC interpreter for Tandy.

The 'Easter' in 'Easter eggs' is, unsurprisingly, named for the traditional Easter egg hunt which is one of the few movable feast days in the Western calendar, determined by algorithm set out by the First Council of Nicaea in the year 325.

```
GOTO 4  : REM Bugs in Jet Set Willy
GOTO 10 : REM PRINT "Always get someone to cheque your work. ";
GOTO 13 : REM Level 13
GOTO 13 : REM ROT
GOTO 14 : REM Canary traps
GOTO 70 : REM Bugs
```

```
GOTO 147 : REM CLS
GOTO 256 : REM The Pac-Man kill screen
GOTO 256 : REM The $2.56 reward program
```

147 : CLS

The CLS command, which clears the screen, would seem to be a fixture in all dialects of BASIC – except two! The Apple preferred the phrase HOME, while Commodore opted to save space by not including the command at all, opting for the less subtle

```
PRINT CHR$(147)
```

This worked because the Commodore 64 had a set of character codes which, instead of printing to the screen, *did* something special like moving the cursor, sounding a bell, or clearing the screen. (The idea of character codes still exists in most modern terminals. The most well-known is when the CTRL+G command triggers a bell sound instead of printing character 7.)

For this 'something special' to happen, the routine which output a character to the screen (at address $E716) needed to check every single input and jump to an appropriate piece of code when a special character was detected. In this case, everything of '128 and above' was considered special, so 128 was subtracted (147 – 128 = 19, or $13 in hex) and a series of comparison checks were made culminating in this one, which jumped to the clear screen subroutine at $E544.

```
Address Machine code hex    Assembly instruction mnemonic
E86A C9 13                  CMP #$13
E86C D0 06                  BNE $E874
E86E 20 44 E5               JSR $E544
```

Although Microsoft had written the first versions of Commodore's BASIC, Microsoft's code diverged in later years so that versions of CLS would also accept a number, which cleared the screen to that specific colour. Once the code was written to support that additional argument, Microsoft sensed a window of opportunity that it could be used for other things.

On the Matra Alice 90, the EF9345 video chip permitted both 40- and 80-column wide displays. So, CLS 40 would instigate the former, whilst CLS 80 triggered the latter – a small optimisation that eliminated the need for additional commands like MODE. There was no 25-column mode, yet the computer was happy to accept a CLS 25 instruction to clear the screen... and print the word 'Microsoft' at the top.

Another surprise was that CLS 32 reproduced the character size of the 40-column mode, but placed the 32x16 character display in the middle of a black box.

Just to be different, the BBC Micro had a VDU 12 command which functioned identically to CLS (which it also provided). The reason for it being the number 12 was that L was the 12th letter of the alphabet, and CONTROL+L on the older mainframe machines would be the character code that cleared the screen.

```
GOTO 4 : REM Bugs in Jet Set Willy
GOTO 13 : REM Level 13
GOTO 14 : REM Canary traps
GOTO 70 : REM Bugs
GOTO 135 : REM Easter eggs
GOTO 256 : REM The Pac-Man kill screen
GOTO 256 : REM The $2.56 reward program
GOSUB 80 : REM Columns
```

```
150 X=10: Y=10: MX=20: MY=20: CATCH=0
```

151 : Pokémon

There are 151 Generation 1 Pokémon.

The CALL address for the Apple 2 monitor program is -151.

A MONitor program is where you can POKE memory.

Coincidence?

```
GOTO 42 : REM The meaning of life
```

199 : Acorn Electron

When this tissue-box-sized machine was released on 23 August 1983, at the promised launch price of £199, it was the only affordable way for many parents to get an educational machine into their home. The Electron's BASIC was mostly compatible with that of the BBC Micro used in most UK schools. Unfortunately, or perhaps fortunately if you were a parent at the time, every other aspect was incompatible! Those games written in machine code needed to be manually converted and, with the machine an unknown quantity at launch, not every publisher was prepared to expend the effort.

Eventually, games appeared. But whereas the rich kids could simply copy the BBC Micro games from school, those with the Electron had to form their own buying cliques or type in listings from magazines. The limited hardware meant that most games had to be rewritten specifically for the machine, and so were somewhat inferior to their BBC originators.

Alas, even with the support of Superior Software, Acorn became an Olivetti subsidiary in 1985, as there were enough supply problems to dampen the spirits of most supporters. But not the spirits of Martin John Callanan and Paul James, who both consider the Electro, affectionately known as the Elk, to be their favourite machine!

GOTO 2 : REM BBC Micro

```
200 A$=GET$
```

201 : Cursor keys

When a manufacturer has to pay for every key they place on a keyboard, there is an obvious temptation to limit their number. Even non-moving membrane keyboards, as found on the Sinclair ZX80 and ZX81, have a cost incurred. So it is perhaps unsurprising that many machines would include the cursor functionality on other, previously existing, keys when used in conjunction with shift. However, the manufacturers could never agree on which keys they were.

The original QWERTY keyboards didn't contain cursors, and so you needed to put your software into a particular mode, and use the letters:

h : left   j : down   k : up   l : right

When viewed on a keyboard these run left-to-right in the middle row and matches the order (although not the position) of the cursor keys on the Sinclair machines, which were 5, 6, 7 and 8. But having all the keys on a single row doesn't provide a good experience, since there is no physical relationship between the on-screen action of 'up' and the real-world position of one key being above the others. (The VT-100 terminals used the order up-down-left-right, but were still placed next to each other in a single row.) Consequently, the idea emerged to position horizontal and vertical controls apart. But no one could agree on how, either.

For those that preferred the vertical to be controlled by the left hand the patterns of QAOP and WASD emerged. (Although I personally find my fingers are cramped when using WASD.)

QAOP

The alternative was for the left hand to control the horizontal with the right handling vertical movement, often with ZXKM, although machines like the Acorn BBC Micro had extra keys to the right of K and M which allowed for * and ? to be used, instead. (And kept M free to display the game's map.)

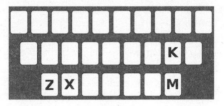

ZXKM

But it wasn't long before more games offered a 'Redefine keys' feature to replace their (seemingly arbitrary choice of) defaults, which kept everyone happy.

When cursor keys were eventually added, designers were in natural agreement that the left cursor would be on the left of the right cursor, but no one agreed on their position on the keyboard as a whole!

But there were always outliers that existed to prove the rule. Maybe by having a special key for up *and* left:

The Exelvision
Photo by the author

Or by having a separate key for every direction:

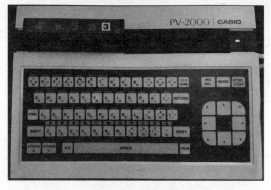

The Casio PV-2000
Photo by the author

This, although apparently redundant, was very helpful since the technical act of scanning the keyboard meant that two keys might be indistinguishable from each other if both were held down.

Ultimately the consensus was to adopt the 1983 'inverse "T"' format; the first keyboard to adopt the layout was the LK201, created by DEC for their VT220 terminals, amongst others. The reason for the layout was that, after studying key stroke logs, the most commonly-used cursor actions (when the key changed) were – in decreasing order of use – down-and-left, then up-and-right, down-and-right, and finally up-and-down. It is easy to see that the keys in each pair can be placed next to each other, and then combined into the inverse T formation.

Inverse T

This position was then cemented by the understanding that the up arrow was the least used of the four cursors, and so was placed above the others.

This format improved on the original IBM layout and was incorporated into their 1985 IBM 3161 terminal. Apple, on the other hand, took a little longer. Steve Jobs had believed that the mouse should be used for cursor positioning, so didn't include *any* cursor keys on the original Macintosh. Although future keyboards had cursors, it was not until 1987 that the M3501 (or Apple Extended Keyboard, to its friends) featured the inverse T.

```
GOTO 5 : REM Keys
GOTO 40 : REM Keyboards
GOTO 80 : REM Sinclair ZX80
GOSUB 64 : REM Custom keyboard for the Commodore 64
```

205.5 : How to draw a maze in one line

This is rather an amusing number, as it forms the foundation of the (in)famous Commodore 64 BASIC program:

```
10 PRINT CHR$(205.5 + RND(1));
20 GOTO 10
```

It prints a random stream of / and \ graphical characters which ultimately form a maze, scrolling up the screen.

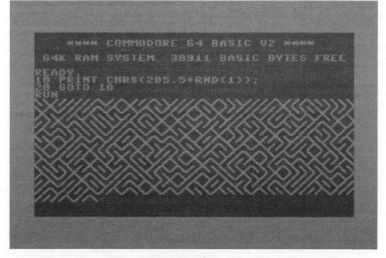

The random maze

It does this by relying on a number of implicit facts about the implementation of Commodore BASIC, V2. Firstly, it uses the fact that all floating point numbers (i.e. those with a fractional part) will be rounded *down* to the nearest whole number, or integer. Down. Never up. It is a process known as 'truncation' and is in contrast with the various rounding techniques used elsewhere in mathematics, such as 'half round up' or common rounding, 'symmetric rounding', or 'banker's rounding'. However, BASIC only performs truncation when it needs to. And it needs to do that in the third step.

The second part, RND(1), indicates that we want a random number between 0 and 1. Again, this is a fraction, making the result somewhere between 205.5 and 206.5. This is one of the three main varieties of the RND instruction used at the time.

The third step passes the sum of 205.5 and the random number between 0 and 1 to CHR$. This is short for character. Every computer has a set of characters where one number maps directly onto one symbol. Most of the time these symbols are recognisable letters of the alphabet or single digits. Sometimes they're graphical images. Since all character sets are integers, the BASIC interpreter running this program spots the floating point number and truncates it, to either 205 or 206, so that CHR$ can generate a sensible character. Characters below 128 are usually – but not always! – in standard ASCII, while those above it are decided by the manufacturer.

By good fortune, the two characters we need for this maze (/ and \) happen to be next to each other in the character set, and so a maze is formed with characters 205 and 206. Other systems weren't so lucky, as the character might be four locations apart, and so needed constructs like RND(1)*4 to make the magic work.

The maze above was rendered from the code on my machine. If you do the same you'll notice that my random maze is exactly the same as yours! Or try it on an emulator. It's the same. It's as if I'd magically predicted what your random numbers would be! I can show this by asking you to boot up a Commodore 64 emulator right now and typing:

```
PRINT RND(1)
```

I should not be able to predict this number, but thanks to (pseudo-)randomness, I think it will be 0.185564016!

```
GOTO 3  : REM Randomness
GOTO 8  : REM CHIP-8
GOTO 84 : REM LCD displays
```

```
GOTO 16509 : REM ZX81 1K Display
GOTO 2455992 : REM The Cathode Ray Tube
GOTO 16777216 : REM Colour
```

```
210 MODE 1: VDU 23;8202;0;0;0;
211 TIME = 0
212 PRINT " CRITTAS : 0 TIME LEFT : "
215 GCOL 0,1
220 S=0: GOSUB 700
```

246 : The Indiana Pi Bill

Thanks to the passing of bill 246 in 1897, the value of Pi was simplified significantly to be exactly 3.2.

It was proposed to the US house of representatives by Edward Goodwin (aka Edwin) who 'proved' you could draw a square with the exact same area as that of a circle – a maths problem known as 'squaring the circle' – if Pi was 3.2, instead of the pesky incidental and transcendental number we known it to be. His proof demonstrates this with a circle of 32 unit circumference and a diameter of 10. Unfortunately for Edwin, this problem had been proven impossible some years earlier. But luckily for him, no one was educated enough to realise the error. So the bill was passed.

His aim was to earn money, in the form of royalties, from anyone outside of Indiana State who used the new value of Pi. By the time the bill had progressed to the Senate, luck, rather than good judgment, had intervened. Professor C. A. Waldo had heard of the proof, and had been able to teach the senators of its fallacy. The bill died here. But the story lives on in various forms that Pi has been proved to be exactly 3, or 4, or some other non-irrational and non-transcendental number.

The author of this book made this standard deviation to make it clear that he is not knowingly related to Edward Goodwin, in any way, although he does celebrate Pi Day, on March 14th, each year. (It's also curious to note the position in the alphabet of the letters in 'Pi day' are the first five perfect squares: 16, 9, 4, 1 and 25.)

```
GOTO 3 : REM Optimising for size
GOTO 80 : REM Sinclair ZX80
```

250 : Acorn Archimedes

When Acorn introduced the Archimedes in June 1987 it made the leap from 8- to 32-bit machines, skipping the 16-bit option, having chosen to bet on their BBC Model B+ and Master systems to maintain the company's relevance. Their continuation of the 8-bit product line resulted in supply chain issues, unfulfilled orders, and unpaid bills, all of which helped cement the death of their company, yet gave birth to the modern era via the ARM chip.

Acorn Archimedes 440/1
Image courtesy of The Centre for Computing History, Cambridge

The origins of the Archimedes began with a series of papers discussing the theoretical idea of RISC (Reduced Instruction Set Computer) from a computing group in Berkeley and Western Design Center who were putting it to practical use. This grandiose design centre was, in fact, a bungalow in the suburbs of Mesa! This inspired the two designers of the BBC Micro, Sophie Wilson and Steve Furber, who realised that building their own silicon wasn't an impossible option. From this they created the ARM as a main CPU for the Archimedes, to be supported by the MEMC (memory controller), IOC (IO controller) and VIDC (video controller).

Speed didn't just come from the RISC architecture. Using a single 32-bit register for both the program counter (PC) and eight condition code flags (CC) meant that the whole CPU state could be saved with just one instruction, making interrupts twice as quick as those with separate PC and CC registers. Having the MEMC control the memory meant that it could prevent the CPU from accessing memory when it wanted, facilitating direct memory access (DMA) to quickly transfer data to and from memory without needing the CPU to do it.

Coupled with the hardware was the software. When jittery management got cold feet, aware of the money spent on a Xerox Parc-like institution called Acorn Research Centre, they switched to plan B and produced an OS called Arthur, and then RISC OS (formally known as RISC OS2). But without anything requiring a strict adherence to system libraries, like the Intuition library of the Amiga, developers *could* customise the user interface as they saw fit, creating a less than uniform interface.

It is difficult to determine whether the Eureka moment belongs to ARM for the chip or Acorn for the computer, as the majority of the benefits of the latter stem from the former. However, there is the infamous story that when a lot of noise was noted on the audio channels – which couldn't be eliminated through normal engineering – the solution was to take the (noisy) output, invert it, and add it back to the input signal, thereby cancelling it out like modern headphones!

By combining the MEMC, IOC and VIDC with the CPU in 1992 to produce the ARM250, Acorn had accidentally invented the 'modern' idea of system-on-a-chip. Which might provide some comfort, knowing they weren't the first to produce commercial RISC chips – that honour goes to the MIPS R2000.

Steve Mars considers this to be their favourite machine.

GOTO 4 : REM Peripherals for processing
GOTO 99 : REM Dots

256 : Nintendo Game Boy Boot ROM

The real-world phrase 'Pull Yourself Up by Your Bootstraps', meaning to improve through your own efforts, has been adopted into computing parlance and shortened to simply boot, or bootstrap. It is a piece of very small software held permanently in a computer so that it knows how to start up, and it appears throughout computing, from the !BOOT file on Acorn DFS diskettes to the PC BIOS, which prepares the machine for use before a user-installed operating system can take over.

At the hardware level a Z80 processor begins with whatever instruction is at memory location 0. On the Game Boy, this location holds a boot ROM to initialise the system. In just 256 bytes this ROM will:

- Initialise the system by setting up a stack and clearing memory
- Initialise the audio
- Initialise the LCD display and colour palette
- Display and animate the Nintendo logo (also stored in these 256 bytes)

- Play the 'ping' sound
- Check the cartridge is valid
- Turn off the boot ROM by writing '1' to the special memory location of 65360 ($FF50)

At this point, the program counter is at memory location 256 ($100) so the cartridge code executes automatically, with access to its first 256 bytes.

However, it is the penultimate step which is most interesting.

To ensure that only licensed developers could release games on the Game Boy, this boot ROM would check that the game cartridge contained a predetermined block of data, as supplied by Nintendo, at a predetermined memory location. If it did, the game would start. If not, the Game Boy simply locked up by jumping back and forth between the same two memory locations of 232 and 233.

What was the data? It was 48 bytes of memory, stored at memory location 260, containing the Nintendo logo. Not coincidentally, its exact same data was used to display the logo when the Game Boy boots up. By requiring that every game included a duplicate of the Nintendo logo, it ensured that any unlicensed products could be taken to court because they:

1. hadn't obtained permission to use their logo (a breach of trademark law) and
2. were using a copy of their data (a copyright violation).

```
GOTO 0 : REM First!
GOTO 6 : REM Nintendo Game Boy
GOTO 256 : REM The $2.56 reward program
GOTO 256 : REM The Pac-Man kill screen
GOTO 1701 : REM Licensed and unlicensed material
```

256 : The $2.56 reward program

In 1962 Donald Knuth began writing a series of books called *The Art of Computer Programming*, covering the fundamentals of computing algorithms. (He still hasn't finished them!) They are as revered in computer science as Einstein's work on relativity are in physics. Such is the precision of his work and writing that anyone finding an original bug is entitled to a reward of at least 0x$1.00 (or 256 cents). This bounty includes uncovering factual errors, typos or software bugs.

Such is the prestige of finding an error that the cheques were rarely cashed. (As Knuth himself says, they are kept and *cached*.)

```
GOTO 1   : REM I'd buy that for a dollar
GOTO 4   : REM Bugs in Jet Set Willy
GOTO 9   : REM Nine Tiles
GOTO 10  : REM New pence
GOTO 13  : REM Level 13
GOTO 14  : REM Canary traps
GOTO 70  : REM Bugs
GOTO 135 : REM Easter eggs
GOTO 147 : REM CLS
GOTO 256 : REM Nintendo Game Boy Boot ROM
GOTO 256 : REM The Pac-Man kill screen
GOSUB 4  : REM The first computer bug
```

256 : The *Pac-Man* kill screen

An 8-bit machine can store 256 distinct values, usually numbered 0 to 255. What it cannot do is store the number 256.

'So what?' you might ask.

Well, since 8-bit machines couldn't represent the numbers 256 or higher, the number 256 would simply 'wrap-around' to 0. And 257 would appear as 1. 258 would be 2. And so on. (This is why it is illegal for trains in Switzerland to have 256 axles, because track detectors use the wheel count to determine information about the train just passed, and a 256-axle train would get counted as 0, and therefore not present!)

So, if an 8-bit value represented the current level in a computer game, for example, but the player was never expected to reach level 256, there would be no problem. But even if they did reach that level, the programmer might believe the game would function as it normally did on level 0. But if that game was *Pac-Man*, and the first level was 1, not 0, then something beautiful happened...

This is the '*Pac-Man* kill screen' which, despite the name, doesn't harm the player. (In contrast, the 22nd level of arcade classic *Donkey Kong* does kill the player.) Instead, it makes the level impossible to finish so you can do nothing more than run around until the ghosts catch you.

However, it isn't the level data which corrupts the screen, it's the level *counter*! *Pac-Man* described each level by a row of (up to seven) fruits, drawn in the bottom right corner of the screen. If that level was 256, the level counter would draw fruits from 1 to 256, which it would view as being from 1 to 0. Since the program code that drew these fruits didn't consider this possibility it didn't stop drawing at seven fruits, and kept going until all 256 were drawn. Because of this, quirks in how the fruit graphics were stored, and how the screen memory is positioned, it meant that non-fruit graphics were used and drawn vertically down the screen, and from right to left.

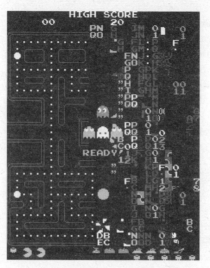

The infamous impasse

What a mess!

PS Even the best programmers I know have, at least once in their lives, tried to fit the number 256 into 8 bits. Yours truly, among them!

```
GOTO 4 : REM Bugs in Jet Set Willy
GOTO 13 : REM Level 13
GOTO 14 : REM Canary traps
GOTO 70 : REM Bugs
GOTO 135 : REM Easter eggs
GOTO 147 : REM CLS
GOTO 256 : REM Nintendo Game Boy Boot ROM
GOTO 256 : REM The $2.56 reward program
GOTO 3333360 : REM Pac-Man Hi Score
```

300 : Kansas City

Also known as the Computer Users' Tape Standard (CUTS), the Kansas City standard was a format for storing data on a cassette tape at between 300 and 2400 baud, i.e. 300 binary bits every second. It began at a *BYTE* magazine symposium in November 1975, when the industry was barely out of short trousers, but was later adopted by companies such as Acorn for their Acorn System 1, Acorn Electron and Acorn BBC Micro range of machines. With a fixed baud rate such as this, you could easily predict how much tape you needed to store your program. A 10 KiB program would be 10240 bytes, or 81920 bits, in size, taking 273 seconds to load. Furthermore, by knowing that a cassette player ran at 1⅞ IPS, you knew that it would require 512 inches of tape.

Some systems, like the Sinclair ZX81 and ZX Spectrum, would have a variable baud rate because they would encode a 0 bit in a different fashion to a 1. In the case of the ZX81, a zero (00000000 in binary) would load in 2/100ths of a second, while 255 (11111111 in binary) would be slower, taking just over 3/100ths of a second. This meant that two programs of identical size could take a different time to load.

So, while there is a common joke that some hardware is heavier than others because there are more data bits in it, it can be strangely true when applied to load times.

```
GOTO 1⅞ : REM IPS
GOTO 15 : REM Saving to tape
GOTO 15 : REM C15, C60, C90
GOTO 33⅓ : REM Revolutions per minute
GOTO 50 : REM Compilations
GOTO 451 : REM Fahrenheit 451
GOTO 65495 : REM Going faster
```

300 REPEAT

301 : REM Video Genie EG3003

Known originally for their TV Pong games, Hong Kong-based electronic company EACA International Ltd let the Video Genie, a rather bulky machine, out in 1980 as an effective clone of the TRS-80 Model I. Like its inspiration, it too had a monochrome 64x16 (or 32x16) text screen, which supported both alphanumeric characters and 2x3 graphical blocks giving a 'high' resolution of up to 128x48.

What might be unique about it, however, is the inbuilt cassette player, capable of loading machine code and BASIC programs... but an *external* cassette port capable of reading only BASIC meant the add-on actually did less!?! (A 'minus-on', perhaps!)

The Video Genie also had wood grain sides, almost unheard of outside of the Atari 2600 (originally called Stella).

The inbuilt power supply unit for these is labelled PS 301.

Nigel Reed considers this to be their favourite machine.

GOTO 80 : REM Tangerine Microtan 65

```
305 COLOUR(1): PRINT TAB(X,Y) CHR$(241)
310 COLOUR(2): PRINT TAB(MX,MY) CHR$(240)
320 PRINT TAB(34,0); INT(61-(TIME/100));" "
```

357 : In-jokes

The number 357, or 1010011010, when reflected in the mirror, is 1010011010 – the number of the beast, 666.

GOTO RND : REM Think of a number and jump to the first entry
greater than or equal to that number

376 : Aquarius MX

When retro hardware becomes difficult-to-impossible to source,
some folk build their own compatible units. This is the Aquarius
MX, a replacement for its original Micro Expander, which features
both traditional ports and a modern CH376S USB interface.

From the personal collection of Mack Wharton

RETURN

399 : Sinclair QL

Just as the Sinclair Spectrum was nicknamed the ZX82 during development, the Quantum Leap (or the QL) was originally called the ZX83. Then, when development slipped, the ZX84. But these names were never official. Sinclair had already realised the value in being able to better brand a *name* as opposed to a *number*. (This idea was later rediscovered by Intel in 1992 when they announced the new processor in their x86 range was to be called Pentium, instead of 586. In Intel's case, a number such as 586 lacked the distinctiveness to acquire a trademark so a formal name was assigned.)

The Quantum Leap was truly that, a 32-bit machine in a sea of 8-bit mediocrity, with mass storage devices built-in, quality graphics with monitor (not just TV) output, software for professional use, networking, prestigious style, and high-quality marketing materials in silver. Even the users' group, known as QLUB, was a users' *bureau*!

But it was also a Sinclair machine...

The 32-bit processor of the moment was the Motorola 68000 (a personal favourite!) but in order for the machine to hit the pre-designated price point, the more limiting 68008 version was used. This meant that all the 32-bit data inside the CPU had to be chopped up into 8-bit pieces in order to go into (or out of) the chip.

As 3.5" floppy discs became the standard for home computers, Sinclair was hoping the microdrive technology originally developed for the Spectrum would win favour. But it didn't. The QL had networking via the QLAN port. Another proprietary gamble that didn't pay off.

When managing director Nigel Searle unveiled the machine to the press at the Continental Hotel in London, a comparison was shown of how much equivalent machines would cost when decked out with all the functionality of the QL. A BBC B cost £1,800, and the Apple II would be £2,150, compared to Sinclair's offering of a mere £399. But it was delivered late (leading to nicknames of 'Quantity Limited' and 'Quite Late'), had unreliable microdrives, and an extra 'dongle' – a 16 KiB ROM cartridge necessary to make the machine work, given that the QDOS and SuperBASIC ROMs didn't fit in the space allocated for them! – meant the machine didn't repeat Sinclair's previous successes.

Colin Murphy considers this to be their favourite machine.

GOTO 1099 : REM SAM Coupé

400 : Atari 400

If Sinclair described the pressure-sensitive keyboard of the ZX80 and ZX81 as 'stylish', the Atari nomenclature for the one on their machine was 'wipe-clean'. This demonstrated that Atari knew their market – gamers! Following up on their arcade roots, they could now ask home gamers, 'Have You Played Atari Today?' and so this machine eschewed an inbuilt version of BASIC and instead provided a machine into which games cartridges could be slotted for play, with immediate effect.

Of course, a games console with four channel sound, sprites, and a 320x192 resolution needs no keyboard, but still, BASIC could be loaded via a cartridge which, like any other software, and made it look like a (potentially) educational computer to parents. It was, at least, easier to program for the novice than the Atari 2600. But how many ever did?

It was known initially as 'Candy', and intended to be a 4 KiB machine (thus the 400) but ultimately became 8 KiB and 16 KiB. Michael Sauers considers this 1979 computer to be their favourite machine.

GOTO 5 : REM Atari 800XL

```
400 A$=INKEY$(0)
```

404 : Entry not found

But countless others exist.

```
410 IF A$ <> "" THEN PRINT TAB(X,Y) " "
420 IF A$="A" X=X-1: IF X=0 THEN X=1
430 IF A$="S" X=X+1: IF X=39 THEN X=38
440 IF A$="K" Y=Y-1: IF Y=1 THEN Y=2
450 IF A$="M" Y=Y+1: IF Y=30 THEN Y=29
```

451 : Fahrenheit 451

In 1953, a dystopian novel by American writer Ray Bradbury called *Fahrenheit 451* was published. Like George Lucas's subsequent *THX 1138*, the unassuming use of a number permeated popular culture. So much so that even if you've never heard the phrase 'temperature for spontaneous ignition' you'll know the number, and that it refers to paper burning.

You might also know it as a keycode in games such as *System Shock*, *Sanitarium* and *Dishonored*, amongst others. When padded to four digits, 0451 is the keycode to an elevator in the game *Mafia III* and a locked door in *BioShock*. Its reverse, 1540, appears in *BioShock 2*. So it is, perhaps, somewhat surprising that 0451 was the security door code to the real-life offices of Looking Glass Studios, the developer responsible for those games. With so many gamers playing these games, and knowing these codes, presumably the game developers have since changed their door code!

However, perhaps most surprisingly, Warren Spector, the game designer of *Deus Ex* (amongst others), has said that the connection between Ray Bradbury's book and the door code is purely coincidental.

So, long before the eventual heat death of the universe, our planet will eventually hit 451°F and all our books, magazines, and periodicals will be lost. Luckily (!?!), floppy discs are made of a laminate plastic called mylar. This has a higher autoignition temperature, meaning our early games will spontaneously ignite at 489.2°F – so, in the future, expect a post-apocalyptic tech-noir book entitled 'Fahrenheit 489.2'!

Cassette tapes, on the other hand, are made from polyester with a gamma ferric oxide coating and are unlikely to last beyond 30 years due to variable environmental effects, such as temperature fluctuations.

If your cassette tapes have been lucky enough to last this long, then it is wise to start archiving them to a digital format now. To maintain existing tapes the best you can manage is to keep them at a constant temperature (50–70° F, about 10–21° C) with 20–40% relative humidity, and rewind after every use. And you should use them. Every 6–12 months you should play them all the way through, or if you're in a rush, fast forward through them. This will prevent each layer of the tape on the spool sticking to the tape that is beside it.

```
GOTO 1⅞ : REM IPS
GOTO 15 : REM Saving to tape
GOTO 15 : REM C15, C60, C90
GOTO 50 : REM Compilations
GOTO 300 : REM Kansas City
GOTO 65495 : REM Going faster
```

```
460 IF X=MX AND Y=MY THEN GOSUB 600
```

464 : Amstrad CPC 464

When you remember Amstrad, you think either of its founder Alan Sugar, the Sinclair takeover, or this machine from 1984. With its red and green buttons, built-in cassette recorder, and dedicated monitor, this was the all-in-one approach that everyone aspired to with the PC, but at a price point that was affordable.

It helped that the machine was very well spec'd, with a resolution of between 640x200 and 160x200 (depending on how many colours you needed), a three-channel sound chip, and 4 Mhz Z80 processor. By initiating its own publishing arm, Amsoft, Amstrad was also able to provide a lot of software at sensible prices. Unlike Sinclair, Alan Sugar realised the value in entertainment so provided both games (including the retrospectively branded Roland series) and a joystick port on the machine itself. He managed to sell over two million computers.

Both James Bland and Stephen Hampshire consider this to be their favourite machine.

GOTO 6128 : REM Amstrad CPC 6128

500 : Commodore Amiga

With a name even more friendly than the VIC-20 (Amiga is Spanish for 'a female friend'), the Amiga is a machine that strides confidently into any conversation. But which Amiga?

The A1000 because it was the first, in 1985? The A500 for being the low-end Amiga which lived in a single case, and consequently looked like a home machine, facilitating Amiga's mass-market breakthrough? The A600 with its enhanced chip set and quirky form factor? (Or because the A600 had been designed as a budget A500 called the A300.)

Don't forget the A2000, A3000 and A4000 as big box and tower variants that allowed PC-like expansion with slots dynamically called Zorro! (Well, calling your expansion slots PCI, ISA, or GDP made you sound like an old crusty, right!?!?!)

Or perhaps you're a fan of the A1200 as a way of getting the AGA (Advanced Graphics Architecture) chipset and standard IDE hard drive controllers, all built-in at a sensible price point. Or maybe you prefer the Amiga CD32 or CDTV because you like to be different.

In any case, the Amiga was not historically originally a Commodore machine. It was built in Los Gatos by Amiga Corporation (formally Hi-Toro), a company who funded their experiments into computer hardware by selling peripherals. When it became clear that Atari weren't going to license the Amiga technology for their games consoles, Commodore stepped in. Luckily for Amiga, the Commodore head office was on the US East Coast and so management interference was significantly less than it might otherwise have been. (Or the hippy-inspired 'Guru Meditation' error that occurred when the computer crashed would almost certainly been removed.)

To conclude I shall fulfil my duty, as whenever the word 'Amiga' is mentioned, one is legally required to utter one of the following phrases:

* 'The first two seasons of *Babylon 5* were made with the Amiga'
* 'Andy Warhol used one, you know'
* 'It's better than the Atari ST'

Both Spencer Shanson and Paul Fearns consider this to be their favourite machine.

GOTO 2.04 : REM Commodore Amiga A500+

```
500 UNTIL TIME >= 6000
510 PRINT TAB(4,6) "GAME OVER!!!"
520 PRINT TAB(4,8) "THANKS FOR PLAYING :)"
530 L=16:M$="UIF!DFOUSF!GPS!DPNQVUJOH!IJTUPSZ":
    GOSUB 1000
540 L=18:M$="DPNF!BOE!WJTJU!VT!": GOSUB 1000
550 COLOUR(2): PRINT TAB(4,24) "PRESS SPACE TO PLAY
    AGAIN"
560 IF GET$= " " THEN GOTO 5
570 GOTO 560
600 CATCH=CATCH+1
610 PRINT TAB(11,0); CATCH
620 SOUND 1,1,1,3
630 MX=RND(36)+1: MY=RND(26)+1
```

640 : 'Ought to be enough for anybody'

This quote, attributed to Microsoft co-founder Bill Gates, was almost certainly never uttered, given that the earliest citation is from 1985, and it was supposedly said at a trade show in 1981. Four years is a long time for someone to suddenly remember it, without reference to any other historical records. Instead, it is more interesting to wonder why 640 KiB is the limit, given that almost every other limit in computing is a power of two.

When IBM introduced the IBM PC 5150 in 1981, it could address a nice round 1,048,576 bytes of memory: 1 MiB. This was an impressive amount of memory by anyone's measure, particularly given that the Intel 8088 chip inside the machine could only address 64 KiB of it. The technique it used to overcome this apparent limitation was one of segments and offsets.

Segments are 64 KiB in size and occur every 16 bytes, so segment 0 is at physical address 0, segment 1 is at 16, and so on. Given that the segment size is larger than the gap between them, some references will clearly overlap. If we write the address as hexadecimal numbers in the form `segment:offset` then `0000:0010` maps to address 16 in the same way that `0001:0000` does. (Each physical address can be written in $2^{12} = 4096$ different segment:offset combinations.) Computing that physical address is nothing more complex than multiplying the segment number by 16 (or shifting it 4 bits to the left) and adding the offset.

The code to retrieve data, via segment 32, might be:

```
MOV AX, 20H    ; set AX to be the value for segment 32 (20 hex)
MOV DS, AX     ; put the value of AX into the data segment
                 register DS
MOV CX, [10H]  ; load the data from the current segment and
                 offset 16 (10 hex) into CX
```

The first two steps are necessary since you cannot assign a value directly to the data segment (DS) register, and the final MOV implicitly uses the data segment unless you specify otherwise. Thus, this accesses address 0020:0010.

Like traditional home machines of the time, the memory in the PC was shared by everything – the OS, the user's programs and data, screen memory, peripherals, and so on. To give some separation of concerns, Microsoft made an arbitrary cut-off point and decreed that the top 384 KiB of memory should be for its own use, handling the screen (such as the loading of device drivers), peripherals, and BIOS, leaving the other 640 KiB available for conventional use by the OS and user software. So while Bill Gates might never have said the attributed quote, he was certainly instrumental in introducing the limit.

As for the reason for a 1 MiB limit, that can be seen by noting that a 20-bit address bus, 2^{20}, is 1 MiB, and that size of bus exists when the 16-bit segment register is shifted left by 4.

GOTO 64 : REM Spanish import law
GOTO 5150 : REM The first personal computer

```
GOTO 38911 : REM Bytes
GOTO 2147483647 : REM Seconds
GOSUB 128 : REM Bytes
```

```
640 RETURN
```

666 : In-jokes

Anything created by individuals or small teams has a sense of those people inside it, whereas large team projects often lose this individuality. When Steve Wozniak, or Woz, creator of the original Apple computer, came to set a price for this new machine he chose $666.66. He has said this was because the wholesale price for the machine was $500 and adding a one-third profit to this gave it a pleasing retail price of $666.66 – one with repeated digits, that was much easier to type, and nothing to do with 'the beast'.

Rule 666, applying the theme of invoking the 'number of the beast', as detailed in the New Testament's Book of Revelation, continues this playfulness by suggesting that every machine which could run *Doom* will, eventually, run *Doom*. 'Can it run *Doom*?' goes the cry whenever a computer is mentioned. So far, this list includes machines which cannot run *Doom* from the original sources, like the ZX Spectrum or a TI-84/83 graphing calculator, but have unofficial ports which claim to be somewhat like its famous predecessor. (Usually implemented with a simpler engine, and all-new bespoke graphics.)

Even seemingly innocent TV shows like *The Simpsons* and *Futurama* are littered with references to maths, science and technology. For example, the *Futurama* episode 'The Honking' hints that Bender might have hexakosioihexekontahexa-phobia. If *you* looked in a mirror and saw the number 0101100101, would you be scared?

To find out why you might, turn to the entry defined by the number above.

Otherwise, total all the numbers on a roulette wheel (0 to 36) to see what total you get!

```
GOTO 4 : REM Peripherals for processing
```

672 : 1K Chess

The transition from board game to computer game has very distinct phases. The first computer games, such as those created back in the 1950s, were for tic-tac-toe and draughts. The process of their creation was simple: take an existing board game and make it available on a computer. This pattern was repeated with each new generation of hardware and wetware (i.e. as new programmers looked for an interesting project). Then, with the process understood, developers started to imagine games that could *only* work on a computer, perhaps because the screen can display moving graphics or require a data store that is too large for a card set or rule book. The third phase happened when networks became prevalent, and all the games that existed on a single machine become network aware. An FPS now becomes a network FPS, for example, and chess is now played by email or on real-time servers.

In the early 1980s, David Horne wrote a version of chess for the ZX81. His was not the first chess game for the machine. Nor was it the best, either in terms of usability or AI. But it was certainly the most memorable because he made everything fit into the unexpanded ZX81, with a total 1 KiB of memory.

The traditional opening of queens pawn, from 1K Chess
Courtesy of Subvert Ltd

Horne self-published the game in early 1982, selling it by mail order from his East Sussex home for £5, but it was soon picked up by Artic Computing, known primarily at this time for their adventure series of games for the ZX range. In turn, it was adopted by Sinclair themselves and re-published under their name. It was then published a third time in late 1982 and early 1983 by *Your Computer*, a UK magazine of news, information, and program listings.

Your Computer published the game as a three-part series. The first part, in December 1982, explained how to generate a game board and write an input system, which allowed two human players to compete against each other. It included the source code and an explanation for those who wished to type it in themselves. In the next issue, part two included code for validating the moves made by each player. Finally, in February 1983, AI was added into the mix. You could, if you wished, type in this program instead of buying the £3 game. But, as those around at the time will remember, magazine listings rarely worked as advertised. The chance of an error in the magazine, or your typing, meant that something would fail – especially for machine code programs. So, if you valued your time and sanity, it was probably worthwhile to simply pay for the cassette.

With such a small memory footprint there were three notable omissions in game play:

- Castling was not permitted
- En passant was not permitted
- When your pawn reached the opposite side of the board, you could only promote it to queen

Consequently, the AI made a technical point that it could be done, rather than providing a challenging game.

It is perhaps intriguing that, despite the game only occupying 672 bytes of memory, you cannot develop 1 K Chess on a 1 KiB machine. In fact, a 3 KiB machine is the bare minimum. One of the main tricks was that the ZX81 would save the screen display along with the program when you typed SAVE. It would also save any variables that existed in memory at the time. This could cut the memory usage in half, since you didn't need to use memory to include code that drew the screen – just the result.

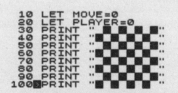

Unnecessary pseudo-code for preparing a game

145

In fact, 1K Chess uses this metaphor throughout. When the AI is contemplating its move, you can see the top left block flickering as the pieces move upon the board. This isn't an aesthetic nicety. This is form following function. The AI is using the screen memory as its own personal representation of the board state to evaluate each position and determine its next move. Once it has done so, the block stops flickering to indicate it is the player's turn. And that same block determines the current player, saving another byte of memory.

Another technique was to use an interface which suited the machine, rather than the human. You needed to type 7D5D to move the black queen's pawn from D7 to D5. Furthermore, it would write this information to the screen backwards:

Moving from D7 to D5

Programmers of Forth will recognise this as being related to Reverse Polish Notation.

By way of a postscript, developers have since overcome this game's various limitations in a similarly confined space. *ChesSkelet* by Alex Garcia, for example, needed 377 bytes for their version, while Olivier Poudade wrote *Chesslin* in just 256 bytes of x86 assembly!

Not to belittle these recent feats of engineering – with enough time and/or money, many things are possible – but the modern versions of compact chess AI benefit from developers who are au fait with so many techniques unavailable to earlier programmers: assembly programming tricks, compact code, compression, improved chess algorithms, etc.

But the ZX81 1K Chess game stands out because it proved that it could be done. Furthermore, having a release early in the machine's life cycle probably inspired other developers to reconsider the possibilities of the unexpanded machine, and convinced potential purchasers that the 1 KiB machine was more capable than they might otherwise have thought.

```
                    O    R    G
                 16514   ;   TKP:
            PUSH HL   ;   PUSH BC
        CALL (KEYBOARD)   ;   LD B,H   ;
        LD C,L   ;   LD D,L   ;   INC D   ;   JR
        Z, (PC+F7H)   ;   CALL (DECODE)   ;   LD
      A,(HL)   ;   POP BC   ;   PUSH BC   ;   CP A,C   ;
      JR Z, (PC+05H)   ;   INC C   ;   DJNZ (PC+FAH)
      ;   POP BC   ;   JR   (PC+E7H)   ;   POP BC   ;   POP HL
      ;   LD (HL),A   ;   RET   ;   KYBD:   LD BC,081DH   ;
        CALL (TKP)   ;   DEC HL   ;   LD C,26H   ;   CALL (TKP)
        ;   INC HL   ;   LD A,(HL)   ;   SUB 1CH   ;   LD B,A   ;
      LD C,08H   ;   XOR A,A   ;   ADD A,C   ;   DJNZ (PC+FDH)
        ;   ADD A,61H   ;   DEC HL   ;   SUB B,(HL)   ;   MOVE:   LD
      C,A   ;   LD L,C   ;   LD H,43H   ;   LD A,(HL)   ;   LD B,01H
      ;   AND 7FH   ;   CP 00H   ;   JR Z, (PC+14H)   ;   INC B   ;
      CP 76H   ;   JR Z, (PC+0FH)   ;   CP 27H   ;   JR Z, (PC+0BH)
      ;   LD A,(HL)   ;   INC B   ;   LD L,37H   ;   ADD A,(HL)
      BIT 7,A   ;   JR Z, (PC+02H)   ;   LD B,00H   ;   LD A,B   ;   LD
      L,C   ;   RET   ;   TABLES:   DC.B 01,08,FF,F5,F6,F4,0C,0A
        ;   DC.B       0D,F3,15,E8,17,E9,F7,09       ;   DC.B
      08,0A,36,0C,37,27,33,35   ;   PIECE:   XOR A,A   ;   LD
      (4046H),A   ;   LD A,(HL)   ;   AND 7FH   ;   CP 35H   ;   JR
        Z, (PC+4FH)   ;   LD C,01H   ;   LD B,08H   ;   LD HL,40E7H   ;
        CP 33H   ;   JR Z, (PC+16H)   ;   LD L,DFH   ;   CP 30H   ;   JR
      Z, (PC+10H)   ;   LD C,B   ;   CP 36H   ;   JR Z, (PC+0BH)   ;
      LD B,04H   ;   CP 37H   ;   JR Z, (PC+05H)   ;   LD L,E3H   ;
      CP 27H   ;   RET NZ   ;   LD A,E   ;   ADD A,(HL)   ;   PUSH
      AF   ;   PUSH HL   ;   PUSH BC   ;   CP 3FH   ;   JR C, (P-
      C+1EH)   ;   CP 94H   ;   JR NC, (PC+1AH)   ;   CALL
      (MOVE)   ;   CP 02H   ;   JR NC, (PC+13H)   ;   PUSH
        AF   ;   CALL (428DH)   ;   POP AF   ;   CP 00H   ;
        JR Z, (PC+0AH)   ;   POP BC   ;   POP HL   ;
        LD A,C   ;   CP 01H   ;   JR Z, (PC+05H)   ;
        POP AF   ;   JR   (PC+DAH)   ;   POP BC
        ;   POP HL   ;   POP AF   ;   INC HL   ;
        DJNZ (PC+D3H)   ;   RET   ;   PAWN:
        LD A,(HL)   ;   AND 80H   ;   LD
      HL,40E4H   ;   JR NZ, (PC+02H)   ;   LD
      L,F1H   ;   LD D,03H   ;   LD A,E   ;   ADD A,(HL)
      ;   PUSH HL   ;   PUSH AF   ;   CP 3FH   ;   JR C, (PC+20H)
      ;   CP 94H   ;   JR NC, (PC+1CH)   ;   CALL (MOVE)   ;   CP 00H
      ;   JR Z, (PC+10H)   ;   CP 01H   ;   JR NZ, (PC+11H)   ;   LD A,D
      CP 01H   ;   JR NZ, (PC+0CH)   ;   CALL (428DH)   ;   LD A,E   ;   CP 52H
      ;   JR C, (PC+13H)   ;   CP 7EH   ;   JR NC, (PC+0FH)   ;   POP AF
      POP HL   ;   DEC HL   ;   DEC D   ;   JR 01H   ;   INC HL, (PC+02H)   ;   RET
        ;   LD A,D   ;   CP 01H   ;   CALL NZ,428DH
        ;   JR   (PC+F1H)   ;   POP AF
        ;   POP HL   ;   LD E,A   ;   JR
        (PC+C5H)   ;   SCORE:   PUSH
        HL   ;   PUSH BC   ;   PUSH DE   ;
        PUSH HL   ;   PUSH BC   ;   LD
        D,L   ;   LD HL,4040H   ;   CALL
        (0724H)   ;   CALL (P5C)   ;
        LD A,B   ;   ADD A,H   ;   LD C,A
        ;   POP AF   ;   CALL (P5C)   ;
        POP HL   ;   CALL (INC)   ;   JR
        NC, (PC+01H)   ;   ADD A,B   ;
        LD C,A   ;   POP HL   ;   POP DE
        ;   LD E,   ;   LD (HL),D   ;
        PUSH HL   ;   LD (HL),D   ;   CALL
        (INC)   ;   JR NC, (PC+01H)   ;
        SUB A,B   ;   PUSH AF   ;   CALL
        (CHGHU)   ;   CALL (CHK)   ;   POP
        BC   ;   JR NC, (PC+02H)   ;   INC
        B   ;   INC B   ;   POP DE   ;   POP HL
        ;   LD (HL),E   ;   POP HL   ;   CALL
        (42FAH)   ;   CALL (INC)   ;   JR
        NC, (PC+01H)   ;   DEC B   ;   CALL
        (42FAH)   ;   CALL (CHGHU)   ;   LD
      A,B   ;   LD HL,403CH   ;   LD (HL),A
      ;   EX DE,HL   ;   LD HL,4041H   ;   CP
      A,(HL)   ;   RET C   ;   LD BC,0005H   ;
      JR (PC+08H)   ;   SHIFT:   LD HL,4063H
      ;   LD DE,4046H   ;   LD BC,TEST_SB
      JR C, (PC+01H)   ;   EX DE,HL   ;   LDIR
      ;   RET   ;   CHK:   LD A, (4337H)   ;   ADD
      A,30H   ;   LD HL,433EH   ;   LD B,A   ;
      CP1R   ;   DEC HL   ;   LD (4080H),HL   ;   SO_
      AT:   LD B,56H   ;   LD HL,4A5EH   ;   INC HL
      ;   PUSH HL   ;   PUSH BC   ;   LD E,L   ;   CALL
      (40BFH)   ;   CP 00H   ;   JR NZ, (PC+19H)   ;
      CALL (CHGHU)   ;   LD L,E   ;   CALL (PIECE)
        ;   CALL (CHGHU)   ;   CALL (TEST_LIST)   ;   JR
        NZ, (PC+F5H)   ;   POP BC   ;   POP HL   ;   SCF   ;   RET
        POP BC   ;   POP HL   ;   DJNZ (PC+D5H)   ;   AND A,A   ;
      RET   ;   DRIVER:   LD B,05H   ;   LD A,08H   ;   LD HL,439FH   ;
      INC HL   ;   LD (HL),A   ;   DJNZ (PC+FCH)   ;   CALL (4A0AH)
      ;   CP 05H   ;   JR NZ, (PC+E2H)   ;   LD (4007H),HL   ;   LD E,L
      ;   CALL (PIECE)   ;   LD HL,43A1H   ;   CALL (40A0H)   ;   CP
      02H   ;   EX DE,HL   ;   JR NC, (PC+DCH)   ;   CALL (4282H)
        ;   JR Z, (PC+D7H)   ;   CP A,C   ;   JR Z, (PC+05H)   ;   CALL
      (PMOVE)   ;   EXX   ;   CALL (CHK)   ;   EXX   ;   JR C, (PC+08H)
      ;   CALL (4286H)   ;   CALL (MPSCAN)   ;   JR (PC+E2H)   ;   LD
      (HL),B   ;   LD A,C   ;   LD (DE),A   ;   JR (PC+F9H)   ;   TEST_LIST
      LD HL,4046H   ;   DEC (HL)   ;   LD A,(HL)   ;   INC A   ;   RET Z   ;   ADD
      A,L   ;   LD L,A   ;   LD A,(HL)   ;   RET   ;   LD HL,4046H   ;   INC (HL)   ;
      LD A,(HL)   ;   ADD A,L   ;   LD L,A   ;   LD (HL),C   ;   RET   ;   MPSCAN:   XOR
      A,A   ;   LD (4041H),A   ;   LD HL,4343H   ;   LD HL,433EH   ;   INC HL   ;   PUSH HL
      ;   PUSH BC   ;   LD E,L   ;   CALL (40BFH)   ;   CP 03H   ;   JR NZ, (PC+22H)   ;   LD
      L,E   ;   LD (4007H),HL   ;   CALL (PIECE)   ;   CALL (TEST_LIST)   ;   JR Z, (PC+1DH)
      ;   LD E,F   ;   LD D,43H   ;   CALL (PMOVE)   ;   EXX   ;   AND A,A   ;   CALL (41F2H)
      (SCORE)   ;   SCF   ;   CALL (41F2H)   ;   JR (PC+DEH)   ;   POP BC   ;   POP HL   ;   DJNZ (PC+C8H)
      ;   LD A, (4041H)   ;   CP 00H   ;   JR C, (PC+FEH)   ;   LD HL,4A45H   ;   LD A,(HL)   ;   DEC HL   ;
      DEC HL   ;   LD E,(HL)   ;   LD D,(HL)   ;   RET   ;   LD HL,   ;   LD L,(HL)   ;   LD H,D   ;   BIT
      0,L   ;   LD (HL),80H   ;   JR Z, (PC+02H)   ;   LD (HL),00H   ;   CALL (CHGHU)   ;   RET   ;   CHGHU:   LD
      A, (4337H)   ;   LD A,(HL)   ;   RRD A,80H   ;   LD (HL),A   ;   RET   ;   PMOVE:   LD HL, (4007H)   ;   LD
      A, (DE)   ;   LD C,A   ;   LD B,A   ;   LD (HL),00H   ;   LD (DE),A   ;   LD B,A   ;   RET   ;   PSC   ;
      AND 7FH   ;   LD HL,40F2H   ;   LD B,05H   ;   CP A,(HL)   ;   RET Z   ;   INC HL   ;   DJNZ (PC+FBH)
      ;   LD A,B   ;   RET   ;   INC:   LD A,L   ;   EXX   ;   LD (4080H),A   ;   CALL (SO_AT)   ;   EXX   ;   LD
      A,C   ;   RET   ;   ORG 4387   ;   LD HL,4343H   ;   LD DE,40004   ;   LD BC,00CDH   ;   LDIR   ;   RET   ;
      ORG 4343   ;   BOARD:   DC.B 128,6,349,193,173,118   ;   DC.B 29,6,55,51,39,48,54,39,51,
      55,118   ;   DC.B 30,8,53,53,53,53,53,53,53,118   ;   DC.B 31,8,0,128,0,128,0,128,0,
      128,118   ;   DC.B 32,8,128,0,128,0,128,0,118   ;   DC.B 33,8,0,128,0,128,0,128,0
      ,128,118   ;   DC.B 34,6,128,0,128,0,128,0,118   ;   DC.B 35,6,181,181,181,181,18
      1,181,181   ;   DC.B 36,6,183,167,176,182,167,179   ;   DC.B 183,118
      ;   DC.B 8,6,45,44,43,42,41,40,39,36,118   ;   DC.B 6,6,8,8,6   ;   ORG 4381   ;   LD BC,0400H
      ;   CALL 05F5H   ;   LD HL,4800H   ;   LD B,6EH   ;   PUSH BC   ;   PUSH HL   ;   LD A (HL)   ;   RST 16
      POP HL   ;   POP BC   ;   INC HL   ;   DJNZ (PC+F7H)   ;   LD HL,407DH   ;   LD (4029H),HL   ;   JP 775
```

The Z80 assembly for 1K Chess

147

GOTO 3 : REM Optimising for size
GOTO 8 : REM Type-in listings
GOTO 16509 : REM ZX81 1K Display
GOTO 31900 : REM With prizes
GOSUB 4 : REM Reverse Polish Notation
GOSUB 128 : REM Bytes

```
700 MOVE 18+S,18+S: DRAW 18+S,975-S: DRAW
   1260-S,975-S
705 DRAW 1260-S,18+S: DRAW 18+S,18+S
710 RETURN
```

720 : Copy protection

With piracy being rife throughout the computer scene, developers and publishers have looked at increasingly complex methods to protect their code, first with tapes, then discs.

A lot of the initial protection methods were to stop you reading and modifying the code since, if you could do this, it was a simple matter to type SAVE to create a perfect copy. In the cassette era, publishers used fast loaders and other technical tricks to load the game in a non-obvious way... all of which could be subverted with a dual tape deck – the analog hole. One of the largest manufacturers of such machines were Amstrad (the same one that made the CPC series, and ultimately bought Sinclair) whose advert proudly claimed, 'It tapes tapes!' For those who couldn't afford a new tape machine, software copiers were available for tape and disc mediums.

Jet Set Willy with custom tape leader and coloured body

But this only affected the casual copier. To prevent commercial piracy, some companies would use a distinctive livery – perhaps a brightly coloured body, or custom printed tape leader. This had two obvious problems: the first was that not all versions of the program would be identical, as fluctuations in stock availability varied over the lifetime of the product. The second was that unless the consumer already knew that a genuine tape should be blue, they'd have no way of knowing. (And this also assumes that the purchasers even cared about the legitimacy of the product they were buying from that dodgy-looking bloke on the market.)

Knowing they couldn't stop folk copying the game, publishers included additional paraphernalia in the box which was necessary to run the software. Items, they hoped, would be less easy to copy. The dongle was one such idea. It would be plugged into your machine and the software would check for its existence. The mechanics of the dongle varied, as each company sought to invent its own techniques, both to reduce licensing costs and to avoid the liability so that if one dongle was cracked it didn't affect the efficacy of all software using it. Some dongles needed to remain in the computer for as long as the program was running while others, like the joystick port dongle *Buzzard Bait* by Tom Mix Software for the Dragon 32, would check its existence only upon load. This was, perhaps, a better approach since you couldn't guarantee that a computer would have a free port.

Lenslok, from ASAP Developments Limited, attempted to solve the piracy issue by supplying a set of small prisms in a plastic case which would refract a scrambled image on-screen to an unscrambled one by the time the light had reached your eyes. Unfortunately, such a real-world device meant real-world problems, such as it not working on TV screens which were too large. Or small. Or ill-positioned. Or not high-quality. Or not configured properly. But for every negative there was a positive, and the computer's inability to generate truly random data meant that the scrambled image (on Elite for the Commodore 64) was always the same. It read AD.

But the most famous system was probably the 720 coloured squares on the Software Protection card which came with the Software Projects game *Jet Set Willy*, and which is accredited to Padlock Systems. The squares were split into a grid, labelled 0–8 and A–R, and the program would start by asking you to enter the four colours at square H7, for example. You were given two attempts to get this right. Failure to do so meant the computer would forcibly restart. At a time when colour photocopiers were expensive, it would not be unusual to find kids spending their maths lessons copying out the whole card! (Since the colours mapped to the numbers 1, 2, 3, 4 on the Spectrum keyboard this didn't take as long as you might think.)

Alas, you can bypass the protection by MERGEing the code, and adding:

```
POKE 34483,195
```

Supplying paper-based products was certainly a cheaper alternative to the various hardware dongles that had existed, particularly when the paper was going to be included anyway. When games, like Geoff Crammond's *Formula One Grand Prix* from MicroProse, needed a large manual to explain the nuances of the simulation, it made sense for the game to start with a question asking for the word from the manual in the form Page-Paragraph-Line-Word. Sometimes the printing was done on Nocopi paper (as in Jack Nicklaus's *Unlimited Golf & Course Design*) or by using low contrasting colours, both of which rendered photocopies poor or useless.

The Secret of Monkey Island featured a 'Dial-A-Pirate' interactive code wheel – in-keeping with the themes of the game, and an unsubtle reference to piracy! This consisted of two pieces of circular card, fixed in the centre, with half a face on both the inner and outer wheels. You would then rotate the outer wheel to match both halves with the pirate shown onscreen and read off the numbers from the inner wheel that needed to be typed into the program.

Such paraphernalia 'worked' with all software, whether on tape or disc. But the move to discs provided new technological opportunities to prevent the software being copied in the first place. *Dungeon Master* on the Atari ST, developed in 1987 by FTL Games, used a 'fuzzy bit'. This section of the disc is neither a 0 or 1 but is indeterminate, so might change whenever it is read. Naturally, if you made a copy of the disc then the computer would *read* the source disc with a random value but *write* it to the target disc with a fixed value. The developers were also smart enough to include other protection methods that not exhibit any ill-effects of a copied game until you had been playing for some time.

Creating such a scheme required custom hardware, and companies like XEMAG could record a 'fat track' which had adjacent tracks containing identical data, all perfectly aligned – something consumer machines could not replicate.

But all software needed to check that the copy protection was in place and so a 'crack' of the game, that didn't include this check, would bypass all the work. Creating such a crack was not necessarily difficult, as custom hardware units (like ISEPIC for the Commodore, or Multiface for the Spectrum) allowed you to save snapshots of the software (e.g. immediately after the copy protection) or watch the game running to see how it was enacting the protection scheme.

```
GOTO 3  : REM Randomness
GOTO 4  : REM Peripherals for processing
GOTO 18 : REM Certificate 18
```

754 : IEEE 754

IEEE 754 is a format specified by the Institute of Electrical and Electronics Engineers which allows a computer to store seemingly infinite numbers in just four bytes of memory. Of course, they are not truly infinite, but being able to store numbers in the range $\pm1.1810^{-38}$ to $\pm3.410^{38}$, instead of 0 to 4 billion, seems like an infinite increase.

It achieves this by moving the decimal point according to the value of the number. When four bytes are used to store an integer (a whole number) between zero and 4 billion, the decimal point is always at the far right. But if the decimal point is allowed to float to any part of the number, then we can increase the range of the number at the expense of accuracy.

For example 123456 has the decimal at the far end and is identical to 123456.0. By moving the point six places to the left we get 0.123456. By storing it in this format, and noting that the actual value needs to be moved six places back (i.e. multiplied by 1,000,000 or 10^6) we can store the number in two parts – called a mantissa (the fractional part of 0.123456) and an exponent (6). The clever part here is that the fraction is always less than one, because as soon as the number exceeds it, the machine simply increases the exponent by one:

```
0.99 * 100 + 1 = 99 + 1 = 100 = 0.1 * 1000
```

Of our 4 bytes, 8 bits hold the exponent and 23 hold the fraction, with one being reserved for the sign bit to indicate whether the number is positive or negative.

The precise mechanisms of IEEE 754 floating point are beyond the scope of this book, but readily available online. Again, not every number is represented, but most people don't need to worry about the difference between 340000000 00000000000000000000000000 and 34000000000000000000000000000 00000000001, so it's a good trade-off. But errors in conversions don't exist only with large numbers. Some people are initially surprised that, using this notation, 0.1 + 0.2 does not equal 0.3. It becomes more apparent when seen in binary:

```
0.1 = 0.00011001100110011010
0.2 = 0.00110011001100110011
0.3 = 0.01001100110011001101
```

Which is 0.3000001907348632815.

Unfortunately for those of us looking for uniformity, many 8-bit machines used a custom format to store their floating point numbers. Sometimes this was because the computer used its own internal format for performance reasons, and sometimes it was because IEEE 754 hadn't been invented yet!

```
GOTO 3  : REM Optimising for size
GOTO 18 : REM Elliott 903
```

```
800 FOR S=1 TO 470 STEP 4: GCOL 0,RND(4): GOSUB 700:
    NEXT S
```

1000 : A kilobyte

There are 1000 bytes in a kilobyte, even though most people believe there are 1024. This confusion most likely originates from a combined misunderstanding. Firstly, computer scientists would always work with powers of two, since they're working with binary machines, so the natural sequence reads 1, 2, 4, 8, 16, 32... up to 1024. Since all memory chips came in sizes that were a power of two it was not unreasonable to assume that a 1 KB chip had 1024 bytes, instead of 1000. Which those chips did.

Secondly, advertising literature on early machines would reference their memory as being 48 KB, or 49152 bytes. Both facts are true. Unfortunately, computer scientists aren't the only scientists on the planet and, in adopting the kilo- prefix, inadvertently promoted the idea to the general public that kilo meant 1024 in computing fields. From a certain point of view, this is a valid point. However, the kilo (with a pre-defined meaning of 1000) uses a lower case 'k', while the computer scientists and advertisers had – by accident or design – used an upper case 'K' to mean 1024. However the difference was too subtle and 'K' was sometimes written as 'k' to further confuse the issue.

Luckily for science, there are standards bodies which oversee such usages and in 1998 the IEC (International Electrotechnical Commission) introduced the kibibyte, represented as KiB, to unequivocally mean 1024 bytes and 1 kB to be 1000 bytes (as it always had done.) But 1998 was too late for the machines released in the 1980s, for which the equivalence of 1 k = 1 K = 1 kB = 1 KB = 1024 bytes had stuck. This means that KB is shorthand for either 1000 bytes if you read it with modern eyes, or 1024 as it was seen in the 1980s (or through our silicon-tinted spectacles of retro).

Perversely, 'k' is the only time the IEC uses a lower-case designation, and it describes a megabyte with MB to mean 1,000,000 bytes.

Even more perversely, JEDEC (the Joint Electron Device Engineering Council) approved the use of KB to mean a 1024-byte kilobyte and MB to reference a megabyte containing 1,048,576 bytes!

Given the complexities of dealing with the changed meaning and understanding of the term 'KB' between the time in which it was used and the present day, this book uses 'KiB' when talking about amounts of memory in the realm of computer science, and 'K' or 'KB' when reflecting the historical designation or naming of machines or software.

```
GOTO 8 : REM Bits in a byte
GOTO 127 : REM 127 or 255?
GOTO 1024 : REM Not a kilobyte
```

1000 : Sega Master System

As a rebrand of the Japanese 'Sega Mark III', the Master System was Sega's first real foray into the US and European markets in 1986 and 1987, respectively. Following the lead of Nintendo, they branded the US arm 'Sega of America' (Cf. 'Nintendo of America') and threw darts at a board to decide the name!

As a machine it follows the standard console design for the time of three main chips, one each dedicated to processing (the Zilog Z80A), audio (the SN76489 programmable sound generator) and graphics (custom).

At a basic level, its legacy is that it provided Sega with a breeding ground from which to launch the Sega Genesis (aka Mega Drive). However, by noting that the Tectoy variant of the Master System sold 8 million units in Brazil alone (compared to 10–13 million across the rest of the world combined) it should be remembered that not all wins are on the home pitch!

The Master System was based upon, and was backwards compatible with, the SG-1000.

Andy Lee considers this to be their favourite machine.

```
GOTO 2 : REM Psion Series 3
```

```
1000 P=4
1010 FOR I=1 TO LEN(M$)
1020 FOR R=1 TO RND(20)
```

1023 : Have you heard of that new band, '1023 Megabytes'?

They're pretty good, but they don't have a gig yet!

GOTO 65 : REM ASCII stupid question...

1024 : Not a kilobyte

Sorry, it's not! There are 1000 bytes in a kilobyte.

GOTO 1000 : REM A kilobyte

```
1030 PRINT TAB(P,L) CHR$(RND(26)+32)
1040 NEXT R
1050 C=ASC(MID$(M$,I,1))
1060 COLOUR (RND(3))
1070 PRINT TAB(P,L) CHR$(C-1)
1080 SOUND 1,-15,RND(100)+100,1
1090 P=P+1: NEXT I
```

1099 : SAM Coupé

This 1989 machine has a 256x192 display with 16 colours, six channels of stereo sound (via the Philips SAA1099 sound chip), 256 KiB memory as standard, disk drives, MIDI, joystick ports, light pen support, and yet... people only want to know about its compatibility with the ZX Spectrum!

Which is a shame since that's its least useful feature! Or perhaps it was its most useful feature, but the one that prevented its growth. The SAM Coupé was not a Spectrum design with extra added magic; it was a machine in its own right, which happened to use the same processor and have a compatible graphics mode. Perhaps the public of the time were not tech-savvy enough to realise this and didn't see that the SAM had other improvements that pushed it up toward the 16-bit machines of the era, rather than dragging it down to its 8-bit heritage. It could have been 'Some Amazing Micro'.

The SAM Coupé was developed by Miles Gordon Technology, with a robot mascot created by Automata's Mel Croucher, and David Woozley considers it to be their favourite machine.

GOTO 16777216 : REM Colour

```
1100 RETURN
```

1200 : BASICODE

Originating in 1973, BASICODE was an attempt at making BASIC programming more universal by removing the vendor-specific syntactical components of each BASIC variant and replacing them with common shared elements. This is much the same as the artificially constructed language Esperanto, from which BASICODE took its slogan, 'Ein Esperanto fuer Computer'. BASICODE did this by limiting the scope of the BASIC commands that could be used, and by providing an abstraction library (in the form of subroutines) for all the machine-specific work.

Take the example of printing a piece of text at a specific position on the screen:

```
PRINT AT 5,12, "GAME OVER"
```

Even in this simple case there are several ways of representing the same thing in BASIC, including the seemingly indifferent

```
PRINT AT 12, 5, "GAME OVER"
```

Also, some developers decided that, since the screen was divided into a grid of 32x24 (i.e. 768) squares, there was no benefit in referring to each area by both its X and Y co-ordinate, and it should simply use the number of the square, with 0 at the top-left and 767 at the bottom-right.

```
PRINT @389, "GAME OVER"
```

Naturally, BASICODE could not allow the programmer to use any variation of the PRINT instruction, so it required BASICODE programmers to write the same line as:

```
HO = 5
VE = 12
GOSUB 110
PRINT "GAME OVER"
```

Line 110 was one of twelve custom routines that would be pre-loaded from tape, written in the machine's native dialect of BASIC. These routines would carry out the necessary work such as clearing the screen, reading the keyboard, and even sending text to a printer.

As you might suspect, this was a lot more work, for very little apparent gain. There were also conventions to follow so that the BASICODE subroutine library and the main program could peacefully coexist. Primarily, the main program was to live at lines 1000 to 19999, and begin with:

```
1000 GOTO 20 : REM Initialise the BASICODE subroutines
1010 REM Main program starts here
```

But this wasn't enough to allow programs from one machine to run on another. There were other, more subtle, problems caused by programmers taking shortcuts available on their machine that did not work on all of them. For example, some machines – such as the Sinclair range – required the keyword LET to assign values to variables. If a developer was not working with such a machine they might be unaware of such a limitation, and inadvertently write:

```
HO=5
```

Instead of the more universally necessary:

```
LET HO=5
```

Another permissible shortcut was to write:

```
IF X THEN 1000
```

Instead of the more verbose:

```
IF X THEN GOTO 1000
```

Both of which tell the computer to continue running the program from line 1000 if the condition X is true. However, the former is not valid syntax in all variants of BASIC. Nor is the seemingly simple

```
HO=5 : VE=12
```

since the ZX81, primarily, did not support multi-line instructions.

Additionally, BASICODE permits a maximum of two-letter names to stop variables becoming confused with built-in function names like SIN and COS which have three letters. But that doesn't stop confusion in the case of AT, of which the programmer might also be unaware.

In short, these programs were an early example of 'write once, debug everywhere'.

But, assuming you understood all these problematic edge cases, you could still not distribute the software to every machine because the cassette interface would save the program in a different and incompatible format.

So, to ensure every computer could load the program, the BASICODE developers created a standardised file format by writing the data at 1200 BPS with FSK (frequency-shift keying) modulation whereby the zero bit was encoded with one period of the 1200 Hz baseband signal, and the one bit was encoded with two periods of the 2400 Hz signal. They then wrote a specific loader program for each computer, again written in its native language. These programs would be distributed on a tape, such as this:

Inlay scan
Courtesy of @annabeep

This has 13 programs (supporting 16 machines) on one side, and 18 BASICODE programs which could be loaded by any supported machine.

Cassette scan
Courtesy of @annabeep

BASICODE 2+ followed in 1984, with loader programs for eight more machines, and BASICODE 3 arrived in 1986. But despite all these considerations (or maybe because of them) BASICODE never took off in the way that other cross-platform languages, like Java, did in more professional environments. Hobbyists programming BASIC would usually do so on only one machine, and machine code software was rewritten by specialists for each new machine.

```
GOTO 8 : REM CHIP-8
GOTO 8 : REM Type-in listings
GOTO 10 : REM BASIC
GOTO 10 : REM Toshiba HX-10
GOTO 30 : REM Storage
GOTO 1200 : REM Acorn BBC Micro baud rate
```

1200 : Acorn BBC Micro baud rate

The baud rate is defined as the number of symbols transmitted every second over an electronic data channel. Although many cassette tapes would be recorded at 300 baud because it was more stable, some software would be recorded at 1200 baud, meaning that four times as much data could be included on the tape, and its loading time would decrease accordingly.

```
GOTO 86 : REM BBC cassettes
GOTO 1200 : REM BASICODE
```

1500 : Computer sounds in music

The idea of computer-generated sounds being used in, and for, music was a long battle. Initial attempts were monophonic square wave beeps that were never *quite* in tune, and so were regarded as a gimmick.

Ironically, when computers were professional enough to generate quality music, the industry used only the noises from retro computer games, like samples of *Pac-Man* on an EP by Power-Pill (one of the many guises of Richard D. James, aka Aphex Twin), or Russian folk song 'Korobeiniki' (as heard in *Tetris*, written by Alexey Pajitnov in 1984) being remixed by Dr Spin, a collaboration between producer Nigel Wright and musical theatre composer Andrew Lloyd Webber. Yes – that one!

Pac-Man was also the inspiration for some literal lyrics on a track called 'Pac-Man Fever' by Buckner & Garcia in 1981. In the US, at least, it was a hit, selling over 500,000 copies, going gold, and reaching number nine on the *Billboard* Hot 100 charts.

One band often credited with bringing computerised music to the masses is German band Kraftwerk. With their futuristic sounds and precise electronic rhythms, they are the poster bots of the field. Ironically, at the time of their ground-breaking 1981 album, *Computer World*, none of them owned a home computer. Nor did they use computers in the studio. Ultimately, one track from the album 'Computer World' was appropriately used by the UK state broadcaster, the BBC, for their TV computer education programme, called *The Computer Programme*.

Yet the computer on the aforementioned album cover did exist. It was the Hazeltine 1500.

```
GOTO 19 : REM Musicians with computers
GOTO 33⅓ : REM Revolutions per minute
GOTO 6581 : REM Sound generation
GOTO 31250 : REM MIDI
```

1701 : Licensed and unlicensed material

On 22 May 1980, Namco released the very first version of *Pac-Man* in the game arcades of Japan. It was an instant hit which alerted and inspired other developers to make their own versions. Sometimes it was a blatant attempt to grab money from public who were unable to buy an official version (since none had been made), and at other times it was an honest homage from those who loved the original. Every version, however, had different names to avoid lawsuits. For example:

- *Zuckman* – the ZX81 version by DJL Software
- *MunchMan* – for TI-99/4A, where the character places pills down instead of eating them
- *Snapper* – Acornsoft's BBC Micro and Acorn Electron version
- *Tax Man* – for Apple II
- *Puck-Man* – the original title of *Pac-Man*, used in some amateur versions

Intellectual property (IP) law extends from copyrights, patents, trademarks, and trade secrets out to almost everything. In motorsport, for example, the Fédération Internationale de l'Automobile (FIA) control all the IP within Formula 1, so the PC strategy game *Grand Prix Manager* had a driver called 'John Newhouse' because they were unable to use the name (or the likeness) of Indy 500 crossover star, Jacques Villeneuve.

For developers unable, or unwilling, to pay the license fees for the character or personnel names, then there is a simple solution – change them! *Motorsport Manager* uses its own team and driver names in place of those found in F1, as does Kevin Toms' *Football Star Manager*. While it does limit the realism some-what, it keeps the authors on the right side of the law and allows you to continue playing.

```
GOTO 64 : REM Spanish import law
GOTO 256 : REM Nintendo Game Boy Boot ROM
```

1729 : Taxicab number

A taxicab number is the smallest integer that can be expressed as a sum of two positive integer cubes, in two or more distinct ways. In this case $1729 = 1^3 + 12^3 = 9^3 + 10^3$. It came about as an offhand remark made by Srinivasa Ramanujan to fellow mathematician Godfrey Hardy in 1919.

By law, every book about numbers must mention 1729! It features as an Easter egg in many episodes of *Futurama*, and therefore must be mentioned here too. Congratulations on finding this interesting number!

1802 : Netronics ELF II

The RCA 1802 CPU was a favourite of magazines like *Popular Electronics*. It began in 1976 when Joseph A. Weisbecker wrote the first of three articles entitled 'Build the COSMAC Elf'. With only 256 bytes of memory his Elf Toggle OPerating System (ETOPS) had to be small – 32 bytes small. For those that didn't want to build their own, there was the Netronics ELF II.

This was an enhanced version of the homebrew machine, supplying value-add in the form of expansion slots, uncommon for this type of machine, into which you could plug accessory cards facilitating colour graphics, EPROM burners, and more RAM. They also sold keyboards, video terminals (supporting 64x14 characters), and programming courses for both Tiny BASIC and 1802 machine code.

With extra memory you could run full BASIC using an additional ROM card, which also acted as a maths co-processor through fast floating point operations and Reverse Polish Notation.

Both Donald Meyer and Todd Decker consider this to be their favourite machine.

GOTO 5 : REM SCRUMPI

1982 : The year 1982

1982 was the peak of the golden age of retro computing. It saw the launch of the Sinclair ZX Spectrum, Commodore 64, Dragon 32, Oric, GCE Vectrex, Jupiter Ace, and many more. *Time* magazine featured video games on its cover for the first time and instead of naming a Person of the Year (a distinction I won in 2006, when Person of the Year was 'You'!), announced 'The Computer' as their Machine of the Year. Even in the cinema, films such as *Star Trek II: The Wrath of Khan* (featuring the first complete computer-generated sequence in a feature film), *Blade Runner* and *Tron* underpinned geek culture of the time. It was if all the planets had aligned!

Such was the prevalence of computing at this time that almost nobody noticed that doctors had implanted the first permanent artificial heart, there was the first International Day of Peace, and there was a syzygy.

With so much to choose from, you could do worse than choosing from the following options:

GOTO 8 : REM Type-in listings
GOTO 82 : REM Sinclair ZX Spectrum+

```
20 GOTO 10
```

```
GOTO 1200 : REM BASICODE
GOTO 31900 : REM With prizes
```

1992 : The year 1992

1992 was the year that id Software released *Wolfenstein 3D*, leading to *Doom*, *Quake* and the creation of the modern first person shooter (FPS). It was also the year when Macromedia was founded, the company which gave us (and then mercifully retired) the accessibility nightmare and security loophole known as Flash.

Unification (not the *Star Trek: The Next Generation* episode of the same name that was broadcast in 1991) was the centre of attention on the world stage, as the European Union was founded through the Maastricht Treaty, while George Bush and Boris Yeltsin formally declared an end to the Cold War, and a South African referendum ended apartheid.

Sadly, the person who popularised the word 'bug', Grace Hopper, passed away on January 1, 1992.

You can make a lot of changes in 30 years, so you have a choice of where to start.

```
GOTO 50 : REM Compilations
GOTO 70 : REM Bugs
```

2000 : The future

Throughout the 1950s, '60s, '70s, and even the '80s, the new millennium seemed a long way away. Far enough, in fact, that anything with the number 2000 written on it was an indication that someone (usually the manufacturer) thought it futuristic. Consequently, there were many devices suffixed with the number 2000 to make it appeal to those expecting the future.

There were computers like the COSMAC Elf 2000, Omnibot 2000, and Tournament 2000 along with watches like the Seiko UC-2000. To go one (or one thousand) better, there was an analogue computer called the Donner 3000! (Although this preceded the microcomputer revolution by being launched in 1955.) Despite geeks fawning over machines which implied they travelled from a Utopian future version of history, there appears to be a direct negative correlation between inclusion of the number 2000 and its commercial success!

```
GOTO 8 : REM CHIP-8
```

2002 : The year 2002

2002 was the year that Microsoft released the very first Xbox in Japan, Europe and Australia. Spurred on by their first foray into game console hardware, Microsoft partnered with Sega on the development of the Dreamcast, resulting in selling, essentially, a PC in a console-shaped box, powered by its DirectX driver software and APIs created, originally, to provide a thin abstraction layer to the PC hardware allowing for faster games.

It was also the year that Napster filed for bankruptcy, LinkedIn was created, and PayPal was acquired by eBay. In the real world, the Euro was introduced, the environmental satellite Envisat was launched, and Jimmy Carter was awarded the Nobel Peace Prize.

You certainly understand that 20 years is old enough to be considered retro, so let's start this journey with that discussion.

GOTO 20 : REM What is retro?

2012 : The year 2012

In 2012, companies like Asus and Samsung released the Chromebox, a headless computer which ran a customised version of Linux called Chrome OS.

It was also the year Tinder was launched, London held the Summer Olympics, and Vladimir Putin was elected President of Russia, again.

And, while the Mayans were wrong that 2012 would be the last year for humanity, it did unfortunately see the passing of Jack Tramiel, the founder of Commodore.

Alas, in no way can we consider 2012 to be a retro year.

Your quest ends here!

5150 : The first personal computer

If it were not already obvious, every computer in this book, which we consider retro, is uniquely different from every other. Not just in terms of its processor, the video chip, or its memory, but in the way it was built. Or the ethos. Or the people that built it – people who were often individuals, but sometimes teams of no more than six or seven engineers working in close proximity. The stories of those teams shine through to this day because, ultimately, these machines were an embodiment of the personality of the people who made them.

So it is perhaps ironic that the machine which ultimately killed the individuality of computing was made in August 1981, just as the industry was about to start.

That machine was the IBM 5150, the first personal computer. Prior to the 5150, IBM's previous machine had cost $13,000 and took the company years to design. IBM engineers had to build each individual component, write all the software, and ship the units to a targeted group of customers. The PC was built with off-the-shelf parts and a third-party OS, and shipped within a twelve-month turnaround. Everything about it was bland, corporate, and lacking in personality.

Although computers not based around the PC architecture were still being made until the 1990s, with versions of the Commodore Amiga and Atari ST (nicknamed the 'Jackintosh') being two of the most popular contenders, there was little hope of them being able to tackle the might of the PC. Sure, the Amiga had astounding sound and graphics chips at a lower price point, but factors such as the raw compute power of the PC and the compatibility of Windows software meant the Amiga would never win against the dominance that had been growing around IBM PCs for over a decade.

The PC spawned a cottage industry all of its own, with well-documented standards providing a lower barrier to entry (and wider customer base) for anyone wanting to enter the marketplace. When Sir Clive Sinclair launched his simple 1 KiB computer, for example, a similar support industry sprung up with add-ons to improve the basic, and rather underpowered, machine. IBM had applied the same learnings that built the (now retro) computer industry in the first place. But, in doing so, it killed it.

Since this book is also an adventure game book, I have designated this to be the equivalent of a 'Game Over' page. Your choices have led you here. You didn't find the POKE for *Jet Set Willy*, or find out what happens when his housekeeper Maria has gone and you're able to complete the game.

Your quest ends here!

6128 : Amstrad CPC 6128

Unusually for a machine designed and built in the UK, the 6128 was originally only sold in the USA, released on 13 June 1985. At least it came back to the UK that August! But otherwise, it was everything you'd expect from an Amstrad machine in 1985 – a 3" floppy drive, 128 KiB of RAM, and supplied with its own monitor. (An important point when the average household had only one TV.)

Like the CPC 664 before it, the Z80 processor and floppy disk combination meant that it could run CP/M, a popular operating system at the time, by Digital Research. This marked it above the usual custom offerings from Amstrad, whose PCW range (also known as 'Joyce') provided all the functionality of a PC word processing system at one quarter of the cost. (Alas, it only included the functionality of the word processor – not the PC!)

Both James Docherty and Paolo Borzini consider this (in its 'plus' form) to be their favourite machine.

GOTO 64 : REM Spanish import law

6581 : Sound generation

It might seem incredible now, but the first generation of microcomputers didn't have sound. Those that did have sound were usually limited to a single monophonic channel, capable of generating one squawkish note at a time. Future machines expanded on this, with modern computers capable of producing music identical to that found on commercial recordings. (For our purposes we separate the ability of a computer to playback an existing piece of pre-recorded music from its ability to generate those sounds in the first place, concentrating on the latter.)

The changes in audio quality have not always been in step with the generational changes in the rest of the hardware. (After all, the 8-bit ZX Spectrum 128 had the same inbuilt sound capabilities as the 16-bit Atari ST.) This difference arose because each manufacturer placed a different priority on the audio experience. Sir Clive Sinclair had originally intended his Sinclair machines to be sold as an education tool that, like the IBM PC and business machines of the day, needed little more than an occasional beep. The Commodore 64, on the other hand, came from the American roots of Atari, which made computers for the masses not the classes, so games were a major selling point; it needed a custom-made chip for game-quality sound and music. This chip was the MOS Technology 6581, the Sound Interface Device or SID for short – and you could tell SID was for Banging Tunes!

Constructing sound waves

Let us backtrack to the basics.

A sound wave is often imagined like this.

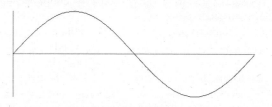

A basic sine wave

Here you can see a fairly smooth sine wave of 440 Hz, or concert pitch A. It is as smooth as Brylcreem because there are 65,536 discrete amplitude levels, at each point in time, along the X-axis. This is a 16-bit sound, or sample. However, if the machine could only generate the amplitude using 1 bit of data, it would have just two discrete levels. That produces a sound like this.

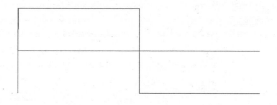

A 1-bit square wave

Naturally, this second waveform will sound nothing like the first, and so a difference in quality is apparent. This sound property is the bit depth. Even before the appearances of the Apple II, ZX Spectrum, and early PCs, with their 1-bit sound resolution, computers could generate basic sounds like this by sending pulses to a connected speaker in a form of bit banging, which controls the hardware speaker directly instead of using a provided library or module. Usually, as with Australia's first digital computer, the CSIR Mark 1 or CSIRAC, the purpose of this audio pulse was to indicate the end of the program. But by carefully timing the pulses, they could be made to occur at regular intervals, thereby creating a steady tone.

The regularity is reflected in the second sound property, playback frequency. Not only do you need to be able to change the amplitude value 880 times a second for a 440 Hz note (one change to go from 0 to 1, and another to go back to 0) you need to be able to do so with a very high accuracy. Any interruption (pun intended for the geeks at the back!) to the timing process of, say, 67 microseconds would change the frequency to 415.30 Hz, resulting in an A♭ and some bleeding ears. Without fast and cycle-accurate code, sound would never be considered high fidelity, and so an alternate method for generation was required.

The solution was through custom chips, such as the aforementioned 6581. Although every chip was different, it would be programmed via similar means and would have a predetermined number of voices, indicating how many concurrent sounds it could generate. The chip would also indicate the types of waveforms each voice could play. Since the programmer no longer sent a stream of numbers to the chip to indicate the shape of the wave, these waveforms would be part of the chip and would usually consist of the main primitive types of sine, square, sawtooth, and pulse (a variation on square).

In theory you can generate any of these using only sine waves, but since you need an infinite number of sine waves to generate a square wave, it is more usual to provide the primitives.

Another common shortcut was that a machine with four channels might only be able to play discernible tones with three of them, so might use the fourth as a noise channel. Noise might not sound useful, but it uses a very cheap circuit to include and control and, when played in very short bursts, can mimic the sound of snare drums and hi-hats.

Consequently, we can say that audio is often described with three parameters:

1. Number of voices, i.e. the polyphony, how many sounds it can play at once
2. Bit depth, i.e. the quality, or clarity, of the sound
3. Playback frequency, i.e. the highest pitch it can play

Affecting the soundwave

But that is only the start of the synthesis story. Some chips might be able to shape the sound, by changing the volume over time. This is the ADSR *envelope* – attack, decay, sustain and release. Real-world instruments have these basic characteristics in varying amounts. An instrument which is struck, like a drum, will have a sharp spike reaching full volume almost immediately (the attack), following by a continual decay.

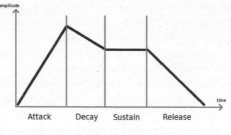

The ADSR envelope

If the audio chip cannot change the volume envelope automatically, then the software might be able to control it manually via the CPU, but only if it has enough processing time to do so. Consequently, on some machines the sound might sound more impressive in a standalone demo when the computer is doing nothing else, compared to when it is trying to run a game with the additional workload of graphics, input and AI.

On the Commodore 64, the SID chip had all of this and more, including a range of filters, effects and modulators to shape the sound from something bland or harsh into something more musical. It also had a 4-bit volume register at address $D418 which could be controlled by feeding it a stream of numbers (just like the bit banging of the early machines) that would simulate a fourth channel, which could be used for playing back sound samples.

Better hardware channels through software

As you can see, with so many parameters, it is very difficult to make quantitative judgments over the sound quality of the various machines... except that the Commodore machines clearly won out! First with the Commodore 64, and then with the Amiga, because only Amiga made it possible to produce music that hit the charts by dance acts like Urban Shakedown and U-U-U-Utah Saints [sic]. Even though, by this time, the machine's custom sound chip, Paula, could generate what was considered four high-quality voices of 8-bit sound onto two stereo channels. There were even tricks to combine the two 8-bit voices on the left-hand channel into one better, high-quality, 12-bit sound (and likewise on the right). The only reason that 8-bit + 8-bit doesn't equal 16 is that there are 4 bits of overlap in the amplitude.

But if by 'better', you mean more channels, instead of higher quality, then there were *other* tricks. One of these was to combine two sounds, of say a kick drum and hi-hat, into one sample. This would occupy only one voice. With careful placement, you could then provide a full-sounding drum kit of kick, snares, toms, and so on, occupying only a single voice. Alternatively, you could combine all three notes of a triad chord into a single sound and achieve a similarly miserly use of voices. Or simply play each note of the chord consecutively (as opposed to concurrently) creating a fast arpeggio where the individual notes would blur slightly into one another.

But in 1989 the Amiga program OctaMED, written by Teijo Kinnunen, managed to use code that would give you eight voices for real. It would change eight 8-bit sounds into eight 4-bit sounds quick enough that two of these 4-bit sounds could then be combined into a single 8-bit channel! This produced eight channels of music. Although it's a simple process, it took the CPU so long to do that there wasn't enough processing power left on a base A500 to run a game at the same time, so this idea was limited to those using the computer exclusively for music production.

The same idea was used in WaveMix, a 1993 Windows API from Microsoft. In this case a single pair of sounds (for the left and right speaker) were played in a loop. Every few milliseconds the computer would combine all the sounds which had requested playback into a single sound, and then insert them into the loop, just ahead of the point the computer was going to play. In this way you could have as many concurrent sounds as your processor speed allowed.

Although turning four voices into eight is an intriguing technique, perhaps the winner is how a machine capable of playing zero notes was coaxed into playing one! This was the Sinclair ZX81 and although unable to play music in the accepted fashion, true, it did generate sound when saving programs to tape. So developers found a way to exploit this idea to produce 1-bit sound via the cassette interface.

Everyone else who wanted sound on the ZX81 simply upgraded to a ZX Spectrum. Or bought a peripheral.

```
GOTO 19 : REM Musicians with computers
GOTO 33⅓ : REM Revolutions per minute
GOTO 1500 : REM Computer sounds in music
GOTO 31250 : REM MIDI
```

6847 : Dragon 32

Wales gets very few mentions in computing literature. When it does, the word Dragon usually follows. Starting as a subsidiary of the toy company Mettoy, Dragon Data Ltd was founded to create a home machine based around the Motorola 6809E in early 1982. The 6809 was less well-known than the incumbents of Zilog Z80 and MOS 6502, but it was generally regarded as a better processor, as witnessed by the 32 K version of *Jet Set Willy* holding 13 more rooms than the 48 K Spectrum version!

One interesting feature is the Synchronous Address Multiplexor (SAM) chip which could be programmed without data. Instead, the SAM mapped pairs of memory addresses to control registers on other chips. Writing a value – *any value* – to location $FFC0 would clear bit 0 of the first control register of the VDG (Video Display Generator). Writing a value to $FFC1 would set bit 0. Consequently, no data need be initialised or transferred, saving time and connectors on the chip, and thereby saving money. The Archimedes would later employ a similar technique.

There are two criticisms often levelled against the Dragon. The first is that it's a copy, or clone, of the Tandy TRS-80 Color Computer (aka the CoCo). This is easily refuted by noting that *both* are taken directly from the Motorola reference design for the 6809E chip.

The second issue is that its default colour scheme includes a lurid (fans might say 'quirky') bright green, reminiscent of luminous socks from the mid-1980s. That is because of the MC6847 chip chosen for graphics. But for that, there is no excuse!

Both Rebecca Bryan and Geoff Campbell consider this to be their favourite machine.

GOTO 3 : REM Tandy TRS 80 Model III

16509 : ZX81 1K Display

Both the Sinclair ZX80 and ZX81 had very limited capabilities. They had a screen able to display 32x24 characters, each one being a graphic block, a letter, number or punctuation symbol. Each of the 24 rows required 33 bytes of memory: 32 for the characters on the screen, and one terminating byte of 118 (0x76) to indicate the end of line. There is also a single byte of 118 to begin the display as a whole, leading us to 33 * 24 + 1 = 793 bytes of memory needed to store a single screen. Given that both machines use the same memory for both the screen and the program, that leaves just 231 bytes for the code, variables and system data. So how were these machines able to store both and do any meaningful work?

Up and to the left.

The trick is to consider the terminating byte of 118. Knowing the screen is always 32 characters wide, it seems superfluous to have a terminating byte, so we must ask ourselves why it's there. In fact, it's there because although the screen is 32 characters wide that's not to say the *display* is. A printer, when faced with a blank page, does not make any attempt to print a series of spaces on the paper. Nor does the ZX81 in a digital form. Instead, it prints each character on a row to the screen until it reaches a 118, and then leaves the rest of the line blank. Consequently, a single (blank) row takes only 1 byte. This is known as a 'compressed display file' where the whole screen uses just 25 bytes.

From this it is also easy to see that any text justified to the left of the screen uses less memory than text on the right, since the latter needs to be prefixed with spaces. And those spaces are charged at 1 byte each.

Why 118? There is a dual reality happening here. The first is that 118 is the character code for newline, or carriage return, meaning that there is nothing that would have been printed anyway and so matches the expectations of a program writing character code 118 to the screen. The second is that both machines used the Zilog Z80 processor, and the Z80 opcode 118 is the HALT instruction. This suspends the processor from doing any more work until it's interrupted by something else. In our case, that interrupt is provided when the screen has finished drawing that line of the display, at which point it can move onto the next line.

Since the memory required by the display grows as necessary it must start immediately after the program memory. (If the display memory was before the program, then the whole program would have to be relocated in memory whilst it was running whenever a new item was drawn on the screen and it needed more memory.) If you have access to a ZX81, or an emulator, you can investigate this phenomenon yourself. Start by finding the value of the display file, DFILE, which is the address of the first byte of screen memory:

```
PRINT PEEK 16396 + PEEK 16397 * 256
```

This will be 16509 on a 1 KiB system that has just been switched on.

Then find the last byte of the screen memory:

```
PRINT PEEK 16400 + PEEK 16401 * 256 - 1
```

You can then write text to the screen, which will cause the screen memory to move, and then PEEK those memory locations (or view them in the emulator's debugger) at your leisure. (Just remember that every time you add a line of program code the first byte of screen memory changes, so you will need to find the value of DFILE again.)

If you do not see this behaviour then it is likely you are using a 16 KiB machine where, by default, the display is 'expanded' with each row consisting of 32 spaces and a carriage return, i.e. character code 118.

As a final note, there is a curious incident with this type of display format – it is possible to have a program that fits in memory, and works perfectly, but cannot be LISTed because that listing would cause the screen display to expand and require more memory than was left. Conversely, it is possible to have a program run fine until it tries to write too many lines of text to the screen, at which point it will stop with an 'out of memory' error.

```
GOTO 84 : REM LCD displays
GOTO 205.5 : REM How to draw a maze in one line
GOTO 672 : REM 1K Chess
GOTO 2455992 : REM The Cathode Ray Tube
GOTO 16777216 : REM Colour
```

31250 : MIDI

MIDI stands for Musical Instrument Digital Interface, and was created as a way for one musical instrument (or computer) to talk about music with another. In this case, it spoke only in notes. This was perfectly acceptable when used by musicians in their recording studios, since they knew which synthesisers would play what sounds when sent a particular MIDI message. When MIDI was introduced onto PC soundcards, the quality of playback was determined entirely by the budget of the end user. So if you wanted the game soundtrack to sound just like the composer wrote it, but using your soundcard's equivalent of a toy keyboard, then you should be so lucky!

The one time when MIDI-based music was truly king was in generative music. Games like *Monkey Island* from LucasArts would have numerous snippets of music that the AI would stitch together, in real time, to form music which would adapt according to how you played the game. A headache for the composer, but a joy to the few game players who noticed it – fewer than you might think, given how seamless the process was.

Ultimately, PC games reverted to type by playing back pre-recorded samples for the effects, and (optionally) using the audio tracks on the accompanying CD for the music, since doing so ensured a consistent high-quality result for all involved and used almost no CPU power.

```
GOTO 19 : REM Musicians with computers
GOTO 33⅓ : REM Revolutions per minute
GOTO 1500 : REM Computer sounds in music
GOTO 5150 : REM The first personal computer
GOTO 6581 : REM Sound generation
```

31900 : With prizes

GCSE Geography Examination. Question 2:

Define and explain the three stages in the creation of an oxbow lake.
(6 marks)

I'm sure that very few of us, when answering that question as a teenager in a school assembly hall, believed it could have any impact in our adult lives. Or that being able to answer such trivia was something we would ever need.

However, as adults, TV quiz shows and pub quizzes have an incredible draw for us. So much so that we might actively revise equally useless trivia (such as the ordering of The Beatles members' birthdates, from oldest to youngest) so that we might win a lukewarm bottle of white wine from the Dog and Duck on a Monday night!

And it's a quiz we're happy to pay to enter!

While the distinction between 'exam' and 'quiz' is an interesting one, it's a question (pun intended) for another time. But where does the traditional quiz intersect with computer games?

Games or quizzes?

Our earliest experiences of quiz-based games on home computers arrived labelled as educational games. Although with questions like '4 + 7' or '12 − 2' they were not games, and barely educational. But they were all we had, since randomly generated maths questions required significantly less memory than the text of a traditional question-and-answer format. Plus, the processing needed to determine whether 'Queen Elizabeth II' was as equally a valid answer as 'Liz Version 2' was too extreme and prone to error. (And multiple-choice questions needed even more memory to store alternate answers.) Those that tried, like *Clever Clogs − Whizz Quiz* by 'Computer Tutor', could only boast 100 questions on a 48K machine, and those would be exhausted (and could be memorised) fairly quickly. In later years developers were able to load questions sets in distinct blocks from tape, a technique which allowed the 1986 game *Trivial Pursuit*, by Domark, to claim 3,000 questions on a 48 K ZX Spectrum. By this time disc drives were more common and the newer machines, such as the Atari ST and Commodore Amiga, came with them built-in, thus making large question sets a real possibility, due to both the disc's capacity and its random (rather than sequential) access. With pub quiz machines sporting around 100,000 questions, 3,000 is still a paltry number, but it perhaps reflects the relative amount of time spent at home in front of the computer versus time spent in the pub!

Instead, the format of brain teaser that was technically feasible was in the related genre named interactive fiction, or adventure games. The basic component was a textual description of several locations connected by twisty little passages that the player could traverse and interact with by typing simple commands like 'GO NORTH', or 'GET LAMP'. (Much like commanding a Big Trak to navigate your parents' kitchen!) Collecting, examining and using specific combinations of items would cause other parts of the game to open up. Perhaps 'USE MATCHES' would create a fire to burn through a prison door, or 'TIE SHEETS' would create a rope that allowed a new exit. Rather than being a true game sandbox, where open-ended and nonlinear play could take place, these had a goal which would be reached by mapping the area onto paper, noting the objects and their properties, and understanding the lateral puzzles presented. Not all the games were played fair, as some had random elements making the navigation more about luck than judgment. Many had tedious sections of maze exits, all alike, which provided cheap but uninspiring game-play. And most had a high level of frustration – one mistake early on in the game could result in a figurative dead-end later on, without any means of being able to backtrack and fix the problem.

But they were universal.

Without the need for sound, high resolution graphics or fast processors, any machine on the market could rely on the power of imagination to present fully-formed worlds with which a player could interact. So much so that adventure games predate most home computers. *Wander*, written in 1974 on a HP 2000 mainframe, even predates its more famous cousin, *Adventure*, based on the real-world Mammoth Cave in Kentucky. As a genre they have gone through many iterations, from text-only, to text and graphics, to graphics only, and even speech-only on Alexa devices. In almost every case, the conclusion of the adventure game resulted in a hearty 'Well done!' message, or simple animation, but nothing you could use to swell the bank account.

So, while many enjoy gaming for the implicit value of winning (the sheer joy of doing so), there is a small group that will only compete for some kind of external reward – like money. But it's not immediately obvious how someone sat at home, physically separated from the prize-giver, could win prizes. The radio was the broadcast medium of choice, with quiz programmes such as *General Knowledge Bee* in April 1938, followed in later years with phone-in shows. But the prizes were rarely large. The key point in all quizzes is that they are essentially live events. Once you've heard the question, there's no challenge. If you can pause the flow, there's time to find a dictionary or encyclopaedia. So how did the genre make its way into games – a medium which can be consumed multiple times? The solution was to limit the quiz element and focusing on the lateral thinking components. More a puzzle than a quiz. More interpretation and less information.

Following the trend

For the mainstream audience this was tried on TV in 1985 with a classic of the lateral-thinking genre, the 'whodunnit', in a film called *Murder in Space* staring Wilford Brimley and Michael Ironside, that offered a £10,000 prize if you posted your correct answer back before the summation was broadcast a few days later. For all the fanfare it was given, the show was a dud. Besides, the non-mainstream audiences knew this approach had already been tried in games. Which is where our part of the story begins. With a 1979 book by Kit Williams.

Kit was an artist. In 1979 he created a book called *Masquerade* that featured 15 of his original fine art prints which, when studied and properly analysed, would point to a specific location in the UK where a treasure was buried. The difference between this armchair treasure hunt and others which came before it was that the treasure was real! A genuine, hand-crafted, 18-carat golden hare pendant had been buried in Ampthill, near Bedford. Spoiler alert: it was by Catherine of Aragon's Cross which casts a shadow, like a sundial, indicating the precise location. But only at midday, on the March or September equinox.

Despite the rather obtuse nature of the puzzle, the prize was won. First by Dugald Thompson, and then again by Mike Barker and John Rousseau. Normally, when only one prize is available, only the first placed winner is of interest. But since Dugald had guessed the location using insider knowledge, the real winners came second – although their only prize was the joy of solving the puzzle, since the hare had already been given to Dugald. The golden hare, however, went onto a second life as we'll see shortly.

Introducing the computer

But we interrupt its tale to introduce a computer. The ZX81. And a 1982 game from Automata called *Pimania* created by Mel Croucher. Mel had taken the ideas of the armchair puzzle game and treasure hunt to build a game which used a surreal sense of humour and lateral clues to determine the date, time and location (also in the UK) of where a golden sundial, said to be valued at £6,000, could be found. The time was necessary because instead of burying the item the developers of *Pimania*, Mel and Christian Penfold (the latter in a Piman costume), would venture to the Litlington White Horse in East Sussex on 22 July every year (i.e. 22/7, an approximation of Pi) to look for any Pimaniacs who were stood at the mouth of the Horse. In 1985 they met Sue Cooper and Lizi Newman who, despite standing at the Horse's rear end, were declared the winners, and received their sundial and a pub lunch.

Anyone who has attempted to play the game will know what an amazing achievement it was to win. What is even more incredible is that the game wasn't solved more quickly given it was written in BASIC! There was no need to hack, crack, reverse engineer or emulate the software. Simply press BREAK when the program starts, and type LIST! Like *Masquerade*, except the clues were included in the game and present in an obfuscated format. In fact, other than a series of PRINT statements indicating the location descriptions, there was almost nothing in the code to guide you.

Let's look at some of the code from the ZX81 version:

```
730 LET Z=D
740 LET T$=M$(GATE)(Z TO Z+D)
750 IF T$="00" THEN GOTO 810
760 IF T$<>P$(D) THEN GOTO 790
770 LET GATE=VAL (M$(GATE)(Z+G
TO Z+S))
780 GOTO 200
790 LET Z=Z+H
800 GOTO 740
```

Pimania ZX81 source extract

Courtesy of Subvert Ltd

Nowhere in the program does it show you the value of D (it's 1, by the way), explain the purpose of M$, or describe why the number 6 is called GATE. And this obfuscation was one way it kept its secrets from the merely curious. The code would also read the character code of the text (which, being a ZX81, wasn't standard ASCII) and subtract 38 from it to do some game logic. It would change program flow based on two variables, preventing any form of static analysis.

```
2510 FOR Q=D TO C*A
2520 IF W$=V$(Q)(S TO ) THEN GOT
O 2550
2530 NEXT Q
2540 RETURN
2550 LET P$(W)=V$(Q)( TO G)
2560 RETURN
2570 LET Y=Y+D
2580 LET GAP=(Y>LEN K$)
2590 IF GAP THEN RETURN
2600 LET GAP=(K$(Y)=" ")
2610 RETURN
```

I would not claim it used every trick in the book, since the machine was too new for a book to have been written, but the code didn't make life easy for anyone trying to solve the game by employing tactics worthy of the no-win simulation of the 'Kobayashi Maru', as found in *Star Trek*.

Furthermore, the ZX81 would save variables in memory alongside the code when committing the program to tape. This was why the program didn't need to explicitly set these variables in code. However, whenever you ran the program, the BASIC interpreter first cleared the memory of all variables, before starting the game. You had to therefore restart the program with GOTO or CONT. Any player who stopped the program running to change or hack it and then carelessly hit RUN would find the game stopping with errors since there were no variables holding that all-important game data.

The game itself was also rather obtuse, using the numbers on a clock face instead of the standard compass points for navigation, and requiring you to type "Pi" to start the game. (Line 190, since you asked.)

Even the win message, although clearly visible in the code, gave no clues.

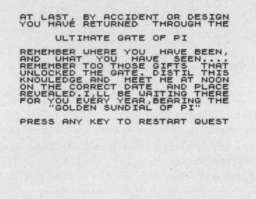

Pimania ZX81 win screen
Courtesy of Subvert Ltd

So, the only way to win was to play the game, and understand the mentality of the puzzle setter.

Of prizes won

Knowing it took three years for Sue Cooper and Lizi Newman to complete *Pimania*, how long would you spend trying to win? And for how much money? When *Pimania* was released in 1982 it retailed for £10, compared to the usual £5.95 price-point for games like *Hungry Horace*. So when BBC Radio 1 DJ Dave Lee Travis put his name to *DLT's Monster Challenge*, with a grand prize of £10,000, you can only wonder whether the £9 price tag was to pay him or the winners.

Oh, and £9 only covered *one* of the games. There were six in total which the publisher, Twig Systems Software, courteously allowed you to purchase at £45 for the set – plus £1 for P&P. Each game would provide a clue, and all six clues would combine to present a riddle for you to solve. Still, £45 was a significant outlay in 1983, before you invested any time with the games. Plus, solving the riddle didn't even win you the prize! It merely put you in a queue, where the first 10 would be finalists in DLT's 'Ten-Grand-Slam'. Whatever that was.

Anyone still keen?

No? Nor was anyone in 1983, either! Despite a few adverts across the 1983–84 Christmas period, listing the games for sale and boasting that it was available for the BBC B, Dragon 32, and ZX Spectrum, there appears to be no surviving copies. This was a shame since the adverts indicated that some of the games could be played with two humans. Presumably you couldn't win a clue from the game in this mode, since you could simply invite the local village idiot to play against.

But these weren't the only games that offered prizes for doing well.

- *Splat!*, a 1983 action game, rewarded James Tant with £500 for scoring over 112,930 points.
- *The Mountains of Ket* Trilogy, an adventure from 1983, won Tom Frost a £4,000 video recorder.
- Automata returned to the prize genre with *My Name is Uncle Groucho, You Win a Fat Cigar*, late in 1983, with an all-expenses paid trip to New York. Phil Daley won.
- *The Staff of Karnath* appeared in 1984 and provided Lee Goldstone and Matthew Porter with a (literal) trophy.

Even the infamous bug in *Jet Set Willy* didn't stop the competition for completion being won by Ross Holman and Cameron Else – although they turned down the champagne, glasses, and helicopter flight to opt instead for cash, to buy new computers.

There seems to be no direct relation between the price of the game and the value of the prize being offered, although the record prize fund at one time was held by *Eureka!* for the ZX Spectrum and Commodore 64, created by Ian Livingstone (now Sir Ian) in 1984. It claimed 250 K of 'pure mystery' and a £25,000 cash prize in return for a £14.95 investment in the software.

We have little further evidence of the real-world treasure format being attempted again until later in 1984, when a hitherto unknown company released a puzzle hunt for the Electron, BBC B, Oric Atmos, Dragon 32, Spectrum 48, Commodore 64, Vic 20 EX, and Amstrad – an impressive cross-platform effort for the time. It was called *Hareraiser*, and had a prize of £30,000 in cash or an 18-carat golden hare pendant. Sound familiar? That's because the company, Haresoft Ltd, was co-founded by Dugald Thompson who 'won' the original *Masquerade* treasure hunt from 1979. The game was released in two parts, *Prelude* and *Finale*, both retailing at an above average £8.95 in July and September respectively. Other than the 'Hare' in the title, the games reflected none of the book's visual or creative aesthetic. Nor did they show any consideration for game play or fairness, with both parts of the game being generally regarded as something of a cynical cash grab. Given the claims of cheating in the original *Masquerade* case, the most telling part of the game, perhaps, lies in the rules for winning the prize. Part 4 of the cassette inlay reads:

> 'No direct or indirect employees of Haresoft Ltd., their families, friends or any person connected with the production of this program is eligible for entry into this competition.'

But the prize was never won, and eventually the golden hare went to auction to recover their company's losses. And the hammer price for the hare at auction? £31,900.

```
GOTO 2 : REM Last!
GOTO 3 : REM The stages of an oxbow lake
GOTO 3 : REM Optimising for size
GOTO 18 : REM Certificate 18
GOTO 33⅓ : REM Revolutions per minute
GOTO 672 : REM 1K Chess
GOTO 69105 : REM Leaves
GOSUB 40404243 : REM The Beatles birthdates
```

35899 : PEEK **and** POKE

There is probably no BASIC instruction more mysterious and beloved than the POKE command!

At its heart, POKE simply writes a single byte of data into a single address in memory. While this is not an uncommon event, since many commands write data to memory, this one does so without any validation checks. If your POKE is to a sensible place in memory, then you might see a character appear on screen. If it's in some memory that's currently unused, it will appear benign. But if it's not, the POKE could either do magical things to the system or just crash the machine, as it rewrites part of the operating system's working area, confusing the OS.

But the real reason enthusiasts remember POKEs is because of instructions printed in magazines like:

```
POKE 35899,0
```

This gives you infinite lives in the ZX Spectrum version of the game *Jet Set Willy*. It worked like this. First, you would load the game into memory in such a way that it didn't automatically start. This was done with:

```
MERGE ""
```

This combined the program on tape with the one in memory. (Not that you had one in memory, but the game didn't realise it was being tricked in this way!) You'd then be able to find the code which loaded the rest of the game, and add the POKE command, or commands, after the code that loads the game, but before it is run.

This specific POKE changed the instruction at location 35899 from 0x35 to a 0. The instruction 0x35 refers to:

```
DEC (HL)
```

It means 'reduce the number stored in the memory location referred to by HL by one'. Naturally HL, in this instance, refers to the number of lives. Because it's close to impossible to remove this instruction, instead the POKE will rewrite the instruction to be NOP or 'No Operation' which is represented by a 0.

By the way, POKE had a sister called PEEK. It would read the contents of memory. But that's rather unimportant given that you have now found the infinite lives POKE for *Jet Set Willy*. Maria, the obstructive housekeeper, has gone. And you can finally get to bed, before throwing up in the toilet shortly afterwards!

You deserve that reward!

```
GOTO 0 : REM NOP
GOTO 4 : REM Bugs in Jet Set Willy
```

38911 : Bytes

Although not every manufacturer lies about the amount of RAM in their machine, some can be a little frugal with the truth. Focusing on the 8-bit era, where machines would generally access memory via a 16-bit address bus, the generally accepted maximum was 2^{16} = 65536 bytes = 64 KiB. But the real number could be higher or lower.

To access *more* memory, the computer, and the programmers, had to do something clever. Using a system called 'banking', a specific portion of the memory address could access any one of a number of different memory banks – but only one bank at a time. So you needed to know in which bank your data (or occasionally code) would reside so you could switch banks, access the necessary data, and then switch back.

The more usual case is when a machine has less memory than advertised. Commodore displayed this at boot-up for all to see: 38911 bytes, or around 59% of the total 64 KiB machine. By a popular comparison, on a par with the battles between wrestlers Big Daddy and Giant Haystacks on *World of Sport* or the question of 'Daddy or chips', the 48 K model of the ZX Spectrum had 41613 bytes, which was larger in both the absolute and relative (85%) sense. (This did, according to the rules of the playground, prove that the Spectrum was superior!) Both machines needed memory for the screen, system variables, and input/output system. A higher resolution screen meant more memory was needed for it. A better IO system needed more space, and so on. But in the case of Commodore, the lion's share of its RAM was hidden in the shadows.

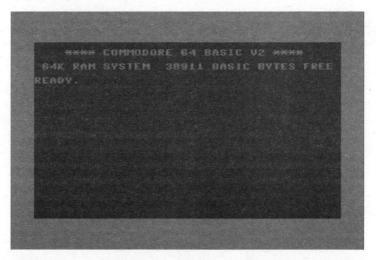

So where is the rest of the RAM that Commodore placed inside the case? To start, there is an 8 KiB Commodore BASIC ROM which lives between memory addresses $A000 and $BFFF (40960–49151). If you want to program in BASIC, then this is necessary. And since the machine boots up into BASIC, this memory is unavailable by default.

There is also a 4 KiB block which lives between $D000 and $DFFF (53248–57343) that is used by the I/O area, and is unavailable.

Finally, there is an 8 KiB Kernal ROM at $E000 and $FFFF (57344–65535) to handle the machine hardware. (Kernal is the *correct* spelling in this context, although it originates from an *incorrect* spelling in one of developer Robert Russell's notebooks.) The Kernal includes machine-specific code that talks to the screen, reads from the keyboard, and so on. This is distinct from the BASIC ROM using an implementation technique known as loose coupling. The origin of Commodore BASIC was in a version created by Microsoft in 1977 who licensed to various companies for their own machines. Given the wide variety of computers, Microsoft's original implementation of BASIC didn't include any code to handle the hardware, such as writing to the screen, or reading from a keyboard. This meant the code could be used on any 6502-based machine with very few, if any, changes. (This has the natural downside of requiring a magical POKE 53280,N to change the colour of the screen border, instead of the more friendly BORDER command which wasn't generic enough to be part of BASIC.) Instead, when the BASIC ROM needed to write OUT a CHaRacter to the screen it would call a specific routine in the Kernal called CHROUT at address $FFD2, and let it do the work. It was then the responsibility of the company making the machine, rather than the BASIC, to ensure that there was a suitable character writing routine at the $FFD2 memory location.

$FFD2 is in a section of memory containing a table of Kernal 'vectors'. Essentially, this is a list of JMP instructions telling the computer to execute code somewhere else. On the Commodore 64 this table begins:

```
Address
FF81    4C 5B FF    JMP $FF5B    ; initalise the screen and keyboard
FF84    4C A3 FD    JMP $FDA3    ; initalise the I/O
FF87    4C 50 FD    JMP $FD50    ; initalise the memory
```

Because the Microsoft BASIC ROM couldn't know how many instructions were needed for the machine-specific 'initialise the screen and keyboard' routine, convention dictated a block at the end memory that would contain only JMP instructions. It was then the responsibility of the Commodore Kernal ROM to find space for the screen routines, and to make sure the instruction at location $FF81 would jump to it.

The implementation for the CHROUT routine was slightly different insomuch as it used an indirect address, denoted with brackets.

```
FFD2   6C 26 03   JMP ($0326)   ; write a character to the
   screen
```

In this case, the CPU would read the data at addresses $0326 and $0327 and then jump to the location that *it* described. $0326 and $0327 were memory addresses in RAM allowing software to take over the print routines if necessary.

This insight gives us an idea of why many versions of BASIC are considered slow. For sure, the time to parse each instruction is expensive, but even the simple and final act of writing a single character to the screen uses multiple steps. In this case specifically:

- A call from the BASIC interpreter to the Kernal ROM code at $FFD2 to write the character
- The code at $FFD2 will read a two-byte memory address, stored in RAM at memory locations $0326 and 0327
- The CPU will then jump to that address (by default, the Kernal ROM routine at $F1CA)
- The printing actually begins

Knowing the Kernal ROM routine for printing a character was at $F1CA, software could always call that routine directly. But it would break when (or if) the ROM was ever updated, or if other software had been loaded into memory at the same time that relied on the redirection at $0326.

Ignoring BASIC

With three blocks of memory unavailable to us, totalling 16 KiB of memory, it seems unfair to call the Commodore 64 a 64 KiB machine. But that is only because it is unavailable to some people – specifically, BASIC programmers. If you're writing in machine code, and not in BASIC, then you don't need the BASIC interpreter and can reprogram the computer to redirect addresses $A000 and $BFFF to access the RAM chip instead of the ROM. If you're happy to develop your own IO routines, then you can also use the area between $D000 and $DFFF as RAM. And finally, using your own code to commune with the hardware, rather than that in the Kernal ROM, means you can use that final 8 KiB as RAM, too. Essentially all three blocks of RAM are hiding in the shadows of the ROM. It is often known as shadow RAM. On the Commodore 64 you could turn off the BASIC ROM with the assembly code:

```
LDA #$36
STA $0001
```

Other 64 KiB machines of the era had similar issues. The Dragon 32, for example, was only 32 KiB and an RS-232 serial port away from being a Dragon 64. Yet, if you programmed only in BASIC, the extra memory you were paying for would be shadowed by the ROM of the BASIC interpreter. By invoking a similar piece of boilerplate assembly, those ROM addresses could be made to reference RAM instead.

This had a surprising benefit to BASIC programmers since it was possible to copy the interpreter into RAM. Being in RAM, rather than ROM, meant that BASIC could now be modified to add new commands to the language.

Full shadows

Improving the implementation of BASIC was also possible with the Sinclair Interface 1 for the ZX Spectrum. Given the rushed implementation of the original ROM, commands intended to support the Sinclair Microdrive were never finished. So, with an Interface 1 plugged in, its 8 KiB ROM would shadow that present in the original Spectrum to provide these necessary commands.

Shadowing also existed with the Sinclair Interface 2, an add-on which provided a cartridge port. In this instance, the ROM cartridge would completely shadow the entire 16 KiB BASIC ROM, between addresses 0 and 16383. This meant developers could not borrow any of the routines in the Sinclair ROM unless they first copied them into the cartridge memory space during the development phase. It also meant they were limited to 16 KiB of code. But they had the advantage of being able to use all 41,613 bytes of the RAM, since none of it was being used by the game code. Unfortunately, the expense of the interface, cartridges, and the inclusion of non-standard joystick ports on the Interface 2, meant that only 10 game cartridges were ever released, and none made use of the extra RAM.

For those wondering, those cartridge games were all originally available on cassette and were:

- *Backgammon* (Psion)
- *Chess* (Psion)
- *Cookie* (Ultimate)
- *Horace and the Spiders* (Melbourne House)
- *Hungry Horace* (Melbourne House)
- *Jetpac* (Ultimate)
- *Planetoids* (Psion)
- *Pssst* (Ultimate)
- *Space Raiders* (Psion)
- *Tranz Am* (Ultimate)

Sometimes, shadow RAM was not a binary choice. The BBC Master allowed you to access shadow RAM in the video memory region, via the Access Control Register, so you could determine on a frame-by-frame basis whether you wanted to display the memory in block A, or block B. This provided a very simple form of double buffering, necessary for smooth scrolling graphics.

```
GOTO 64 : REM Spanish import law
GOTO 640 : REM Ought to be enough for anybody
GOTO 49152 : REM SYS 49152
```

49152 : PEEK 49152

49152 is the first memory address of the system ROM in the Commodore PET. To stop users from reading this code, the PEEK instruction was tweaked to prevent users from accessing it.

Of course, users could write machine code to avoid this limitation – as could those who upgraded to BASIC 2.0.

```
GOTO 49152 : REM  SYS 49152
```

49152 : Commodore PET

By selling a stone in a box, Gary Dahl created the 'Pet Rock', a collectable toy fad around Christmas 1975, which mimicked a real-life pet in that it came in a box with straw bedding and air holes. Andre Souson considered that if a rock could become a pet, why not a computer? Thus we have the Commodore PET.

Over its lifespan, 1977 to 1982, the PET had helped move the fortunes of Commodore from a failing calculator company to world-leader computer powerhouse. Commodore did this by, first, purchasing MOS who made the 6502 microprocessor, then by failing to buy the Apple II which actually used it! Instead, Chuck Peddle and his team had to build Commodore their own computer. It took six months to produce the first machine, the 2001, using the 6502 chip he had designed at MOS.

The hardware in the 2001 was a single board affair, with 4 KiB of RAM, a 40x25 character-based monochrome display, and tape interface which ran at 750 baud. (It technically ran at 1500, but everything was recorded twice, such was the 'reliability' of tape.) Over time every component was upgraded, as Commodore released more machines than a numerophile could shake a slide rule at!

(And for European audiences, the name changed from PET to CBM, to avoid a Philips trademark.)

```
20 GOTO 10
```

Eventually, Dahl opened a bar in Los Gatos, California, where another computer company would be based – Amiga.

Arnold considers this to be their favourite machine.

```
GOTO 40 : REM Commodore 64
```

49152 : SYS 49152

The Commodore 64 had 4096 bytes of memory in the address range $C000–$CFFF (49152–53247) called the upper RAM area. This is interesting to note because it is separate from the memory used by BASIC, at $0800–$9FFF (2048–40959), so even if your BASIC program fills up the 38911 bytes available to it, it cannot accidentally overflow and corrupt this area. (Compare this to most other machines, where your memory would be shared between all parts of the system, and you had to manually manage the boundaries between them.)

Consequently, it was used to store small pieces of machine code that would speed up a BASIC game, or provide simple utilities. It would be executed by the SYS command which begins with the machine code instruction at the address which followed. Therefore, code in this upper RAM area could be run with:

```
SYS 49152
```

```
GOTO 38911 : REM Bytes
GOTO 49152 : REM PEEK 49152
```

65495 : Going faster

Users always want faster machines. Nowadays, you usually need to buy a new laptop if you want it to go faster. Not so in the 8-bit era! The Sinclair ZX81, for example, had a 'fast' mode which made your BASIC programs actually run faster. This worked because the CPU had two jobs: updating the screen and running your program. By turning off the screen the computer didn't need to think about how to draw the graphics (a surprisingly time-consuming process), so it would spend that time processing something else: your program. This would cause a speed increase of up to 400%. While it is not always obvious why it's useful to have a computer which is unable to draw to the screen, many programmers used this mode for compute-intensive tasks like generating random worlds and mazes, or drawing complex backgrounds, without the user being able to see the magical process happening.

The Dragon 32 also had a fast mode, although it was still able to update the

186

screen because its method was to change the rate at which the hardware ran by doubling the processor speed from 0.89 mhz to 1.7 mhz. Everything would run twice as fast. But not every Dragon computer could handle this faster mode because it was being forced to run outside of its normal operating parameters and would sometimes suffer what was called 'heartburn'. Those brave souls that risked their machine would type:

```
POKE 65495,0
```

And revert with:

```
POKE 65494,0
```

Which would return the computer to normal. Here be dragons, however, because if you accidentally saved the program to tape whilst in this double speed mode, the resultant audio was also too fast! Instead of a high-pitched whine, all you could hear was a *very* high-pitched whine that couldn't be loaded in the normal way, even in fast mode. In case you were interested, the solution was an equally magical:

```
POKE 146,8: POKE 147,4: POKE 148,8
CLOAD
```

For the super brave, there was an 'even faster' fast mode, which also turned the screen off like the Sinclair ZX81.

```
POKE 65497,0
```

Since the screen image was lost one used it with extreme caution, because if you can't see the screen, it's difficult to know when/if you've entered the command correctly! The mode turned off with:

```
POKE 65496,0
```

Given the risk to the hardware it was rare for commercial software to use it, but that wouldn't stop nefarious programs (or curious users) from doing so. The Commodore PET also had a speed POKE which, on some later machines, was said to damage the CRT as it caused the whole bottom half of the screen to be drawn as a single line, halfway down the display. The excessive wear on the 74LS08 chip as this one line was continually overwritten could have led to the monitor's slow and gradual demise.

```
POKE 59458,62
```

Creating similar situations on modern machines is somewhere between 'hard as a conker in the oven' to 'very difficult' to 'almost impossible', because any program which runs on your computer is protected by the OS which validates all requests, such as those for disc access. The OS in turn is protected by the device drivers, which do a similar job. In fact, the worst thing you can usually do is waste printer paper. Most older machines had similar protections, but since user programs were treated with as much reverence as the OS software, there was very little to stop your program from implementing a bad version of the safe code in ROM.

The Commodore 1541 disc drive, for example, had protection code to stop the drive head from moving outside its safe range of tracks 0 to 39… but only if you used the official routines. There was nothing to stop you trying to send the drive head to track 40, causing it to hit the internal stop barrier and permanently push the head out of alignment.

This is true of anything with moving parts, as they wear out. Relays are small electrical switches which consist of an electromagnet that opens or closes a set of metal contacts by having them attracted to the electromagnet. Machines with relays, often as part of the cassette interface and used to start and stop the tape at the appropriate time, could be instructed to turn on and off many hundreds of times a second, thus significantly (and quickly) destroying them.

As a final note, it must be remembered that early model PCs had a button on the front of the machine to switch between normal and high-speed mode. This was called 'Turbo mode'. However, instead of increasing the speed when it was pressed, it actually slowed down the computer when it wasn't pressed! This was for backwards compatibility with old software (mostly games) that didn't correctly determine the passing of time between successive frames.

```
GOTO 1⅚ : REM IPS
GOTO 15 : REM Saving to tape
GOTO 15 : REM C15, C60, C90
GOTO 50 : REM Compilations
GOTO 70 : REM Bugs
GOTO 300 : REM Kansas City
GOTO 451 : REM Fahrenheit 451
GOTO 6847 : REM Dragon 32
```

69105 : Leaves

According to the 1977 text-only adventure game *Zork*, from Infocom, this is the number of leaves on the ground at one point in the game. This information is only shared with the player if they decide to count them with the traditional verb-noun instruction of:

COUNT LEAVES

Amusingly 69 in hex is 105 in decimal.

And 69 in decimal is 105 in octal.

This is not the only number to have such properties. Ignoring the trivial examples, like 1,001, the first one is 64,100.

Like many in-jokes, it gets repeated and honoured in many places, sometimes literally as the number of leaves in a sack (in Steve Meretzky's 1986 game, *Leather Goddesses of Phobos*) or in the book in the cottage (as per *Trinity*), and sometimes as more esoteric items such as the ticket number in *Bureaucracy* or the gun receipt in *The Witness*.

Unfortunately, you have been wondering around in the dark, and are eaten by a grue.

Your quest ends here!

1000000 : Sales

Alongside questions of 'What was the most popular...?' and 'What was the first...?', another common inquiry is 'What sold the most?', with the implicit belief that sales meant quality, or popularity. Unfortunately, getting sales figures is difficult. Companies had no obligation to disclose their sales figures, only their profits. Some would intentionally inflate the numbers – sometimes slightly, sometimes wildly – for the purpose of bumping their share price, or personal egos. Even the best-selling machines, with comparatively good accounting, have a margin of error.

However, we have confidence that the Commodore VIC-20 was the first to sell a million units (one of which was Elon Musk's first computer) but its follow-up, the Commodore 64, has estimated sales anywhere from 12.5 to 30 million. These variations are dependent on how you count, and from where you get the numbers. So, although we know the Commodore 64 was the best-selling home computer (until 2018 when the combined sales of the Raspberry Pi topped it) we might never have a definitive answer.

Commodore VIC-20

*Courtesy of The Centre for
Computing History, Cambridge*

Commodore VIC-20,
rear ports

GOTO 1 : REM First!
GOTO 20 : REM A friendly number

2455992 : The Cathode Ray Tube

The idea of a CRT stretches back to the late 19th century, with an electron beam hitting a phosphor-coated tube to illuminate portions of this 'screen' for very short periods of time, while relying on the persistence of vision in humans to see all the portions visible at once. By deflecting the beam with electromagnets the beam could appear anywhere on the screen (which were initially circular) to trace out shapes. This is what we now think of as 'vector displays', since the movement would be continuous and could illuminate any arbitrary position on the screen, whereas the raster (i.e. more modern) versions could illuminate only discrete areas. The GCE Vectrex home console used this type of display, as did the 1979 Atari arcade cabinet *Asteroids*. While Atari, who also brought the computer age home, could afford to add a 'shadow mask' to the CRT to give their *Star Wars* arcade game colour (although they described it as 'Quadrascan technology'), the Vectrex had to adopt a simpler method – plastic! It provided a colourful translucent overlay that could be placed over the screen so that each game could be given some semblance of colour for less monetary outlay. This idea had been used on the Magnavox Odyssey, but was less successful since it fitted to a domestic TV set and the manufacturer had no control over the size of that screen.

Although vector displays are easily emulated on raster displays, you *need* to see it on an original display to appreciate its smoothness and brightness, as well as the pleasant glow around closely rendered lines, and the subtle fading of the phosphor.

Sometimes you can spot the technical difference – drawing a line from X1,Y1 to X2,Y2 to X3,Y3 on raster looks normal, but the vectorised version can show a brighter dot at X2,Y2 as there are essentially two draw commands focusing the beam on the same point!

The CRT was also part of the very first computer game, a 'CRT amusement device' patented in 1947 as number 2455992. However, since no evidence exists for it being built, does it still count?

```
GOTO 1 : REM First!
GOTO 84 : REM LCD displays
GOTO 205.5 : REM How to draw a maze in one line
GOTO 16509 : REM ZX81 1K Display
GOTO 16777216 : REM Colour
GOSUB 4 : REM The first computer bug
```

3333360 : *Pac-Man* Hi Score

Given the definite end of *Pac-Man* on level 256, it is possible to compute the maximum possible score.

On levels 1 to 255 you can earn

- 2400 points for the dots
- 200 for all four energizers
- 200, 400, 800, 1600 for eating all the ghosts (x4 for each power pill) on levels 1–17 and 19
- 100–5000 for the fruit (which appear twice per level)

The broken level 256 only has

- 1120 for the dots
- 100 for the two energizers
- 5000 for the single fruit
- 540 for the 9 dots hidden in the glitch area

In the case of the latter, the dots reappear every time you die, so you need to use all six lives to earn the maximum total of 3,333,360. Reaching this total is considered a perfect game and has been achieved many times, the first claim being made in 1999, 19 years after its initial release.

```
GOTO 256 : REM The Pac-Man kill screen
```

16777216 : Colour

On a raster display, like a standard TV, every dot on-screen requires memory. For a black-and-white display, that requires 1 bit of memory. For a black and white display with 256 shades of grey, you require 8 bits of memory. Or 1 byte. A coloured dot also requires 1 byte... if you limit yourself to 256 colours. The problem then becomes: which colours do you choose?

One solution is the palette, a lookup table with 256 entries each describing the colour in some notation, such as RGB888. That is, each colour is described in terms of 256 shades of red, followed by 256 shades of green, and 256 shades of blue, in that order. RGB, each with 8 bits of colour depth, has 16,777,216 possible colours and is known as 'true colour'.

An alternative method is to encode the varying shades of red, green and blue into the byte itself. One such format might be RGB232, where the first two bits give you four shades of red, the next bits describe eight shades of green, and finally four shades of blue. The specific shades are determined by some other mechanism, usually baked into the hardware.

In both cases, any transparency must be handled separately. This can be by assigning a specific palette entry, such as 0, to be transparent (meaning your image can now only display 255 different colours) or by modifying the format to, say, ARGB1222 with a specific bit to indicate transparent or not.

The arcade implementation of *Pac-Man*, for example, saved a lot of precious memory by using 2-bit images for the map pieces, fruits and pills, giving a maximum of four possible colours within each graphic. Since these specific images never overlapped, they were stored in a grid of 28x36 tiles. Each tile used one byte which held details of which graphic image to draw, and an attribute determining the palette colours used for that instance of the image. Thus, you could have a full-colour 224x288 display, using around 1 KiB of memory instead of the expected 1.5 MiB!

```
GOTO 6 : REM The ZX Spectrum Screen Display
GOTO 84 : REM LCD displays
GOTO 205.5 : REM How to draw a maze in one line
```

GOTO 16509 : REM ZX81 1K Display
GOTO 2455992 : REM The Cathode Ray Tube

40404243 : The Beatles' birthdates

All four Beatles were born between 1940 and 1943 and, ordered oldest to youngest are:

- Ringo Starr (July 7, 1940)
- John Lennon (October 9, 1940)
- Paul McCartney (June 18, 1942)
- George Harrison (February 25, 1943)

RETURN

824545201 : PEEK

This nonsensical PEEK address, outside the 16-bit address range, was the title of a track from the 1996 *Richard D. James Album* by Aphex Twin, which also contained the computer-influenced title 'Inkey$' on its American release. If you found this entry, you're obviously a fan, so I need not regurgitate all the well-known rumours and stories about his work, or the technical wizardry and in-jokes he employs, and will instead let you explore further.

GOTO 19 : REM Musicians with computers

1597463007 : Inverse Square Root

Two of the most computationally expensive operations for computers to, er, compute are divisions and square roots. So it is probably surprising to know that both can be combined into one function and computed using only multiplications, subtraction and bit shifts. (All comparatively cheap operations.) Even more surprisingly, this code runs about four times as fast, all thanks to the magic constant, 1597463007 (0x5f3759df).

```
float InvSqrt(float x){
   float xhalf = 0.5f * x;
   int i = *(int*)&x;           // store floating-point bits
                                in integer
   i = 0x5f3759df - (i >> 1);   // initial guess for Newton's
                                method
   x = *(float*)&i;             // convert new bits into float
   x = x*(1.5f - xhalf*x*x);    // One round of Newton's method
   return x;
}
```

Although credited to id Software's John Carmack as part of the *Quake* source code, the original idea was believed to have belonged to Terje Mathisen, also of id. Yet Gary Tarolli of NVIDIA had been using it before this, but even he didn't know the origin. An investigation by Rys Sommefeldt eventually revealed Greg Walsh, who created it for the Titan graphics minicomputer in the 1980s, as the likely originator. Although that is still unproven, as both Chris Lomont and Charles McEniry have claims to similar code with the mathematical ideas behind the algorithm going back further – possibly to Velvel Kahan and K. C. Ng in 1986.

What this shows is that if you don't need an exact result, an approximation will do, and a fast approximation can be intriguing, yet totally non-obvious, code.

RETURN

2147483647 : Seconds

Storing integers in 32 bits gives us a signed range of between -2147483648 and 2147483647 that includes around four billion numbers. This used to be enough to represent a company's bank balance. But no longer. It used to be enough for personal wealth. But no longer. It is perhaps forgivable that these limits were once deemed 'big enough' as the 2147483647 limit appears in many forms of software – such as the maximum number of copper coins in the original Blizzard game *World of Warcraft*. Yet, 32-bit numbers were always incapable of expressing the infinity of time. Worse still, when computer scientists were working out how to represent time, they used a number of bits they knew would run out. And they could work out exactly when the computer would determine that time ends:

19 January 2038.

It's a Tuesday.

This is because 'they' decided that time would be measured in the number of seconds since 1 January 1970, with positive numbers being dates after that, and negative numbers representing times earlier. It is this use of negative dates that prevents most computer systems from simply reframing the range as 0 to 4294967295. So, 3:14:07 in the morning will be the final second it knows and by 3:14:08, any unfixed computers will have reset back to zero and display the time as being midnight on New Year's Day, 1970. (The fact that this time, 3:14, represents pi is surely a coincidence.)

Of course, the identity of 'they' is still a mystery so we can't assign blame. But just because the Unix operating system (and those descended from it) elected to use 'seconds from 1970' as their pulse, doesn't mean everyone does. The designers behind the programming language Java used 64-bit long integers so that their code would work for longer. Much longer. For nearly one-third of a trillion years. But they then decided to shorten the units from seconds to milliseconds. Consequently, Java programs will lose track of time somewhere around the year 292 million.

But this is not the only epoch in computing. Famously, developers who stored the year as a two-digit number (counting from 1900) inadvertently created the 'Year 2000' or 'Y2K' problem (known to most as the Millennium Bug) where the year following 1999 was 1900. Again.

Storing the year as a 4-bit number gives a range of just 0 to 15 giving a year span from 1980 to 1995, as happened with the Apple Lisa (a machine described by some as drop-dead ugly).

Those who count the years in binary coded decimal (BCD) had a similar problem 10 years later. Software which stored the year as two bytes, such as 20 and 10, would have the 10 (mis-)interpreted as being a hexadecimal number. The hex for 10 is 16, so some text messages sent via SMS in 2010 would have the year marked as 2016.

```
GOTO 10 : REM Seconds
GOTO 640 : REM Ought to be enough for anybody
```

Appendix O : Computing Terms

What follows are brief descriptions of many of the terms from this book. It is not intended to be exhaustive in scope or depth, which is to say each definition is closer to advisory. Indeed, many of the explanations are kept purposefully short and simplistic to help the reader through the specific instances covered here, avoiding the caveats, edge cases, and rabbit holes which a full description would necessitate. (The extensive use of 'usually' and 'often' highlights the wide design variations in retro machines, and hints at the way the terms and technology have changed in the modern era.)

AI

Artificial intelligence has changed its scope of meaning over the years. In the era currently known as 'retro', it refers to a fixed program which makes seemingly intelligent decisions, within a very small problem domain. Usually, AI is controlling non-player characters in a computer game, to such an extent that it would be better named 'Algorithms Implemented'. In modern parlance it often refers to machine-generated art, self-learning algorithms, and more.

Assembly instructions

These carry many forms. There are instruction bytes, the raw hexadecimal numbers (like A5 20) which represent the machine code or opcode which is executed by the CPU. There are the assembly mnemonics (like lda $20) that the human writes as part of their program. The assembler is the software which converts the latter into the former.

Throughout the book, whenever a piece of assembly is shown it will generally be in form:

```
Address Machine code hex     Assembly instruction mnemonic
0100    A5 20                lda $20
```

The first number (0100) is the address of the instruction, in memory, written in either hex or decimal.

The second is the raw hex of the instruction, also written in hex, and usually with spaces for clarity.

Finally, there is the instruction.

Sometimes the address is omitted for brevity if it has no bearing on the instruction.

BASIC

When most 8-bit machines first started up you were presented with a cursor. This allowed you to type in BASIC commands which were executed immediately. If you began typing a number followed by a command on the same line, the number was considered a line number and upon pressing RETURN (or ENTER) that line would become part of the current program in memory. You could then type RUN to see the results of that program.

Early versions of BASIC, notably from Sinclair, would tokenise the keywords (such as PRINT and GOTO) into a single byte. This saved space obviously, but also time, since the BASIC interpreter didn't need to read through each letter in the keyword and then spend more time determining whether it was valid, and what to do with it.

Typical BASIC instructions, included in this book, are:

CLS An instruction used in the BASIC language to clear the screen. Some versions of BASIC support clearing the screen to a specific colour, or resolution. Sometimes it would trigger an Easter egg.

CONT Continue the execution of a program which had previously stopped.

DATA A way of storing information in a program. Such data is usually constant and stored in one of more lines of comma separated values. e.g. DATA 16,10,"Welcome to the game!" There is a data pointer which remembers which item of data can be READ next.

DIM Short for DIMension. Specifies a variable name which is to be used as an array, storing multiple values. e.g. DIM A(10). Different BASIC dialects would interpret this range as either 0 to 9, 1 to 10, or even 0 to 10. Individual elements of the array can be retrieved with round brackets (parentheses) with A(5), in contrast to non-BASIC languages which prefer square brackets.

END Terminate the program on the current line. STOP is sometimes also used.

FOR   Start a loop, which repeats all the code from here until the first NEXT instruction. The loop would have a variable name to indicate the iteration it was on, e.g. FOR X=0 TO 32 STEP 2. FOR loops can be nested.

GOSUB   Enter a program SUBroutine on the line number given. (If the line doesn't exist, most dialects of the language would jump to the next line that did.) The program continues at this point until the word RETURN is found, at which point execution reverts to the next instruction after the GOSUB.

GOTO   Jump to the line number given, as per GOSUB. But unlike GOSUB, it continues work through subsequent lines.

IF   A conditional branch, taking one of two paths depending on whether an expression is TRUE or FALSE, e.g. IF LIVES=0 THEN GOTO 1000 ELSE GOTO 2000.

INPUT   Allow the user to type in text, followed by the ENTER or RETURN key. The program could force the user into typing only numbers (INPUT A) or permit full text strings (INPUT A$).

LET   Assign a value, to a variable, in the form LET LIVES = 3. The value need not be a constant number but can be any valid mathematical expression. Many variations eventually dispense with the need to use the word LET.

LIST   Show the current BASIC program in memory.

NEW   Clear the memory holding the BASIC program. BBC BASIC also supported OLD, which recovered the previous program.

NEXT   Return to the previously found FOR loop and continue with the next iteration. Some dialects required the variable name from the FOR loop to be explicitly mentioned here.

POKE   Write a piece of data into a specific memory address. It can be used to write machine code programs into memory, change hardware settings, or amend programs already in memory. See also: PEEK and GOTO 35899 : REM PEEK and POKE.

PEEK   Read a piece of data from a specific memory address. See also: POKE and GOTO 35899 : REM PEEK and POKE.

PRINT   Write information to the screen at the current cursor position. If the instruction ended with a semicolon, it would also move the cursor to the end of the text printed, whereas a comma would move the cursor to the next tab stop. If neither was present, new text would appear on the next line.

READ   Take the next value from the DATA statements, as indicated by the data pointer, then move the pointer to the next value.

REM   An instruction used in the BASIC language to indicate a REMark or a REMinder. It had no effect on the program as, in interpreted languages, the computer simply ignored it. For a human, however, it would help explain what the program was doing, and how it worked. Some programmers would write their comments with graphic characters or white-on-black text to make them stand out. Modern languages refer to such code as comments.

RESTORE   Move the data pointer, used to reference DATA statements, to the start of the data.

RETURN   Go to the line after the previously executed GOSUB instruction. All GOSUB line numbers are stored on a stack, so RETURN simply looks at the one on the top and removes it. This allows nested routines where one subroutine can GOSUB into another. And so on.

RND   An instruction or function to generate a random number. (Although it is never truly random since that is impossible for a deterministic machine!) The range of this number is often between 0 and 1, although that is determined by the implementation of BASIC involved.

RUN   Start interpreting the program in memory, from the lowest numbered line number. The program only stops running if it encounters an END or STOP instruction, if the user presses a suitable break/escape key, or if there are no more lines left.

Binary
A number base (or radix) involving 2 symbols: 0–1. Such numbers are usually postfixed with b to distinguish them from numbers in other bases. Appendix 256, Numbers, provides a handy conversion table.

Bit

A binary digit, either 0 or 1, which can be thought of a false or true, off or on. It is the smallest amount of data a computer can process when performing calculations. However, it is generally impossible to read, or write, a single bit to memory, and so they are combined into sets called bytes or words.

Bootstrap

Originating with the phrase 'Pull Yourself Up by Your Bootstraps', this is a piece of very small software held permanently in a computer so that it knows how to start, and consequently load larger software (such as an OS) into memory.

Bus

The internal route that electronic signals use to travel from one part of a circuit to another. Data is passed between the CPU and memory, for example, on a bus which contains the same number of routes as the number of bits in a piece of data, so 8-bit data is passed in parallel along an 8-bit bus. How fast the data can traverse this bus is governed by a piece of hardware known as a bus controller, which might use a clock to quantise time into slots and only allow data to travel along that bus at specific intervals.

Byte

A set of bits, usually 8. Sometimes termed an octet to formally specify the use of 8 bits. The contents of a byte can be treated as a number between 0 and 255, -128 and 127, or a collection of 8 on/off boolean values. When written in binary, such as 00001111, the left-hand side digit (0) is referred to as the most significant bit (MSB) since when converted to a number it has the largest effect on its magnitude. Similarly, the rightmost digit (1) is the least significant bit (LSB).

Compiler

A piece of software which converts source code into machine code, in its entirety. The resultant program can then be run without access to, or knowledge of, the original source code.

Computer architecture

A bus is a way of moving information from one chip to another, say from a CPU to memory. A bus consists of multiple lines, each one carrying a single bit. Eight of these lines carrying eight bits, or one byte, of data at once (i.e. in parallel) is called an 8-bit bus.

Condition code, CC register, condition flags

These are a series of bits, stored in the CC register of the processor, that reflect the state of the most recent instruction (or opcode). Each code will be typically labelled by a single letter. The CC of Z, for example, would indicate that the last instruction produces an answer that was zero. Or a CC of N highlights the result was negative. Having a register hold these results makes it very quick to determine if the program needs to jump, or branch, to a separate section of code to handle this type of result. Every instruction on every processor affects the CC register slightly differently.

CP/M, Control Program/Monitor

An operating system originally developed for Intel 8080 processors, created by Gary Kildall of Digital Research, Inc. It famously lost out to PC-DOS from Micro-Soft when IBM were looking for an OS for its new Personal Computer.

CPU, Central Processing Unit

The brain of the computer. It runs programs, performs logical and arithmetic instructions, and controls many other aspects of the machine. Often shortened to just 'processor'. Some CPUs of the era can be found in Appendix 4.

Decimal, or denary

A number base (or radix) involving 10 symbols: 0–9. Beings with 10 fingers (and, oddly, The Simpsons!) use this system as it comes naturally to them. Appendix 256, Numbers, provides a handy conversion table.

EEPROM, electrically erasable programmable read-only memory

A ROM-like memory which holds its data when the power is removed, i.e. non-volatile. Unlike a ROM, however, its contents can be written, and rewritten, with special hardware known as a burner.

Exponent

See float.

Firmware

Software which forms part of a computer's internal workings. It is often read-only, to prevent it from being tampered with by user software. This protection is usually afforded by hardware, either because the chip itself cannot be changed, or because special connections need to be made to the circuit board.

Float, or floating point

A number that, optionally, may have numbers after the decimal point, such as 1.2. They are usually stored in IEEE-754 format, consisting of an exponent, mantissa and sign bit as: $N = (-1)^S * 2^{exponent} * mantissa$. Compare with: Integer.

Heap

A way of organising data within a program in a structured manner so that it can be found later, e.g. in a tree. To retrieve the data, the computer needs to understand this structure and spend some time working through it. Compare with: Stack

Hex, or hexadecimal

A number base (or radix) involving 16 symbols: 0–9, followed by A–F. Such numbers are usually prefixed with 0x or $ to distinguish them from numbers in other bases. Give that each hex digit requires 4 bits, every 8-bit byte needs only two characters to represent it. This makes it more efficient than the usual base 10 (decimal) system used by humans in their day-to-day lives. It is often used to describe the machine code representation of assembly instructions. Appendix 256, Numbers provides a handy conversion table.

High-level

A type of language that people want to program in, like Python, C++, and even BASIC. It provides sensible human-readable forms of text that is converted, via compilation or interpretation, into something a computer can understand.

Homebrew

A home-made computer built by an enthusiast, rather than a company. Usually a one-off (or perhaps made in small batches) these are often built from individual chips and discrete components. They were first popular in the 1970s when computers were big – in both physical size and cost – as it provided the only way individuals could explore the technology. There was a resurgence in the 2000s as the maker movement demonstrated the low barrier to entry for DIY electronics with processors like the Arduino.

IDE, Integrated Drive Electronics

Also known as Parallel ATA (PATA), or AT Attachment, this is a standard for connecting peripheral devices, hard disks and CD drives, to computers. Although it arrived later than SCSI, in 1986, its use in IBM PC-compatibles, along with its consequent lower price, meant it become the standard for many years.

IO, Input/Output
Any elements of a computer system not directly involved in computation, such as keyboards, screens and so on. Can also refer to the input and output systems of a processor connected to other chips.

Integer
A whole number, such as 1, 2, 0, or -100. Compare with Float.

Interpreter
A piece of software which reads program source code one line at a time and which feeds alternate instructions to the processor to fulfil the original intent.

Low-level
A type of language that almost no one wants to program in, like assembly. Computers understand this level natively, so no conversion is necessary for the human – at the expense of its human readership.

LSB, least significant bit
See: Byte.

Machine code
See: Opcodes.

Mantissa
See: Float.

Memory
Memory is usually measured in bytes or kilobytes. The latter might be represented by KB, Kb, or KiB, with any of the units referencing 1000 or 1024 bytes. In an attempt to avoid confusion, when documenting an actual number of bytes, we used KiB (meaning 1024 bytes) whereas in contrast we use KB to reflect its usage in a historical context, when it appeared as such in the historical literature.

Memory address
See: Memory location.

Memory location
In order for a computer to store or recall data from memory, it must know the place where that data lives. That place is known as the memory address, or location.

A machine with 64 KiB of memory might refer to each location with a single number, 0 to 65535, with 0 being the smaller address and considered the bottom of memory. Having a single number is known as having a flat address space. In contrast, a segmented address space would usually have two: the segment number, and the offset within that segment. In some segmented systems, such as the IBM PC 5150, the same location in memory can be addressed by two different numbers. See 640 : Ought to be enough for anybody

MSB, Most significant bit
See: Byte.

Opcodes, operation code
A machine code instruction which instructs the CPU to do something, be it arithmetic, or memory accesses, or to jump to a different part of the program. These are usually represented as hex numbers, and converted from the assembly language written by a human.

RAM, Random Access Memory
A chip that holds data that, unlike ROM, can be changed by programs. This data is usually lost when power is removed from the device. Contrast ROM.

Register
An internal data store inside a processor used for calculations, where each register holds a single number. They often have names like A, accumulator, B, X, and so on.

RISC, Reduced instruction set computer
A way of designing CPU opcodes so that they are as simple as possible so that even if more instructions were needed to write a particular program, it would be a saving overall. Furthermore, by making the size of each opcode identical it would reduce the effort the chip needed to do to decode and execute those opcodes and improve the ability for instruction to be run in parallel with other similarly sized instructions or in a pipeline. Also, they traditionally have a much lower power footprint. The ARM chip inside most mobile phones uses RISC.

ROM, Read Only Memory
A chip that holds unchangeable data. A computer may have any number of these, but there is usually at least one which contains the BASIC interpreter and other firmware necessary for a computer to work. As the name suggests, a user program

cannot change the data on this chip. It retains its contents when power is removed. Contrast with RAM.

SCSI, Small Computer System Interface (pron. scuzzy)

A set of standards for connecting peripheral devices, usually hard disk drives, to computers. Although created in 1979, and announced in 1981, it wasn't until 1986 that it was fully standardised and became prominent via the Commodore Amiga, Atari ST and Apple Mac.

Source code

The textual form of a computer program, which a developer will type into the machine. This version of source is then converted (by assembling, compiling or interpreting) into a code which the computer can understand and process directly, known as its machine code.

Stack

A way of organising data so that the last thing which is added to it is the first thing removed. (As opposed to a queue, where the first thing added is the first to be removed.) Because the computer doesn't need to search for the data, because of any intermediate structure, this is comparatively fast to access. Compare with: Heap.

Variables

A named store to hold a number, or string of text, in a programming language. Can usually be changed throughout its lifetime, to reflect the state of the program, e.g. SCORE = SCORE + 25.

Wetware

Any biological life form, but usually refers to the functioning of a human brain. Although originating in the 1950s, its use in Cyberpunk to contrast both hardware and software has seen an uptick in modern adoption.

Word

A set of bits which are operated upon by the processor. The word size refers to the quantity of data bits that can be transferred, as a unit, by the computer. To avoid confusion with the byte, these quantities are known as 16-bit words, 32-bit words, and so on.

Appendix 1 : Character sets

These character sets have been generated from the order of characters in their respective chips, and usually map to the character index that appears if you were to POKE it into memory. Printing the same character index with CHR$ will, on some machines, produce a completely different image.

Amstrad CPC

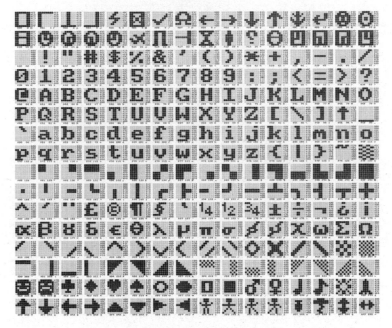

Stored as 6x10, but interpolated by hardware to 12x20, this is used for Mode 7. It is more formally the Teletext font, as generated by the SAA5050 chip.

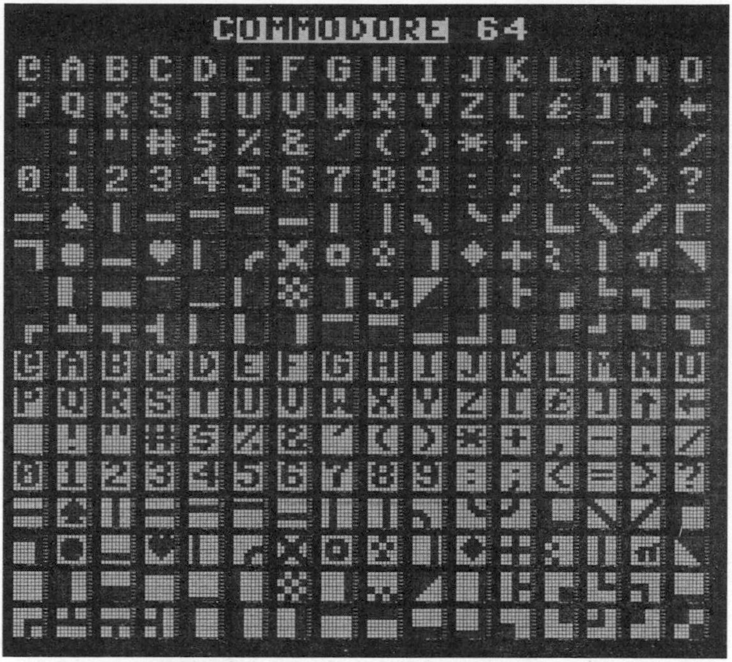
COMMODORE 64

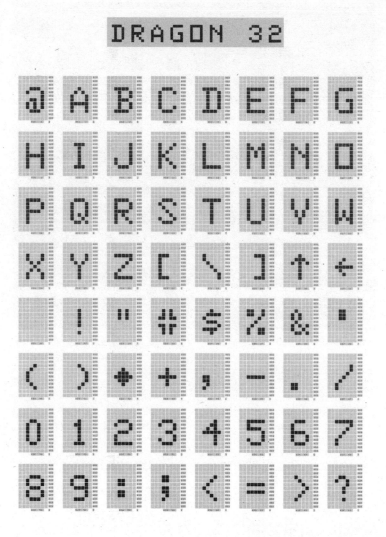

DRAGON 32

There were various clones of the 6847 graphics chip. This is the more common, and original, MC6847.

Jupiter Ace

The eight block characters are repeated four times when written to the screen with instructions, such as EMIT, although when using characters most of these represent control codes, e.g. carriage return.

211

Oric 1

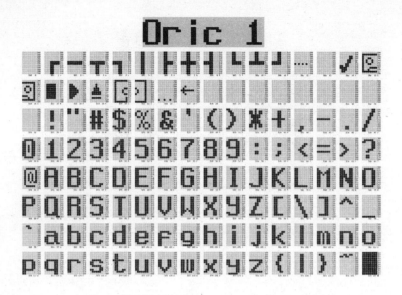

Tandy Color

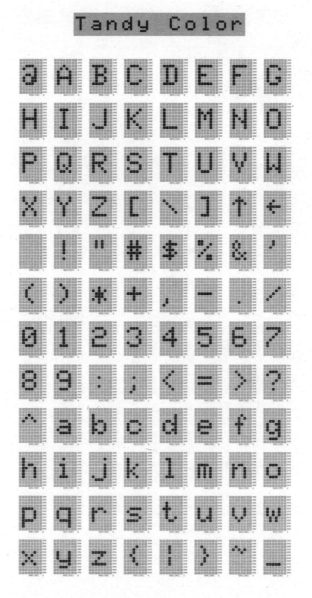

SINCLAIR ZX80

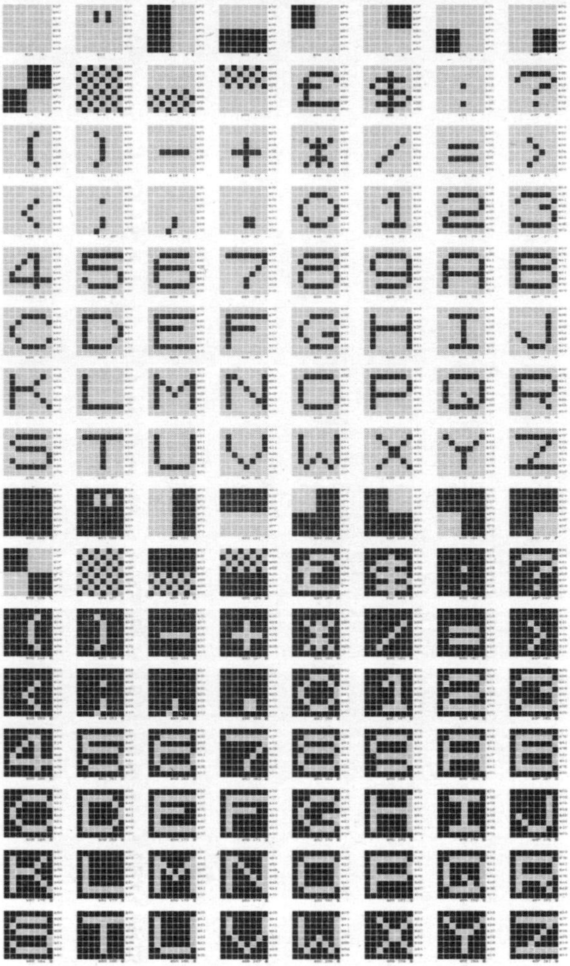

$0E00 — 0FFF

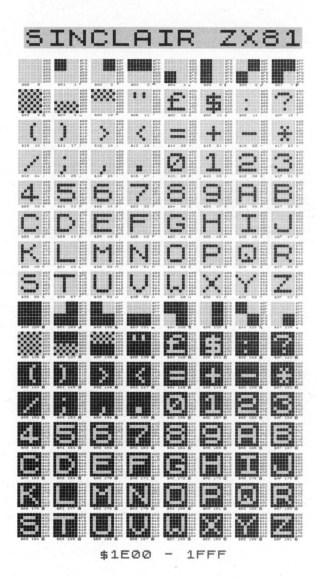

SINCLAIR ZX81

$1E00 - 1FFF

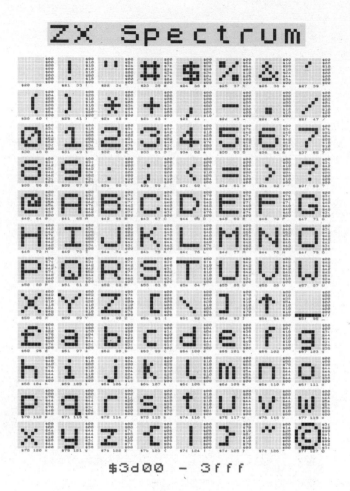

$3d00 — 3fff

Appendix 2 : Keys on a keyboard

In all the following charts, a selection of 100 or so machines was taken from the 1975–1990 era and their stats entered. The choice of machines was arbitrary, to include both popular and lesser-known machines. The choice was also to list machines in the same family separately. This means a slight bias when the Matra Alice, for example, has three entries whereas the significantly more influential Commodore 64 has just one. Knowing that you can never please everyone with this sort of data, it is presented only as a rough guide to the industry, rather than a definitive analysis.

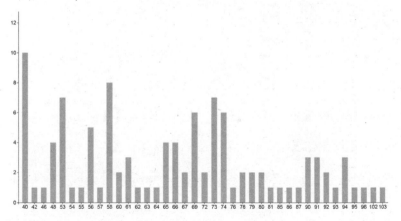

An obvious bias here is in the 40-key machines, given it is the bare minimum of keys necessary (26 letters, 10 numbers, space, return, and two shifts) and formed the basis of all the first Sinclair machines.

Appendix 3 : Year of release

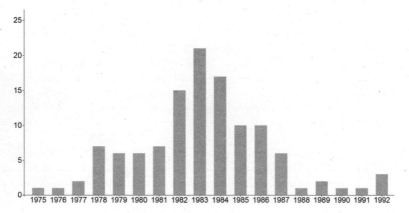

It is perhaps surprising that 1983 appears to be the most popular year, but that is probably a consequence of 1982 being the breakthrough year – it saw the launch of the Commodore 64 and ZX Spectrum (from companies that had some prior success in the market) along with the Dragon, Oric, Sord and Jupiter Ace (companies that didn't). It is likely that new competitors (such as Camputers, Memotech and Mattel) saw this groundswell in 1982 and pushed harder to get their products onto shelves before the bubble burst, as existing companies (Acorn, Atari and Apple) wanted to remind folk that they were still a force to be taken seriously.

Appendix 4 : CPUs in use

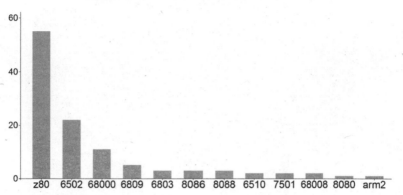

The Zilog Z80 was always going to top a poll based on quantity. It was the work-horse of everything Sinclair did, and it created a legacy. After all, if you had learned about the Z80 by working for Sinclair (as the Jupiter Ace creators, Richard Altwasser and Steven Vickers, had done), if you had cloned it (Microdigital), or if it was simply for your own amusement, then it made sense to apply those skills when creating your next (or first) computer.

Appendix 5 : CPU families

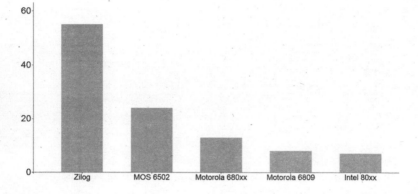

Appendix 6 : Inflation

To get an accurate idea of how much a £199 computer from 1982 would cost now is a difficult task. How was the UK price determined? If it was imported, what was the exchange rate between the two currencies? Were there hidden import duties or other costs? What was the spending power of £1 in 1982? And so on.

Therefore, the best we can do in the general case is provide a basic inflation calculator, based on the numbers from the Bank of England which (at the time of writing) end in 2021.

Begin on the column which matches the year for the original price. Then move down that column and note the value of £1 for each successive year, until you reach the target year. Finally, multiply the cost you're trying to find. For example, the cost of a Sinclair ZX80 in 1980 was £99.95. Its equivalent cost in 1987 would be multiplied by 1.52, making it £151.92. Or – in 2021 – multiplied by 4.56, making it £455.77.

	1975	1976	1977	1978	1979	1980	1981	1982	1983	1984	1985	1986	1987	1988	1989	1990	1991	1992	1993	1994
1975 :	1																			
1976 :	1.17	1																		
1977 :	1.35	1.16	1																	
1978 :	1.46	1.25	1.08	1																
1979 :	1.66	1.42	1.23	1.13	1															
1980 :	1.96	1.68	1.45	1.34	1.18	1														
1981 :	2.19	1.88	1.62	1.50	1.32	1.12	1													
1982 :	2.38	2.04	1.76	1.63	1.43	1.22	1.09	1												
1983 :	2.49	2.13	1.84	1.70	1.50	1.27	1.14	1.05	1											
1984 :	2.61	2.24	1.93	1.78	1.57	1.33	1.19	1.10	1.05	1										
1985 :	2.77	2.38	2.05	1.89	1.67	1.42	1.27	1.16	1.11	1.06	1									
1986 :	2.86	2.46	2.12	1.96	1.73	1.46	1.31	1.20	1.15	1.10	1.03	1								
1987 :	2.98	2.56	2.21	2.04	1.80	1.52	1.36	1.25	1.20	1.14	1.08	1.04	1							
1988 :	3.13	2.68	2.32	2.14	1.89	1.60	1.43	1.32	1.26	1.20	1.13	1.09	1.05	1						
1989 :	3.37	2.89	2.50	2.31	2.03	1.72	1.54	1.42	1.36	1.29	1.22	1.18	1.13	1.08	1					
1990 :	3.69	3.17	2.73	2.52	2.23	1.89	1.69	1.55	1.48	1.41	1.33	1.29	1.24	1.18	1.09	1				
1991 :	3.91	3.35	2.89	2.67	2.36	2.00	1.79	1.64	1.57	1.50	1.41	1.36	1.31	1.25	1.16	1.06	1			
1992 :	4.05	3.48	3.00	2.77	2.44	2.07	1.85	1.71	1.63	1.55	1.46	1.42	1.36	1.30	1.20	1.10	1.04	1		
1993 :	4.12	3.53	3.05	2.82	2.48	2.11	1.88	1.73	1.66	1.58	1.49	1.44	1.38	1.32	1.22	1.12	1.05	1.02	1	
1994 :	4.22	3.62	3.12	2.88	2.54	2.16	1.93	1.77	1.70	1.62	1.52	1.47	1.41	1.35	1.25	1.14	1.08	1.04	1.02	1
1995 :	4.36	3.74	3.23	2.98	2.63	2.23	1.99	1.84	1.76	1.67	1.58	1.52	1.46	1.39	1.29	1.18	1.12	1.08	1.06	1.03
1996 :	4.47	3.83	3.31	3.06	2.70	2.28	2.04	1.88	1.80	1.71	1.61	1.56	1.50	1.43	1.33	1.21	1.14	1.10	1.09	1.06
1997 :	4.61	3.95	3.41	3.15	2.78	2.36	2.11	1.94	1.85	1.77	1.66	1.61	1.55	1.47	1.37	1.25	1.18	1.14	1.12	1.09
1998 :	4.77	4.09	3.53	3.26	2.88	2.44	2.18	2.01	1.92	1.83	1.72	1.67	1.60	1.52	1.41	1.29	1.22	1.18	1.16	1.13

	1975	1976	1977	1978	1979	1980	1981	1982	1983	1984	1985	1986	1987	1988	1989	1990	1991	1992	1993	1994
1999 ::	4.84	4.15	3.59	3.31	2.92	2.47	2.21	2.04	1.95	1.85	1.75	1.69	1.62	1.55	1.44	1.31	1.24	1.19	1.18	1.15
2000 ::	4.98	4.28	3.69	3.41	3.01	2.55	2.28	2.10	2.00	1.91	1.80	1.74	1.67	1.59	1.48	1.35	1.28	1.23	1.21	1.18
2001 ::	5.07	4.35	3.76	3.47	3.06	2.59	2.32	2.13	2.04	1.94	1.83	1.77	1.70	1.62	1.50	1.37	1.30	1.25	1.23	1.20
2002 ::	5.16	4.42	3.82	3.53	3.11	2.64	2.36	2.17	2.07	1.98	1.86	1.80	1.73	1.65	1.53	1.40	1.32	1.27	1.25	1.22
2003 ::	5.31	4.55	3.93	3.63	3.20	2.71	2.42	2.23	2.13	2.03	1.92	1.85	1.78	1.70	1.57	1.44	1.36	1.31	1.29	1.26
2004 ::	5.46	4.69	4.05	3.74	3.30	2.79	2.50	2.30	2.20	2.09	1.97	1.91	1.83	1.75	1.62	1.48	1.40	1.35	1.33	1.30
2005 ::	5.62	4.82	4.16	3.84	3.39	2.87	2.57	2.36	2.26	2.15	2.03	1.96	1.88	1.80	1.67	1.52	1.44	1.39	1.36	1.33
2006 ::	5.80	4.97	4.29	3.96	3.50	2.96	2.65	2.44	2.33	2.22	2.09	2.03	1.94	1.85	1.72	1.57	1.48	1.43	1.41	1.37
2007 ::	6.05	5.19	4.48	4.13	3.65	3.09	2.76	2.54	2.43	2.32	2.18	2.11	2.03	1.93	1.79	1.64	1.55	1.49	1.47	1.43
2008 ::	6.29	5.39	4.66	4.30	3.79	3.21	2.87	2.65	2.53	2.41	2.27	2.20	2.11	2.01	1.86	1.70	1.61	1.55	1.53	1.49
2009 ::	6.25	5.37	4.63	4.28	3.77	3.20	2.86	2.63	2.52	2.40	2.26	2.18	2.10	2.00	1.85	1.69	1.60	1.54	1.52	1.48
2010 ::	6.54	5.61	4.85	4.47	3.95	3.34	2.99	2.75	2.63	2.51	2.36	2.29	2.19	2.09	1.94	1.77	1.67	1.61	1.59	1.55
2011 ::	6.88	5.91	5.10	4.71	4.15	3.52	3.15	2.90	2.77	2.64	2.49	2.40	2.31	2.20	2.04	1.86	1.76	1.70	1.67	1.63
2012 ::	7.10	6.10	5.26	4.86	4.28	3.63	3.25	2.99	2.86	2.72	2.57	2.48	2.38	2.27	2.11	1.92	1.82	1.75	1.73	1.68
2013 ::	7.32	6.28	5.42	5.01	4.41	3.74	3.34	3.08	2.94	2.80	2.64	2.56	2.45	2.34	2.17	1.98	1.87	1.81	1.78	1.74
2014 ::	7.49	6.43	5.55	5.12	4.52	3.83	3.42	3.15	3.01	2.87	2.71	2.62	2.51	2.40	2.22	2.03	1.92	1.85	1.82	1.78
2015 ::	7.57	6.49	5.60	5.18	4.56	3.87	3.46	3.18	3.04	2.90	2.73	2.64	2.54	2.42	2.24	2.05	1.94	1.87	1.84	1.79
2016 ::	7.70	6.61	5.70	5.26	4.64	3.94	3.52	3.24	3.10	2.95	2.78	2.69	2.58	2.46	2.28	2.09	1.97	1.90	1.87	1.83
2017 ::	7.97	6.84	5.91	5.45	4.81	4.08	3.64	3.35	3.21	3.06	2.88	2.79	2.67	2.55	2.37	2.16	2.04	1.97	1.94	1.89
2018 ::	8.24	7.07	6.10	5.64	4.97	4.21	3.77	3.47	3.31	3.16	2.98	2.88	2.76	2.63	2.44	2.23	2.11	2.03	2.00	1.95
2019 ::	8.45	7.25	6.26	5.78	5.10	4.32	3.86	3.56	3.40	3.24	3.05	2.95	2.83	2.70	2.51	2.29	2.16	2.09	2.05	2.00
2020 ::	8.58	7.36	6.35	5.87	5.17	4.39	3.92	3.61	3.45	3.29	3.10	3.00	2.88	2.74	2.54	2.32	2.20	2.12	2.08	2.03
2021 ::	8.93	7.66	6.61	6.10	5.38	4.56	4.08	3.76	3.59	3.42	3.22	3.12	2.99	2.85	2.65	2.42	2.28	2.20	2.17	2.12

Appendix 7 : What type of retro fan are you?

Whenever you visit an entry, fill in the appropriate area. Then check the images opposite for your Rorschach-inspired result! (For more clarity, a high resolution version can be found online at https://marquisdegeek.com/20goto10/.)

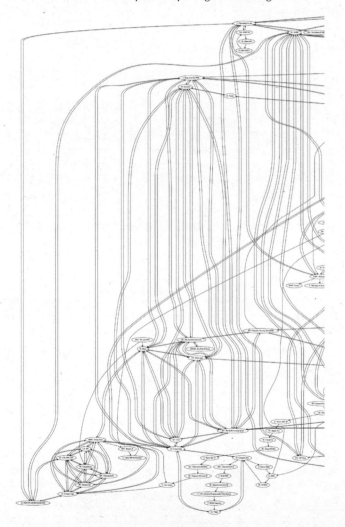

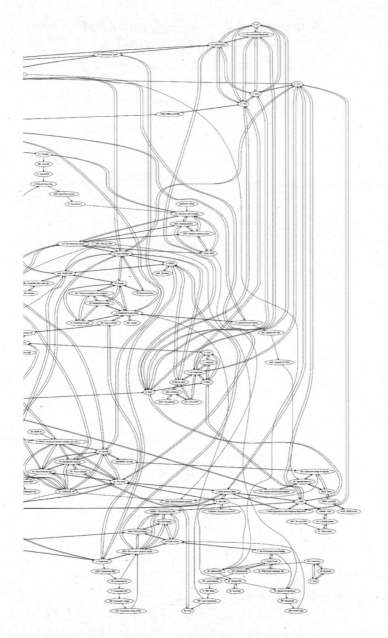

225

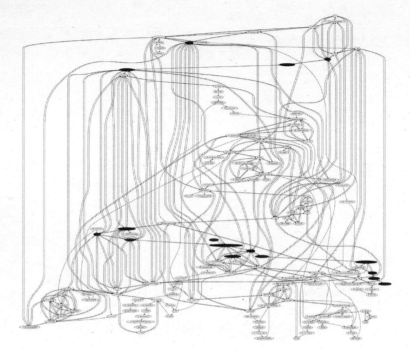

Targeted: you have a goal, and you head to it with the minimal of distractions!

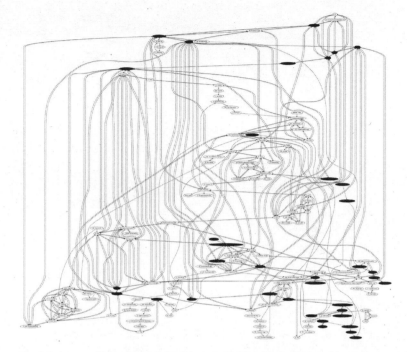

Sinclair fan: you even (begrudgingly) worked through the Amstrad hazards to get there!

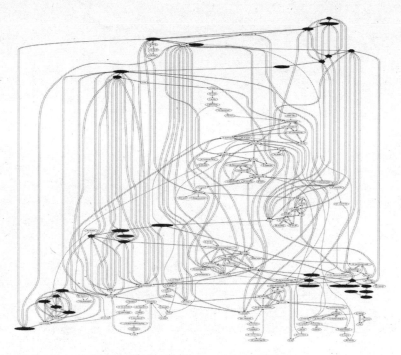

Aimless: you were guided by curiosity more than loyalty!

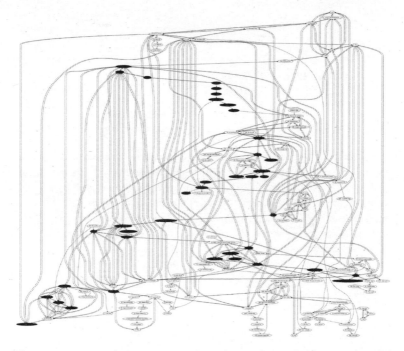

The gamer: you sought out every gaming reference but probably never found the *Jet Set Willy* POKE yourself, because it could only be access via arcane law and PC references!

Appendix 50 : Cascade
Cassette 50 - Contents

A true determination of the titles is currently an unsolved problem, as the names listed on the cassette inlay often do not match those presented on the title screen in-game. In fact, they sometimes don't even match the names promised by the advertisements, with the BBC version being promoted with a game called *Evasive Action*, instead of the released version *Ivasive Action*. Moreover, the game listed on the cover might be completely wrong where, for example, loading *Do Your Sums* shows up as *Die Thrower*.

Also, for reasons best left forgotten, Cascade considered it worthwhile to release a *second* version of their Cassette 50 for the Dragon 32 in 1984, and in doing so renamed *Jet Mobile* to *Jetmobile*.

#	Amstrad	Apple II	Atari	Acorn BBC Micro	Commodore 64	Dragon 32
1	Maze Eater	Maze Eater	Maze Eater	Maze Eater	Maze Eater	Maze Eater
2	Cylons	Galactic Attack	Galactic Attack	Galactic Attack	Galactic Attack	Galactic Attack
3	Handicap Golf	Space Mission	Space Mission	Space Mission	Space Mission	Space Mission
4	Rush Hour Attack	Lunar Lander	Lunar Landing	Lunar Lander	Lunar Landing	Lunar Lander
5	Royal Rescue	Plasma Bolt	Plasma Bolt	Plasma Bolt	Plasma Bolt	Plasma Bolt
6	Star Trek	Startrek	Star Trek	Star Trek	Star Trek	Startrek
7	Whirly	Radar Landing	Radar Lander	Radar Lander	Radar Landing	Radar Lander
8	Attacker	Attacker	Attacker	Attacker	Attacker	Attacker
9	Fighter Command	Galactic Dog Fight	Defend the Fortress	Galactic Dogfight	Galactic Dog Fight	Galactic Dogfight
10	Draughts	Zion Attack	Zion Attack	Psion Attack	Psion Attack	Zion Attack
11	Evasive Action	Ivasive Action	Ivasive Action	Ivasive Action	Ivasive Action	Ivasive Action
12	Noughts & Crosses	Noughts And Crosses	Noughts and Crosses	Noughts & Crosses	Noughts and Crosses	Noughts And Crosses
13	The King's Orb	Boggles	Boggles	Boggles	Boggles	Boggles
14	Play Your Cards Right	Pontoon	Pontoon	Pontoon	Pontoon	Pontoon
15	Creepy Crawley	Ski Jump	Ski Jump	Ski Jump	Ski Jump	Ski Jump
16	Hangman	Hangman	Maths Hop!	Hangman	Hangman	Hangman
17	Pontoon Bet	Old Bones	Old Bones	Old Bones	Old Bones	Old Bones
18	Fireman Rescue	Thin Ice	Baby Chase!	Thin Ice	Thin Ice	Thin Ice
19	3D-Maze	Orbitter	Orbitter	Orbitter	Orbitter	Orbitter
20	Colony-9	Motorway	Motorway	Motorway	Motorway	Motorway
21	Backgammon	Force Field	Rabbit Raid	Forcefield	Force Field	Forcefield
22	Solit	Nim	Nim	Nim	Nim	Nim
23	Yamzee	Tunnel Escape	Tunnel Escape	Tunnel Escape	Tunnel Escape	Tunnel Escape
24	Three Card Brag	Barrel Jump	Barrel Jump!	Barrel Jump	Barrel Jump	Barrel Jump
25	Trucking	Space-ship	Cannon Ball Battle	Cannon Ball	Cannon Ball	Cannon Ball Battle
26	Rally 3000	Overtake	Overtake	Overtake	Overtake	Overtake
27	Sitting Target	Databank Snooker	Sitting Target	Sitting Target	Sitting Target	Sitting Target
28	Nemesis IV	Smash The Windows	Smash the Windows	Smash the Windows	Smash the Windows	Smash the Windows
29	Space Ship	Space Ship	Space Ship	Spaceship	Space Ship	Spaceship
30	Jet Flight	Jet Flight	Jet Fighter	Jet Flight	Jet Flight	Jet Flight
31	Dragona Maze	Space Wars	Phaser	Phaser	Phaser	Phaser
32	Intruder	Startrek-1	Intruder!	Intruder	Intruder	Intruder
33	Inferno	Inferno	Inferno!	Inferno	Inferno	Inferno
34	Ghosts	Ghosts	Ghosts	Ghosts	Ghosts	Ghosts
35	Fantasy Land	Submarines	Sea Alert	Submarine	Submarines	Submarines
36	Space Base	Rocket Launch	Planets	Rocket Launch	Rocket Launch	Rocket Launch
37	Planets	Planets	Rocket Launch	Planets	Planets Defender	Planets
38	Hopping Herbert	Black Hole	Black Hole	Black Hole	Black Hole	Black Hole
39	Dynamite	Dynamite	Dynamite	Dice Thrower	Dynamite	Dynamite
40	Timebomb	Die Thrower	Do Your Sums	Dynamite	Do Your Sums	Dynamite
41	Day at the Races	Derby Dash	Derby Dash	Derby Dash	Derby Dash	Derby Dash
42	Lunar Lander	Space Search	Space Search	Space Search	Space Search	Space Search
43	Space Mission	Universe	Universe	Universe	Universe	Universe
44	Rats	Rats	Rats	Rats	Rats	Rats
45	Motorway	Tanker	Tanker	Tanker	Tanker Rescue	Tanker
46	Dungeon Adventure	Parachute	Parachute	Parachute	Parachutist	Parachute
47	Space Pod Rescue	Jet Mobile	Jetmobile	Jet Mobile	Jetmobile	Jet Mobile
48	High Rise	High Rise	High Rise	High Rise	High Rise	High Rise
49	Craps	The Force	The Force	The Force	The Force	The Force
50	Exchange	Exchange	Exchange	Exchange	Exchange	Exchange

#	Acorn Electron	Oric 1	VIC-20	Sinclair ZX81	Sinclair ZX Spectrum
1	Maze Eater	Maze Eater	Maze Eater	Maze Eater	Muncher
2	Galactic Attack	Galactic Attack	Star Trek	Galactic Attack	Ski Jump
3	Space Mission	Space Mission	Noughts & Crosses	Space Mission	Basketball
4	Lunar Lander	Lunar Lander	Nim	Lunar Lander	Frogger
5	Plasma Bolt	Plasma Bolt	Pontoon	Plasma Bolt	Breakout
6	Star Trek	Star Trek	Hangman	Star Trek	Crusher
7	Radar lander	Radar lander	Space Search	Radar lander	Star Trek
8	Attacker	Attacker	Do Your Sums	Attacker	Martian K.O.
9	Galactic Dogfight	Galactic Dogfight	Mole Hole	Galactic Dogfight	Boggles
10	Psion Attack	Psion Attack	Radar Landing	Psion Attack	Alien Attack
11	Ivasive Action	Ivasive Action	Lite Bikes	Ivasive Action	Lunar Lander
12	Noughts & Crosses	Noughts & Crosses	Grid Racer	Noughts & Crosses	Maze Eater
13	Boggles	Boggles	One Armed Bandit	Boggles	Microtrap
14	Pontoon	Pontoon	Golf	Pontoon	Motorway
15	Ski Jump	Ski Jump	Skull Castle	Ski Jump	Labyrinth
16	Hangman	Hangman	Balloon Dodger	Hangman	Skittles
17	Old Bones	Old Bones	Lunar Lander	Old Bones	Race Track
18	Thin Ice	Thin Ice	Knight Out	Thin Ice	Ski Run
19	Orbitter	Orbitter	Orbitter	Orbitter	Tanks
20	Motorway	Motorway	Jet Flight	Motorway	Solar Ship
21	Forcefield	Forcefield	Plasma Bolt	Forcefield	Ten Pins
22	Nim	Nim	Submarines	Nim	Cars
23	Tunnel Escape	Tunnel Escape	Force Field	Tunnel Escape	Stompers
24	Barrel Jump	Barrel Jump	Intruder	Barrel Jump	Pinball
25	Cannon Ball	Cannon Ball	Jet Mobile	Cannon Ball	Cavern
26	Overtake	Overtake	Ski Run	Overtake	Laser
27	Sitting Target	Sitting Target	Bank Raid	Sitting Target	Alien
28	Smash the Windows	Smash the Windows	Bomber	Smash the Windows	Cargo
29	Spaceship	Spaceship	Dustman Dan	Spaceship	The Race
30	Jet Flight	Jet Flight	Planetoids	Jet Fighter	The Skull
31	Phaser	Phaser	Cupid's Arrow	Phaser	Orbit
32	Intruder	Intruder	Sentinel-1	Intruder	Munch
33	Inferno	Inferno	Krazy	Inferno	Bowls
34	Ghosts	Ghosts	Meteoroids	Ghosts	Raiders
35	Submarine	Submarine	Turtle Bridge	Submarine	Field
36	Rocket Launch	Rocket Launch	Super Hi-Low	Rocket Launch	Dragon's Gold
37	Planets	Planets	Houses	Planets	Space Search
38	Black Hole	Black Hole	Three Card Brag	Black Hole	Inferno
39	Do Your Sums	Do Your Sums	PanAttack	Do Your Sums	Nim
40	Dynamite	Dynamite	Super Vaders	Dynamite	Voyager
41	Derby Dash	Derby Dash	Flesh Eaters	Derby Dash	Sketch Pad
42	Space Search	Space Search	Soccer	Space Search	Blitz
43	Universe	Universe	Minotaur's Treasure	Universe	Fishing Mission
44	Rats	Rats	Thin Ice	Rats	Mystical Diamonds
45	Tanker	Tanker	Motorway	Tanker	Galaxy Defence
46	Parachute	Parachute	Derby Dash	Parachute	Cypher
47	Jet Mobile	Jet Mobile	Galactic Dogfight	Jet Mobile	Jetmobile
48	High Rise	High Rise	Spaceship	High Rise	Barrel Jump
49	Exchange (*)	Exchange	Exchange	Exchange	Attacker
50	The Force (*)	The Force	Star Falls	The Force	Space Mission

Games listed on the inlay, that are not present on the cassette

Appendix 256 : Number conversions

Dec	Hex	Bin	8080	Z80	6502	6809
0	00	00000000	NOP	NOP	BRK B	NEG
1	01	00000001	LXI B,D16	LD BC,HHLL	ORA (D,X)	ILLEGAL
2	02	00000010	STAX B	LD (BC),A	COP B	ILLEGAL
3	03	00000011	INX B	INC BC	ORA D,S	COM
4	04	00000100	INR B	INC B	TSB D	LSR
5	05	00000101	DCR B	DEC B	ORA D	ILLEGAL
6	06	00000110	MVI B, D8	LD B,NN	ASL D	ROR
7	07	00000111	RLC	RLCA	ORA [D]	ASR
8	08	00001000	-	EX AF,AF'	PHP	LSL/ASL
9	09	00001001	DAD B	ADD HL,BC	ORA #	ROL
10	0A	00001010	LDAX B	LD A,(BC)	ASL A	DEC
11	0B	00001011	DCX B	DEC BC	PHD	ILLEGAL
12	0C	00001100	INR C	INC C	TSB A	INC
13	0D	00001101	DCR C	DEC C	ORA A	TST
14	0E	00001110	MVI C,D8	LD C,NN	ASL A	JMP
15	0F	00001111	RRC	CA	ORA AL	CLR
16	10	00010000	-	DJNZ NN	BPL R	PAGE1+
17	11	00010001	LXI D,D16	LD DE,HHLL	ORA (D),Y	PAGE2+
18	12	00010010	STAX D	LD (DE),A	ORA (D)	NOP
19	13	00010011	INX D	INC DE	ORA (D,S),Y	SYNC
20	14	00010100	INR D	INC D	TRB D	ILLEGAL
21	15	00010101	DCR D	DEC D	ORA D,X	ILLEGAL
22	16	00010110	MVI D, D8	LD D,NN	ASL D,X	LBRA
23	17	00010111	RAL	RLA	ORA [D],Y	LBSR
24	18	00011000	-	JR NN	CLC	ILLEGAL
25	19	00011001	DAD D	ADD HL,DE	ORA A,Y	DAA
26	1A	00011010	LDAX D	LD A,(DE)	INC A	ORCC
27	1B	00011011	DCX D	DEC DE	TCS	ILLEGAL
28	1C	00011100	INR E	INC E	TRB A	ANDCC
29	1D	00011101	DCR E	DEC E	ORA A,X	SEX
30	1E	00011110	MVI E,D8	LD E,NN	ASL A,X	EXG
31	1F	00011111	RAR	RRA	ORA AL,X	TFR
32	20	00100000	RIM	JR NZ,NN	JSR A	BRA
33	21	00100001	LXI H,D16	LD HL,HHLL	AND (D,X)	BRN
34	22	00100010	SHLD ADR	LD (HHLL),HL	JSL AL	BHI
35	23	00100011	INX H	INC HL	AND D,S	BLS
36	24	00100100	INR H	INC H	BIT D	BHS/BCC
37	25	00100101	DCR H	DEC H	AND D	BLO/BCS
38	26	00100110	MVI H,D8	LD H,NN	ROL D	BNE
39	27	00100111	DAA	DAA	AND [D]	BEQ
40	28	00101000	-	JR Z,NN	PLP	BVC
41	29	00101001	DAD H	ADD HL,HL	AND #	BVS
42	2A	00101010	LHLD ADR	LD HL,(HHLL)	ROL A	BPL
43	2B	00101011	DCX H	DEC HL	PLD	BMI

Dec	Hex	Bin	8080	Z80	6502	6809
44	2C	00101100	INR L	INC L	BIT A	BGE
45	2D	00101101	DCR L	DEC L	AND A	BLT
46	2E	00101110	MVI L, D8	LD L,NN	ROL A	BGT
47	2F	00101111	CMA	CPL	AND AL	BLE
48	30	00110000	SIM	JR NC,NN	BMI R	LEAX
49	31	00110001	LXI SP, D16	LD SP,HHLL	AND (D),Y	LEAY
50	32	00110010	STA ADR	LD (HHLL),A	AND (D)	LEAS
51	33	00110011	INX SP	INC SP	AND (D,S),Y	LEAU
52	34	00110100	INR M	INC (HL)	BIT D,X	PSHS
53	35	00110101	DCR M	DEC (HL)	AND D,X	PULS
54	36	00110110	MVI M,D8	LD (HL),NN	ROL D,X	PSHU
55	37	00110111	STC	SCF	AND [D],Y	PULU
56	38	00111000	-	JR C,NN	SEC	ILLEGAL
57	39	00111001	DAD SP	ADD HL,SP	AND A,Y	RTS
58	3A	00111010	LDA ADR	LD A,(HHLL)	DEC A	ABX
59	3B	00111011	DCX SP	DEC SP	TSC	RTI
60	3C	00111100	INR A	INC A	BIT A,X	CWAI
61	3D	00111101	DCR A	DEC A	AND A,X	MUL
62	3E	00111110	MVI A,D8	LD A,NN	ROL A,X	RESET*
63	3F	00111111	CMC	CCF	AND AL,X	SWI
64	40	01000000	MOV B,B	LD B,B	RTI	NEGA
65	41	01000001	MOV B,C	LD B,C	EOR (D,X)	ILLEGAL
66	42	01000010	MOV B,D	LD B,D	WDM	ILLEGAL
67	43	01000011	MOV B,E	LD B,E	EOR D,S	COMA
68	44	01000100	MOV B,H	LD B,H	MVP S,D	LSRA
69	45	01000101	MOV B,L	LD B,L	EOR D	ILLEGAL
70	46	01000110	MOV B,M	LD B,(HL)	LSR D	RORA
71	47	01000111	MOV B,A	LD B,A	EOR [D]	ASRA
72	48	01001000	MOV C,B	LD C,B	PHA	LSLA/ASLA
73	49	01001001	MOV C,C	LD C,C	EOR #	ROLA
74	4A	01001010	MOV C,D	LD C,D	LSR A	DECA
75	4B	01001011	MOV C,E	LD C,E	PHK	ILLEGAL
76	4C	01001100	MOV C,H	LD C,H	JMP A	INCA
77	4D	01001101	MOV C,L	LD C,L	EOR A	TSTA
78	4E	01001110	MOV C,M	LD C,(HL)	LSR A	ILLEGAL
79	4F	01001111	MOV C,A	LD C,A	EOR AL	CLRA
80	50	01010000	MOV D,B	LD D,B	BVC R	NEGB
81	51	01010001	MOV D,C	LD D,C	EOR (D),Y	ILLEGAL
82	52	01010010	MOV D,D	LD D,D	EOR (D)	ILLEGAL
83	53	01010011	MOV D,E	LD D,E	EOR (D,S),Y	COMB
84	54	01010100	MOV D,H	LD D,H	MVN S,D	LSRB
85	55	01010101	MOV D,L	LD D,L	EOR D,X	ILLEGAL
86	56	01010110	MOV D,M	LD D,(HL)	LSR D,X	RORB
87	57	01010111	MOV D,A	LD D,A	EOR [D],Y	ASRB
88	58	01011000	MOV E,B	LD E,B	CLI	LSLB/ASLB
89	59	01011001	MOV E,C	LD E,C	EOR A,Y	ROLB
90	5A	01011010	MOV E,D	LD E,D	PHY	DECB
91	5B	01011011	MOV E,E	LD E,E	TCD	ILLEGAL
92	5C	01011100	MOV E,H	LD E,H	JMP AL	INCB
93	5D	01011101	MOV E,L	LD E,L	EOR A,X	TSTB
94	5E	01011110	MOV E,M	LD E,(HL)	LSR A,X	ILLEGAL
95	5F	01011111	MOV E,A	LD E,A	EOR AL,X	CLRB
96	60	01100000	MOV H,B	LD H,B	RTS	NEG
97	61	01100001	MOV H,C	LD H,C	ADC (D,X)	ILLEGAL
98	62	01100010	MOV H,D	LD H,D	PER RL	ILLEGAL

Dec	Hex	Bin	8080	Z80	6502	6809
99	63	01100011	MOV H,E	LD H,E	ADC D,S	COM
100	64	01100100	MOV H,H	LD H,H	STZ D	LSR
101	65	01100101	MOV H,L	LD H,L	ADC D	ILLEGAL
102	66	01100110	MOV H,M	LD H,(HL)	ROR D	ROR
103	67	01100111	MOV H,A	LD H,A	ADC [D]	ASR
104	68	01101000	MOV L,B	LD L,B	PLA	LSL/ASL
105	69	01101001	MOV L,C	LD L,C	ADC #	ROL
106	6A	01101010	MOV L,D	LD L,D	ROR A	DEC
107	6B	01101011	MOV L,E	LD L,E	RTL	ILLEGAL
108	6C	01101100	MOV L,H	LD L,H	JMP (A)	INC
109	6D	01101101	MOV L,L	LD L,L	ADC A	TST
110	6E	01101110	MOV L,M	LD L,(HL)	ROR A	JMP
111	6F	01101111	MOV L,A	LD L,A	ADC AL	CLR
112	70	01110000	MOV M,B	LD (HL),B	BVS R	NEG
113	71	01110001	MOV M,C	LD (HL),C	ADC (D),Y	ILLEGAL
114	72	01110010	MOV M,D	LD (HL),D	ADC (D)	ILLEGAL
115	73	01110011	MOV M,E	LD (HL),E	ADC (D,S),Y	COM
116	74	01110100	MOV M,H	LD (HL),H	STZ D,X	LSR
117	75	01110101	MOV M,L	LD (HL),L	ADC D,X	ILLEGAL
118	76	01110110	HLT	HALT	ROR D,X	ROR
119	77	01110111	MOV M,A	LD (HL),A	ADC [D],Y	ASR
120	78	01111000	MOV A,B	LD A,B	SEI	LSL/ASL
121	79	01111001	MOV A,C	LD A,C	ADC A,Y	ROL
122	7A	01111010	MOV A,D	LD A,D	PLY	DEC
123	7B	01111011	MOV A,E	LD A,E	TDC	ILLEGAL
124	7C	01111100	MOV A,H	LD A,H	JMP (A,X)	INC
125	7D	01111101	MOV A,L	LD A,L	ADC A,X	TST
126	7E	01111110	MOV A,M	LD A,(HL)	ROR A,X	JMP
127	7F	01111111	MOV A,A	LD A,A	ADC AL,X	CLR
128	80	10000000	ADD B	ADD A,B	BRA R	SUBA
129	81	10000001	ADD C	ADD A,C	STA (D,X)	CMPA
130	82	10000010	ADD D	ADD A,D	BRL RL	SBCA
131	83	10000011	ADD E	ADD A,E	STA D,S	SUBD
132	84	10000100	ADD H	ADD A,H	STY D	ANDA
133	85	10000101	ADD L	ADD A,L	STA D	BITA
134	86	10000110	ADD M	ADD A,(HL)	STX D	LDA
135	87	10000111	ADD A	ADD A,A	STA [D]	ILLEGAL
136	88	10001000	ADC B	ADC A,B	DEY	EORA
137	89	10001001	ADC C	ADC A,C	BIT #	ADCA
138	8A	10001010	ADC D	ADC A,D	TXA	ORA
139	8B	10001011	ADC E	ADC A,E	PHB	ADDA
140	8C	10001100	ADC H	ADC A,H	STY A	CMPX
141	8D	10001101	ADC L	ADC A,L	STA A	BSR
142	8E	10001110	ADC M	ADC A,(HL)	STX A	LDX
143	8F	10001111	ADC A	ADC A,A	STA AL	ILLEGAL
144	90	10010000	SUB B	SUB A,B	BCC R	SUBA
145	91	10010001	SUB C	SUB A,C	STA (D),Y	CMPA
146	92	10010010	SUB D	SUB A,D	STA (D)	SBCA
147	93	10010011	SUB E	SUB A,E	STA (D,S),Y	SUBD
148	94	10010100	SUB H	SUB A,H	STY D,X	ANDA
149	95	10010101	SUB L	SUB A,L	STA D,X	BITA
150	96	10010110	SUB M	SUB A,(HL)	STX D,Y	LDA
151	97	10010111	SUB A	SUB A,A	STA [D],Y	STA
152	98	10011000	SBB B	SBC A,B	TYA	EORA
153	99	10011001	SBB C	SBC A,C	STA A,Y	ADCA

Dec	Hex	Bin	8080	Z80	6502	6809
154	9A	10011010	SBB D	SBC A,D	TXS	ORA
155	9B	10011011	SBB E	SBC A,E	TXY	ADDA
156	9C	10011100	SBB H	SBC A,H	STZ A	CMPX
157	9D	10011101	SBB L	SBC A,L	STA A,X	JSR
158	9E	10011110	SBB M	SBC A,(HL)	STZ A,X	LDX
159	9F	10011111	SBB A	SBC A,A	STA AL,X	STX
160	A0	10100000	ANA B	AND B	LDY #	SUBA
161	A1	10100001	ANA C	AND C	LDA (D,X)	CMPA
162	A2	10100010	ANA D	AND D	LDX #	SBCA
163	A3	10100011	ANA E	AND E	LDA D,S	SUBD
164	A4	10100100	ANA H	AND H	LDY D	ANDA
165	A5	10100101	ANA L	AND L	LDA D	BITA
166	A6	10100110	ANA M	AND (HL)	LDX D	LDA
167	A7	10100111	ANA A	AND A	LDA [D]	STA
168	A8	10101000	XRA B	XOR B	TAY	EORA
169	A9	10101001	XRA C	XOR C	LDA #	ADCA
170	AA	10101010	XRA D	XOR D	TAX	ORA
171	AB	10101011	XRA E	XOR E	PLB	ADDA
172	AC	10101100	XRA H	XOR H	LDY A	CMPX
173	AD	10101101	XRA L	XOR L	LDA A	JSR
174	AE	10101110	XRA M	XOR (HL)	LDX A	LDX
175	AF	10101111	XRA A	XOR A	LDA AL	STX
176	B0	10110000	ORA B	OR B	BCS R	SUBA
177	B1	10110001	ORA C	OR C	LDA (D),Y	CMPA
178	B2	10110010	ORA D	OR D	LDA (D)	SBCA
179	B3	10110011	ORA E	OR E	LDA (D,S),Y	SUBD
180	B4	10110100	ORA H	OR H	LDY D,X	ANDA
181	B5	10110101	ORA L	OR L	LDA D,X	BITA
182	B6	10110110	ORA M	OR (HL)	LDX D,Y	LDA
183	B7	10110111	ORA A	OR A	LDA [D],Y	STA
184	B8	10111000	CMP B	CP B	CLV	EORA
185	B9	10111001	CMP C	CP C	LDA A,Y	ADCA
186	BA	10111010	CMP D	CP D	TSX	ORA
187	BB	10111011	CMP E	CP E	TYX	ADDA
188	BC	10111100	CMP H	CP H	LDY A,X	CMPX
189	BD	10111101	CMP L	CP L	LDA A,X	JSR
190	BE	10111110	CMP M	CP (HL)	LDX A,Y	LDX
191	BF	10111111	CMP A	CP A	LDA AL,X	STX
192	C0	11000000	RNZ	RET NZ	CPY #	SUBB
193	C1	11000001	POP B	POP BC	CMP (D,X)	CMPB
194	C2	11000010	JNZ ADR	JP NZ,HHLL	REP #	SBCB
195	C3	11000011	JMP ADR	JP HHLL	CMP D,S	ADDD
196	C4	11000100	CNZ ADR	CALL NZ,HHLL	CPY D	ANDB
197	C5	11000101	PUSH B	PUSH BC	CMP D	BITB
198	C6	11000110	ADI D8	ADD A,NN	DEC D	LDB
199	C7	11000111	RST 0	RST 00	CMP [D]	ILLEGAL
200	C8	11001000	RZ	RET Z	INY	EORB
201	C9	11001001	RET	RET	CMP #	ADCB
202	CA	11001010	JZ ADR	JP Z,HHLL	DEX	ORB
203	CB	11001011	–	CB OPCODES	WAI	ADDB
204	CC	11001100	CZ ADR	CALL Z,HHLL	CPY A	LDD
205	CD	11001101	CALL ADR	CALL HHLL	CMP A	ILLEGAL
206	CE	11001110	ACI D8	ADC A,NN	DEC A	LDU
207	CF	11001111	RST 1	RST 08	CMP AL	ILLEGAL
208	D0	11010000	RNC	RET NC	BNE R	SUBB
209	D1	11010001	POP D	POP DE	CMP (D),Y	CMPB

Dec	Hex	Bin	8080	Z80	6502	6809
210	D2	11010010	JNC ADR	JP NC,HHLL	CMP (D)	SBCB
211	D3	11010011	OUT D8	OUT (NN),A	CMP (D,S),Y	ADDD
212	D4	11010100	CNC ADR	CALL NC,HHLL	PEI D	ANDB
213	D5	11010101	PUSH D	PUSH DE	CMP D,X	BITB
214	D6	11010110	SUI D8	SUB A,NN	DEC D,X	LDB
215	D7	11010111	RST 2	RST 10	CMP [D],Y	STB
216	D8	11011000	RC	RET C	CLD	EORB
217	D9	11011001	–	EXX	CMP A,Y	ADCB
218	DA	11011010	JC ADR	JP C,HHLL	PHX	ORB
219	DB	11011011	IN D8	IN A,(NN)	STP	ADDB
220	DC	11011100	CC ADR	CALL C,HHLL	JML (A)	LDD
221	DD	11011101	–	DD OPCODES	CMP A,X	STD
222	DE	11011110	SBI D8	SBC A,NN	DEC A,X	LDU
223	DF	11011111	RST 3	RST 18	CMP AL,X	STU
224	E0	11100000	RPO	RET PO	CPX #	SUBB
225	E1	11100001	POP H	POP HL	SBC (D,X)	CMPB
226	E2	11100010	JPO ADR	JP PO,HHLL	SEP #	SBCB
227	E3	11100011	XTHL	EX (SP),HL	SBC D,S	ADDD
228	E4	11100100	CPO ADR	CALL PO,HHLL	CPX D	ANDB
229	E5	11100101	PUSH H	PUSH HL	SBC D	BITB
230	E6	11100110	ANI D8	AND NN	INC D	LDB
231	E7	11100111	RST 4	RST 20	SBC [D]	STB
232	E8	11101000	RPE	RET PE	INX	EORB
233	E9	11101001	PCHL	JP (HL)	SBC #	ADCB
234	EA	11101010	JPE ADR	JP PE,HHLL	NOP	ORB
235	EB	11101011	XCHG	EX DE,HL	XBA	ADDB
236	EC	11101100	CPE ADR	CALL PE,HHLL	CPX A	LDD
237	ED	11101101	–	ED OPCODES	SBC A	STD
238	EE	11101110	XRI D8	XOR NN	INC A	LDU
239	EF	11101111	RST 5	RST 28	SBC AL	STU
240	F0	11110000	RP	RET P	BEQ R	SUBB
241	F1	11110001	POP PSW	POP AF	SBC (D),Y	CMPB
242	F2	11110010	JP ADR	JP P,HHLL	SBC (D)	SBCB
243	F3	11110011	DI	DI	SBC (D,S),Y	ADDD
244	F4	11110100	CP ADR	CALL P,HHLL	PEA A	ANDB
245	F5	11110101	PUSH PSW	PUSH AF	SBC D,X	BITB
246	F6	11110110	ORI D8	OR NN	INC D,X	LDB
247	F7	11110111	RST 6	RST 30	SBC [D],Y	STB
248	F8	11111000	RM	RET M	SED	EORB
249	F9	11111001	SPHL	LD SP,HL	SBC A,Y	ADCB
250	FA	11111010	JM ADR	JP M,HHLL	PLX	ORB
251	FB	11111011	EI	EI	XCE	ADDB
252	FC	11111100	CM ADR	CALL M,HHLL	JSR (A,X)	LDD
253	FD	11111101	–	FD OPCODES	SBC A,X	STD
254	FE	11111110	CPI D8	CP NN	INC A,X	LDU
255	FF	11111111	RST 7	RST 38	SBC AL,X	STU

Appendix 4294967295 : Everything

This is an incomplete list of numbers, with an incomplete list of facts. They range from the intriguing to the dull, to the completist, to the amazing – such than none deserved to be left out.

Num	Category	Notes
0	Book	CC (public domain)
0	Book	Dewey Decimal Classification
0	Book	False
0	Book	First!
0	Book	NOP
0	Book	Abbreviations
0	Index	First Amiga disc, DF0
0	Index	First BBC Micro disc, Drive 0
0	Random	First line number in Atari BASIC
0	Random	GOTO 0 is faster version of RUN
1	Book	I'd buy that for a dollar
1	Book	First!
1	Book	REM Captain Blood Kill 5 Duplicate Planet Find?
1	Book	True
1⅛	Book	IPS
1	Machine	System 1 (ordinal of release)
1	Machine	Nascom 1 (ordinal of release)
1	Machine	Oric-1 (ordinal of release)
1	Machine	Osborne 1 (ordinal of release)
1	Machine	Tatung Einstein TC-01 (ordinal of release) – could play (or develop) Spectrum games with a £50 'Speculator' hardware emulator add-on
1	Hardware	Acorn Electron Plus 1 provided expansion
1	Hardware	The issue of the ZX Spectrum to have light-grey keys, all other rubber-keyed variants had blue-grey
1	Machine	Tulip 1
1	Machine	IMKO-1, a Bulgarian clone of the Apple II
1	Machine	Sirius 1, an 8088-based PC, sold as the Victor 9000 in the United States
1	Machine	John V Blankenbaker created the Kenbak-1 using TTL logic, since the microprocessor hadn't been invented, contained 128 bytes of memory. 50 were made. 44 were sold. And 14 might still exist.
1	Machine	MOS, the manufacturers of the 6502, produced a single board computer called the KIM-1 (Keyboard Input Monitor) to demonstrate their chip

Num	Category	Notes
1	Machine	Using the same case as the IMSAI 8080, the Cromemco Z-1 originated from Stanford University, Crothers Memorial
1	Machine	Sphere 1, made by Sphere Corporation, released in 1975, contained an IO interface and full keyboard which contained a hard reset feature when two keys were pressed simultaneously (predating CONTROL-ALT-DELETE)
1	POKEs	POKE 1,53 crashes the Commodore 64 in a spectacular way
1	Random	The only number where its letters appear in reverse alphabetical order (see also 40)
1	Limits	Highest signed number with 2 bits, meaning that 2 becomes −2
1.3591409	Book	The square root of 0.25 (according to the ZX81)
2	Book	Alignment
2	Book	2's complement
2	Book	First!
2	Book	Last!
2	Machine	Nascom 2 (ordinal of release)
2	Machine	ZX Spectrum +2
2	Machine	ZX Spectrum +2A
2	Random	The number of consecutive spaces in a ZX80 program which triggers a bug
2	Random	A BBC Micro will start echoing all text to the printer after invoking VDU 2
2	Random	Number of hidden registers in the Z80, nicknamed W & Z
3	Book	Optimising for size
3	Book	Randomness
3	Machine	Ivel Z3
3	Machine	ZX Spectrum +3
3	Hardware	An unused bit in the CC register of the Z80
3	Random	A BBC Micro will stop echoing all text to the printer after invoking VDU 3
3	Random	A number that Valve can't count to!
3	Limits	Highest unsigned number with 2 bits, meaning that 4 wraps to 0
4	Book	Amstrad numeric notation
4	Book	Bugs in *Jet Set Willy*
4	Book	Peripherals for processing
4	Machine	Commodore Plus/4
4	Index	Computer Buffs, UK TV show
4	Random	Amiga's exec base, the one constant
4	Random	Bits in a nibble (written with an 'i', despite being clearly derived from 'byte' with a 'y')
4	Random	Number of paging schemes in the MSX: ASCII 8kb, ASCII 16kb, Konami, and Konami with SCC
4	Random	'GAMESTAPE 4' by J.K. Greye Software is better known as the ZX81's killer app, *3D Monster Maze*. (It was later sold by New Generation Software under its named title only)
4	Random	The ZX81 FAST mode is four times faster than SLOW mode, because the machine doesn't 'waste' time drawing the screen

239

Num	Category	Notes
4	Random	The speed increase a Spectrum owner could gain by using a Sprint cassette player over an ordinary one. (According to the adverts!)
5	Book	Keys
5	Machine	Sord M5, a distant relation to The Ultimate Computer
5	Hardware	Another unused bit in the CC register of the Z80
5	Random	Number of different commands on a single key of the Sinclair Spectrum keyboard
5	Random	Address to CALL to perform CP/M functions
6	Book	King's Parade
6	Book	The ZX Spectrum Screen Display
6	Machine	Thomson MO6
6	Random	Page 6 on an Atari is protected memory for user's machine code. Also, the name of a magazine
6	Random	Number of segments in a Semigraphics character
6	Random	Total number of countries in Europe that made computers in the 1980s
7	Machine	FM 7
7	Random	Graphics mode on the Super NES
7	Random	Text mode on the BBC Micro
7	Random	Maximum number of characters allowed in an Acorn DOS filename
7	Random	The character which often produces a beep when printed
7	Random	The number of companies approached to design and build a computer for the UK's BBC. Ultimately, Acorn won
7	Random	The number of distinct tetrominoes in Tetris. Their official names are Orange Ricky, Cleveland Z, Rhode Island Z, Blue Ricky, Hero, Teewee and Smashboy
7	Limits	Highest signed number with 4 bits, meaning that 8 becomes -8
8	Book	Bits in a byte
8	Book	CHIP-8
8	Book	Type-in listings
8	Book	DEC PDP-8
8	Machine	DEC PDP-8, 12-bit computer
8	Machine	Orel BK-08
8	Machine	Pravetz 8D, a Bulgarian Oric from 1990 with alternate ROM and font
8	Machine	English Electric (later merged into ICL) KDF8 which sold 13 units, a version of the RCA 501
8	Random	The Hut at Bletchley Park used by the code breakers
8	Random	Number of display modes on the BBC Micro
8	Random	The 8-bit era is represented by machines with an 8-bit data bus like the Spectrum, Commodore, and Acorn BBC Micro. Of these, only the Commodore really made an impact in the US, alongside the Apple II
8	Random	The number of traitorous employees who, in 1957, left Shockley Semiconductor Laboratory to form Fairchild Semiconductor
9	Book	Nine Tiles
9	Hardware	Pins on most early joysticks

Num	Category	Notes
9	Hardware	Pins on a DE-9 serial port
9	Hardware	Pins on the head of a dot-matrix printer
9	Index	Billboard position of 'Pac-Man Fever' by Buckner & Garcia
9	Machine	English Electric (later merged into ICL) KDF9 which sold 29 units
9	Random	You would get a free Sinclair Spectrum for every £4,645 purchase of a Renault 9 car between April 1st and May 31st 1984
10	Book	BASIC
10	Book	Disabling the break key
10	Book	Tales of *Chuckie Egg*
10	Book	Toshiba HX-10 (MSX)
10	Book	New pence
10	Book	PRINT "Always get someone to cheque your work. ";
10	Book	Seconds (booting the Macintosh)
10	Machine	Casio MX-10
10	Machine	Toshiba HX-10
10	Hardware	The first Japanese all-transistorised desk calculator, Sharp Compet CS-10A, from 1964
10	Index	Typical cassette length
10	Machine	CER-10 from Yugoslavia
11	Random	Character to print which clears the screen on the Aquarius
11	Random	The machine supposedly under the desk when the Sinclair QL was being demonstrated was a PDP-11
11	Machine	DEC PDP-11, 16-bit computer
12	Book	Celebrity
12	Random	The number of *Pac-Man* clones on the ZX Spectrum, alone, according to Issue No.1 of *Crash Magazine* in February 1984. They were: *Egg Farm, Ghost Hunt, Gnasher, Gobble a Ghost, Gulpman, Haunted Hedges, Hungry Horace, Mazechase, Mazeman, Monster Muncher, Muncher, Paseman.*
13	Book	ROT 13
13	Book	Level 13 (*Minestorm*)
13	Book	Points (Sir Clive Sinclair and Mastermind)
14	Book	Canary traps
14	Book	Chips
14	Book	Computer kits
14	Machine	MK-14
14	Random	Number of trucks needed to take unsold ET cartridges to their desert graveyard
15	Book	C15, C60, C90
15	Book	REM SNAKESNAKESNAKE
15	Book	Saving to tape
15	Hardware	Pins on the PC game port
15	Hardware	Pins on a VGA port
15	Index	Typical cassette length
15	Random	Bytes in the header of Sinclair Spectrum tape file
15	Limits	Highest unsigned number with 4 bits, meaning that 16 wraps to 0
16	Book	RAM Pack
16	Machine	Sinclair ZX Spectrum (16K)

Num	Category	Notes
16	Machine	Epson QX-16
16	Random	The 16-bit era is represented by machines with a 16-bit data bus. In the UK they were home computers like the Amiga and Atari ST. The US these machines were considered part of the professional arena (with the Amiga and its Video Toaster being used for TV graphics) so their 16-bit era focused more on the consoles, the Sega Genesis (aka Mega Drive), SNES, and TurboGrafx-16.
16	Random	The answer to 8 * 2, the first calculation performed on the Sinclair Executive prototype
16	Random	SWEET16, a set of byte-code instructions intended to work with 16-bit pointer data in the 8-bit Apple II
18	Book	Certificate 18
18	Hardware	Word size, in bits, for the PDP-1
18	Hardware	Word size, in bits, for the Elliott range
19	Book	Musicians with computers
19	Random	The chapter of the Spectrum manual which suggests the reader might like to program the computer to play 'the rest of Mahler's first symphony'
20	Book	What is retro?
20	Book	A friendly number (the VIC-20)
20	Machine	Canon V20
20	Machine	Commodore VIC-20
20	Machine	VC-20, or VolksComputer, as the VIC-20 was known in Germany
20	Random	Number of Activision games re-released as Firebird Silver budget titles
22	Hardware	Columns on the VIC-20
22	Index	Donkey Kong kill screen
22	Random	Pence cost of the GB postage stamp marked 'Babbage – Computer'
22	Random	The first disc in the game *The Secret of Monkey Island* to be inserted after Guybrush climbs down into the stump. Followed by discs 36 and 114
23	Machine	Sord M23 Mark II
24	Hardware	Pins on the head of a dot-matrix printer
25	Book	Willis Road, Cambridge, UK
25	Hardware	Pins on a DB-25 serial port
25	Hardware	Pins on a DB-25 parallel port
26	Random	Pence cost of one of the two UMIST-related GB postage stamps released for Information Technology year, 1982. (The other was 15½p)
28	Book	Peripherals for output
28	Random	The number of Earth days most mail order companies would promise delivery of your item. Given Sinclair's reputation in this area, with delivery times stretching into months, they might have meant Venus days!
28	Random	Total number of original games released for the Vectrex
29	Index	Tetris screen (original NES version)
30	Book	Monmouth Street
30	Book	Storage

Num	Category	Notes
30	Random	The number of hours the BBC said it would take to learn BASIC in their course
31	Book	Peripherals for input
31	Limits	Highest signed number with 6 bits, meaning that 32 becomes -32
32	Machine	Dragon 32 (memory)
32	Machine	Matra Alice 32
32	Machine	Pecom 32
32	Random	Cent cost of the US postage stamp marked 'Computer Technology'
33⅓	Book	Revolutions per minute
33	Random	Cent cost of the US postage stamp marked 'Personal Computers'
35	Hardware	Tracks on a Commodore DOS format disc
35	Index	Number of opcodes in CHIP-8
36	Hardware	Word size, in bits, for the PDP-10
36	Index	Issue of *Computer & Video Games* with The Thompson Twins flexidisc
37	Random	Cent cost of the US postage stamp marked 'John von Neumann'
40	Book	Keyboards
40	Hardware	Tracks on an Acorn BBC format disc, selectable by a toggle switch
40	Random	Commodore 64 was originally to be called the VIC-40
40	Random	The only number whose letters appear in alphabetical order (see also 1)
40	Prices	The cost of the MK-14 (Science of Cambridge) was £39.95 (1978)
42	Random	Number of Apollo guidance computers built
43	Random	Percentage stake in Sinclair Radionics, taken by National Enterprise Board (NEB) in 1976
48	Machine	Sinclair ZX Spectrum (48 K)
49	Book	Optimising for speed
50	Book	Compilations
50	Book	Signetics Instructor 50
50	Machine	Signetics Instructor 50
50	Prices	The cost of the Sinclair ZX81 (Sinclair Research) was £49.95 (1981) – built version
60	Machine	Bit 60
60	Machine	Electronika 60. Russian machine on which Alexey Pajitnov wrote the original Tetris
60	Hardware	'There's only one thing wrong with the ZX81. Its keyboard. Or rather its lack of one.' Thus ran the advert for the add-on Filesixty keyboard. So, given the infinite range of keyboards they could have sold, what type did they choose? Yep, a rubbery dead flesh one!
60	Index	Typical cassette length
60	Random	Number of rooms in the Spectrum version of *Jet Set Willy* (because four didn't work properly, so Matthew Smith removed them)
63	Limits	Highest unsigned number with 6 bits, meaning that 64 wraps to 0
64	Book	Spanish import law (CPC 472)

Num	Category	Notes
64	Machine	Commodore 64 (memory)
64	Machine	Commodore SX-64 (memory)
64	Machine	Dragon 64 (memory)
64	Machine	Enterprise 64 (memory)
64	Hardware	The Commodore 64GS, short for Games System, was a cartridge-based console released in 1990. It failed
64	Machine	Pecom 64
64	Machine	Oric nova 64, an Oric Atmos
64	Random	UK games publication *Edge* has given few games 10/10 – *Super Mario 64* was the first. (Although Elite was retroactively appraised as such)
65	Machine	Atari 65XE
65	Machine	Aim-65
65	Machine	Commodore 65, a machine that almost no one has!
65	Machine	Tangerine Microtan 65
70	Book	Bugs
70	Prices	The cost of the Sinclair ZX81 (Sinclair Research) was £69.95 (1981) – assembled version
71	Random	Commands available in C64 basic 2.0
73	Random	Number of rooms in the Dragon 32 version of *Jet Set Willy*, 13 more than the original on the larger 48 K Spectrum
77	Random	Memory location of the Atari attract mode
80	Hardware	Zilog Z80
80	Machine	Advanced Basic Computer 80 (CPU)
80	Machine	Sharp MZ-80K (CPU)
80	Machine	Sinclair ZX80 (CPU)
80	Machine	Radio Shack TRS-80 Color Computer 2 (ordinal of release)
80	Machine	TRS-80 Model I (CPU)
80	Machine	TRS-80 Model II (CPU)
80	Machine	TRS-80 Model II (CPU)
80	Hardware	Tracks on an Acorn BBC format disc, selectable by a toggle switch
80	Machine	An Australian clone of the TRS80, but incorporating a cassette recorder, called the 'Dick Smith System 80'
80	Prices	The cost of the Sinclair ZX80 (Science of Cambridge) was £79.95 (1980) – kit version
80	Prices	The cost of the Timex Sinclair 1500 (Timex Sinclair) was $79.95 (1983) – built version
81	Machine	Sinclair ZX81
84	Book	LCD displays
85	Machine	Hewlett-Packard HP-85
85	Machine	Misedo 85, a Tandy CoCo 2
85	Prices	The cost of the Minivac 601 (Scientific Development Corporation) was $85 (1961)
86	Book	BBC cassettes
87	Machine	Robotron KC 87
88	Machine	Cambridge Z88
90	Machine	Bit 90
90	Machine	Matra Alice 90
90	Machine	Microdigital TK90X

Num	Category	Notes
90	Index	Typical cassette length
90	Machine	Alice 90
90	Prices	The cost of the Jupiter Ace (Jupiter Cantab) was £89.95 (1982)
96	Machine	Camputers Lynx 96 (memory)
99	Book	Press to continue
99	Book	Dots (the owl logo)
99	Machine	TI-99/4A
100	Book	The extent of computer upgrades (the S100 bus)
100	Machine	Franklin Ace 100
100	Index	*Duck Hunt* kill screen
100	Random	Baud rate
100	Random	The dollar rebate offered by Commodore, in January 1983, for anyone that traded in another console or computer. Since Timex computers were retailing at $50 it was easy to hack the system, artificially inflating the sales figures of both machines
100	Random	The number of bytes used by the KIM-1 tape interface as a SYN marker (each byte is 0x16)
100	Random	A label on some games would proudly claim '100% machine code' which, knowing that most machines had frustratingly slow BASIC, was a given
100	Prices	The cost of the Atari 65XE (Atari Corporation) was $99.95 (1985)
100	Prices	The cost of the Sinclair ZX80 (Science of Cambridge) was £99.95 (1980) — built version
100	Prices	The cost of the Timex Sinclair 1000 (Timex Sinclair) was $99.95 (1982) — built version
108	Random	Section 108 of Title 17 of the US Code of Laws is used to protect archive.org by classing it as a library which provides for exceptions in copyright and fair use, making it one of the few legal online repositories for retro software and material
110	Book	Fulbourn Road
113	Index	The Dragon 32 reset vector
116	Machine	Commodore 116 (memory)
118	Index	HALT instruction, used in generating the ZX81 screen
120	Prices	The cost of the Acorn Atom (Acorn Computers) was £120 (1980) — kit version
125	Hardware	Designation of the Quickshot joystick
125	Random	Memory size of KITT, from the TV show *Knight Rider*, in megabytes
125	Prices	The cost of the Sinclair ZX Spectrum (16 K) (Sinclair Research) was £125 (1982)
126	Index	Samples on the very first soundtracker disc
127	Book	127 or 255?
127	Limits	Highest signed number with 8 bits, meaning that 128 becomes -128
128	Machine	Acorn BBC Master 128
128	Machine	Camputers Lynx 128 (memory)
128	Machine	Commodore 128 (memory)
128	Machine	ELAN Enterprise 128 (memory)
128	Machine	Sinclair Spectrum 128
130	Machine	Atari 130 ST, which never shipped

Num	Category	Notes
130	Prices	The cost of the Memotech MTX512 (Memotech Corporation) was £130 (1985)
135	Book	Easter eggs
141	Random	The character code to create double height characters on the BBC Micro
147	Book	CLS
150	Hardware	Opcodes in a 6502
150	Random	Millions of dollars invested in Apple stock, by Microsoft, in 1997. They had sold it all by 2003
150	Prices	The cost of the Acorn Atom (Acorn Computers) was £150 (1980) – built version
160	Prices	The cost of the Mattel Aquarius (Mattel) was $160 (1983)
165	Prices	The cost of the Atari 800 (Atari Inc.) was $165 (1983)
170	Hardware	Kilobytes on a Commodore 64-formatted disk
175	Prices	The cost of the Sinclair ZX Spectrum (48K) (Sinclair Research) was £175 (1982)
180	Hardware	A Zilog processor, the Z180, was a backward-compatible successor to the Z80
180	Prices	The cost of the Enterprise 64 (Enterprise Computers) was £180 (1985)
186	Hardware	The Intel 80186 was a 55,000 transistor chip with a 16-bit data bus, and 20-bit addressing
188	Hardware	The Intel 80188 was a 55,000 transistor chip with an 8-bit data bus and 20-bit addressing
195	Prices	The cost of the Sord M5 (Sord Computer Corportion) was £195 (1982)
197	Hardware	In hex this is represented as C5, which can be interpreted as a musical note. The second one played by an Acorn BBC Micro when it switched on, and was used to indicate an error when COPY was pressed without moving the cursor to a target location
198	Prices	The cost of the Nascom 1 (Nascom) was £197.50 (1978)
199	Random	The price (in UK new pence) of the Mastertronic budget range
199	Prices	The cost of the ZX Spectrum +3 (Amstrad) was £199 (1988)
200	Machine	Dragon 200
200	Machine	Sinclair PC 200
200	Machine	VTech Laser 200
200	Machine	Number of Apple 1s made
200	Prices	The cost of the Sinclair ZX80 (Science of Cambridge) was $199.95 (1980) – built version
200	Prices	The cost of the Timex Sinclair 2068 (Timex Sinclair) was $199.95 (1983)
201	Book	Cursor keys
205.5	Book	How to draw a maze in one line
220	Random	Common Soundblaster setting in the autoexec.bat, BLASTER=A220 I5 D1 H6 T6 P330
225	Prices	The cost of the Camputers Lynx (Camputers) was £225 (1983)

Num	Category	Notes
228	Random	Number of colour cycles, per line, that NTSC computers *actually* wrote. (The specific requires 227.5)
229	Prices	The cost of the Amstrad CPC 6128 (Amstrad) was £229 (1984) – colour monitor version
232	Hardware	Serial protocol
235	Prices	The cost of the Acorn BBC Model A (Acorn Computers) was £235 (1981)
239	Prices	The cost of the Amstrad CPC 464 (Amstrad) was £239 (1984) – colour monitor version
240	Random	White dots in a level of *Pac-Man*
244	Hardware	In hex this is represented as F4, which can be interpreted as a musical note. The first one played by an Acorn BBC Micro when it switched on
246	Book	The Indiana Pi Bill
249	Prices	The cost of the ZX Spectrum +3 (Amstrad) was £249 (1987)
250	Hardware	First microcontroller, the GI 250, used in the Royal digital III calculator
255	Limits	Highest unsigned number with 8 bits, meaning that 256 wraps to 0
256	Book	Nintendo Game Boy Boot ROM
256	Book	The $2.56 reward program
256	Book	The *Pac-Man* kill screen
256	Machine	Tatung Einstein 256 (memory)
256	Index	Size, in bytes, of the zero page on the 6502
256	Index	Size, in bytes, of the Apple 1 ROM
256	Index	*Galaga* kill screen
256	Index	*Dig Dug* kill screen
256	Index	Size, in bytes, of the Apple I ROM containing its memory monitor
256	Random	Size, in bytes, of most disc sectors
256	Random	Size, in bytes, of the Sinclair MK-10 RAM
275	Prices	The cost of the Memotech MTX500 (Memotech Corporation) was £275 (1983)
280	Prices	The cost of the Canon V20 (Canon) was £280 (1984)
286	Hardware	The Intel 80286 was a 134,000 transistor chip with a 16-bit data bus and 24-bit addressing
287	Hardware	The Intel 80287 was a math co-processor for the 80286
288	Hardware	RPM of Atari floppies
299	Prices	The cost of the Camputers Lynx 96 (Camputers) was £299 (1983)
299	Prices	The cost of the Sinclair PC 200 (Sinclair Research) was £299 (1988)
300	Book	Kansas City
300	Machine	The original name for the Amiga 600, before it was upgraded to 600 (as it was of lower spec than the A500)
300	Random	Baud rate of Atom cassettes, amongst others
300	Random	The number of original customers allegedly affected by the ZX81 SQRT bug. (The true answer was nearer half a million, since the problem was slow in being fixed)

Num	Category	Notes
300	Prices	The cost of the Cambridge Z88 (Cambridge Computer) was £300 (1987)
300	Prices	The cost of the Commodore Plus/4 (Commodore Business Machines) was $300 (1984)
300	Prices	The cost of the Nascom 2 (Nascom) was £299.5 (1979)
308	Random	Frequency of the hum on a Vectrex at boot
310	Random	Buffer Micro Shop, possibly the first UK computer games shop, traded at 310 Streatham High Road, London SW16
315	Prices	The cost of the Memotech MTX512 (Memotech Corporation) was £315 (1983)
321	Random	UK TV quiz show, and computer game, featuring Ted Rogers whose recorded voice is on the tape introducing each game
328	Machine	Spectravideo SVI-328 Mk II
328	Machine	Spectravideo SVI-328
335	Prices	The cost of the Acorn BBC Model B (Acorn Computers) was £335 (1981)
345	Prices	The cost of the Camputers Lynx 128 (Camputers) was £345 (1983)
349	Prices	The cost of the Amstrad CPC 464 (Amstrad) was £349 (1984) – green monitor version
357	Book	In jokes
360	Hardware	The IBM System/360 was a family of mainframes available between the mid-1960s and the late 1970s
360	Machine	IBM System/360 was a family of mainframes from the mid-1960s which set the standard for compatibility and progression
375	Prices	The cost of the Aim-65 (Rockwell) was $375 (1978)
380	Machine	Research Machines 380Z
386	Hardware	The Intel 80386 was a 275,000 transistor chip with a 32-bit data bus and 32-bit addressing (the SX version had 16- and 24-bit buses, respectively)
399	Prices	The cost of the Amstrad CPC 6128 (Amstrad) was £399 (1984) – green monitor version
399	Prices	The cost of the Amstrad PC1512 DD (Amstrad) was £399 (1986) – monitor version
399	Prices	The cost of the Amiga 1200 (Commodore International) was £399 (1992)
399	Prices	The cost of the ICL Merlin Tonto M1800 (International Computers Limited) was £399 (1984)
399	Prices	The cost of the Sinclair QL (Sinclair Research) was £399 (1984)
400	Machine	Atari 400 (memory)
400	Hardware	Maximum length, in meters, of an Econet network cable
400	Machine	IBM Application System/400 was a family of computers which succeeded the System/36 and 38 in the late 1980s
400	Prices	The cost of the TRS-80 Model I (Tandy Corporation) was $399.95 (1977)
404	Book	Entry not found
410	Hardware	Designation of the Atari tape recorder
423	Prices	The cost of the Sharp MZ-80K (Sharp Corporation) was £423 (1978)

Num	Category	Notes
425	Prices	The cost of the Genie II EG 3008 (EACA) was £425 (1981)
432	Hardware	Serial protocol
438	Random	The number of electoral votes that the UNIVAC computer predicted Eisenhower would win by in the 1952 Presidential Election. However, since this is the complete opposite of what had been previously suggested, it was decided to not announce for fear of it being wrong
439	Prices	The cost of the Altair 8800b (Micro Instrumentation and Telemetry Systems) was $439 (1975) – kit version
440	Machine	Acorn Archimedes A440
450	Random	The number of staff of UK newsagent W.H. Smith who received training to turn a computer on and off, load software, and write basic BASIC programs
451	Book	Fahrenheit 451
464	Machine	Amstrad CPC 464 – a colour computer which came with a green-screen monitor
472	Index	Amstrad machine for Spain
479	Prices	The cost of the Minivac 6010 (Scientific Development Corporation) was $479 (1962)
480	Machine	Link 480Z
486	Hardware	The Intel 80486, or i486, was a 1.2–1.6 million transistor chip with a 32-bit data bus and 32-bit addressing
499	Prices	The cost of the Tatung Einstein TC-01 (Tatung Corporation) was £499 (1984)
500	Machine	Commodore Amiga 500
500	Machine	Commodore Amiga 500 Plus
500	Machine	Memotech MTX500
500	Machine	Acorn Archimedes A500
500	Random	Price of the first Apple kit, in dollars, before tax pushed it to $666
500	Random	The dollar amount Elon Musk earned for his VIC-20 BASIC game, Blastar
500	Random	Thousands of dollars invested in Amiga by Atari, in the hope of having access to their new chipset
501	Machine	A transistor-based computer from 1958 called the RCA 501 used pluggable cards
511	Limits	Highest signed number with 10 bits, meaning that 512 becomes -512
512	Machine	Memotech MTX512
520	Machine	Atari 520 ST FM
525	Prices	The cost of the TI-99/4A (Texas Instruments) was $525 (1981)
550	Index	The ZX81 BASIC ROM, revision 1
550	Prices	The cost of the Atari 400 (Atari Inc.) was $549.95 (1978)
560	Random	The line in Altair BASIC which read 'PAUL ALLEN WROTE THE NON-RUNTIME STUFF.'
580	Random	The line in Altair BASIC which read 'BILL GATES WROTE THE RUNTIME STUFF.'
596	Prices	The cost of the Amiga 600 (Commodore International) was $595.95 (1992)

Num	Category	Notes
600	Machine	Atari 600XL (memory)
600	Machine	Commodore Amiga 600
600	Random	Baud rate
600	Random	The line in Altair BASIC which read 'MONTE DAVIDOFF WROTE THE MATH PACKAGE.'
601	Machine	Minivac 601 (memory)
618	Random	The phone number (technically 'short code') to dial for the UK's videotex system, Prestel. (918 was also available in some areas)
621	Prices	The cost of the Altair 8800b (Micro Instrumentation and Telemetry Systems) was $621 (1975) – built version
640	Book	Ought to be enough for anybody
666	Book	In-jokes
667	Prices	The cost of the Apple I (Apple Computer Company) was $666.66 (1983)
672	Book	1K Chess
699	Prices	The cost of the Amiga 500 (Commodore International) was $699 (1987)
699	Prices	The cost of the Amiga 500 Plus (Commodore International) was $699 (1991)
699	Prices	The cost of the TRS-80 Model II (Tandy Corporation) was $699 (1980)
700	Machine	Sharp MZ-700
700	Random	Amount of dollars Jobs and Wozniak were paid for *Breakout* for Atari (according to Jobs)
700	Random	The first of eight pages of 'Telesoftware', available on BBC 2's Ceefax service
720	Book	Copy protection
720	Hardware	Kilobytes on a PC-formatted disk, single density
754	Book	IEEE 754
775	POKEs	Commodore 64, POKE 775,200 protects BASIC from LISTing
795	Prices	The cost of the Pet 2001 Series (Commodore International) was $795 (1977)
800	Machine	Atari 800 (memory)
800	Random	Amount of dollars Ronald Wayne earned for his 10% stake in Apple
800	Random	One telesoftware service providing a form of online magazine in the early 1980s, via Prestel, was called Micronet 800. Like all walled gardens, information placed on it could be removed at the whim of the owners. When, in late 1984, the pages relating the UK Labour Party were removed recriminations started about whether it was BTs walled garden or sub-licensees Telemap that was to blame – citing that religion and politics were classified as prostitution and crime
805	Hardware	The first calculator to use an LCD, the Sharp EL-805
808	POKEs	Commodore 64, POKE 808,225 disables RUNSTOP/RESTORE
808	POKEs	Commodore 64, POKE 808,237 enables RUNSTOP/RESTORE
810	Hardware	Designation of the Atari floppy drive
880	Hardware	Kilobytes on an Amiga-formatted disk

Num	Category	Notes
895	Prices	The cost of the Sorcerer (Exidy) was $895 (1978)
903	Machine	Elliott 903
1000	Book	A kilobyte
1000	Machine	Commodore Amiga 1000
1000	Machine	Tandy 1000
1000	Machine	Tandy 1000 EX
1000	Machine	Timex Sinclair 1000
1000	Hardware	The first Amiga, whose case included signatures of the designers and a dog's pawprint
1000	Random	The monthly royalty of a Logic 3 programmer, according to their adverts entitled 'Game to earn £1,000?'
1000	Prices	The cost of the Atari 800 (Atari Inc.) was $999.95 (1978)
1000	Prices	The cost of the Commodore SX-64 (Commodore Business Machines) was $1000 (1984)
1001	Machine	Japan sold the VIC-20 as a VIC-1001
1023	Limits	Highest unsigned number with 10 bits, meaning that 1024 wraps to 0
1024	Book	Not a kilobyte
1024	Random	First location of screen memory on the Commodore 64
1200	Book	BASICODE
1200	Book	Acorn BBC Micro baud rate
1200	Machine	Commodore Amiga 1200
1200	Random	Baud rate of BBC Micro cassettes, amongst others
1200	Prices	The cost of the Matra Alice (Matra Hachette) was Francs 1200 (1984)
1200	Prices	The cost of the Tandy 1000 (Tandy Corporation) was $1200 (1984)
1200	Prices	The cost of the VTech Laser 200 (Video Technology) was 1200 French Francs (1984)
1234	Random	The insecure default password in too many situations. (Even now!) See also: 2222222222
1285	Prices	The cost of the Commodore Amiga 1000 (Commodore International) was $1285 (1985)
1292	Machine	1292 Advanced Programmable Video System
1351	Hardware	Commodore mouse
1395	Prices	The cost of the Apple IIe (Apple Computer, Inc.) was $1395 (1983)
1400	Prices	The cost of the Advanced Basic Computer 80 (Luxor) was $1400 (1978)
1495	Prices	The cost of the Amiga 2000 (Commodore International) was $1495 (1987)
1500	Book	Computer sounds in music
1500	Machine	Timex Sinclair 1500
1510	Machine	IBM 1510
1512	Machine	Amstrad PC1512 DD (memory)
1530	Hardware	Commodore 64 tape unit
1541	Hardware	Commodore 64 disk drive, followed by the 1541C and then 1541-II
1565	Prices	The cost of the IBM 1510 (IBM) was $1565 (1981)
1600	Hardware	The first clean-room BIOS, which reverse engineered the IBM PC, was in the Compaq 1600
1701	Book	Licensed and unlicensed material

Num	Category	Notes
1735	Index	The address of the ZX81 square root bug
1770	Hardware	Disk controller in the Acorn DFS 2.10
1795	Prices	The cost of the C/WP Cortex (C/WP) was £1795 (1983)
1795	Prices	The cost of the Osborne 1 (Osborne Computer Corporation) was $1795 (1981)
1800	Machine	ICL Merlin Tonto M1800
1802	Hardware	The TMS 1802 from Texas Instruments was a microcontroller chip which predated Intels MCU. Used in calculators
1802	Hardware	The RCA 1802 ran the original CHIP-8 interpreter
1843	Random	On Tuesday 21st March Hansard, the official report of all UK Parliamentary debates, included the first mention of the 'computer', albeit in reference to a person
1951	Random	On Monday 12th March Hansard, the official report of all UK Parliamentary debates, included the first mention of the 'computer', in the modern meaning in a debate on North Atlantic Defence, by Mr. Richard Fort
1970	Prices	The cost of the Superbrain (Intertec Data Systems) was $1970 (1979)
2000	Book	The future
2000	Machine	Commodore Amiga 2000
2000	Hardware	A receiver to take broadcast teletext signals and make them ingestible by the Sinclair Spectrum. (Not be to be confused the VTX 5000, which used an identical case)
2000	Random	The cost paid to Ian Williamson by Sinclair, in sterling, for the MK-14 manual after using his idea for the SC/MP based MK-14, but not his design. An early demonstration of the power of good documentation
2001	Machine	Pet 2001 Series
2047	Limits	Highest signed number with 12 bits, meaning that 2048 becomes −2048
2048	Random	MicroAce, a clone of the ZX80 by CompShop, was identical in everything except its colour scheme and memory. It had 2 KiB. To save an extensive court case, Sinclair licensed the machine
2049	Random	*Miner 2049er* was the Atari 800 game that inspired Matthew Smith to create *Manic Miner*
2068	Machine	Timex Sinclair 2068
2084	Random	The twin joystick was popularised by Robotron: 2084
2101	Hardware	A memory chip, providing access to 1024 individually addressable bits
2105	Machine	BT Merlin M2105
2149	Hardware	Yamaha sound chip in the Atari SI, MSX and 128K Spectrum which produced three tone channels and one noise channel
2200	Machine	The Datapoint 2200, released in November 1970
2200	Machine	The Wang 2200, released in May 1973
2400	Random	Baud rate
2400	Random	The KIM-1 uses a tone of this frequency, in Hz, for the '1' bit on its tape interface
2495	Prices	The cost of the Apple Macintosh (Apple Computer, Inc.) was $2495 (1984)

Num	Category	Notes
2496	Index	Frequency of the ZX Spectrum header tone
2496	Random	Frequency of the Spectrum's sync tone
2600	Random	Frequency of a whistle found in Cap'n Crunch cereal, which inspired a hacker culture
2600	Machine	Atari 2600, also known as the Atari VCS between 1977 and 1982
3000	Machine	Commodore Amiga 3000
3000	Machine	Business computer from Xerox, the Diablo 3000
3000	Random	Amount paid for the Commodore 64 version of *Jet Set Willy*
3003	Machine	Video Genie EG3003
3003	Machine	Genie I EG 3003
3008	Machine	Genie II EG 3008
3200	Machine	Genie III EG 3200
3250	Prices	The cost of the Hewlett-Packard HP-85 (Hewlett-Packard) was $3250 (1980)
3379	Prices	The cost of the Amiga 3000 (Commodore International) was $3379 (1990)
3450	Prices	The cost of the TRS-80 Model II (Tandy Corporation) was $3450 (1979)
3500	Random	The initial number of TRS-80 machines built because the manufacturer, Radio Shack, had 3500 stores and could use them internally if they didn't sell
3699	Prices	The cost of the Amiga 4000 (Commodore International) was $3699 (1992)
3700	Random	The KIM-1 uses a tone of this frequency, in Hz, for the '0' bit on its tape interface
4000	Machine	Commodore Amiga 4000
4000	Machine	Jupiter Ace 4000
4000	Machine	Amstrad GX4000
4000	Machine	Inex made a machine called the Total Microcomputer Model 4000, which has an external appearance similar to the Sphere 1
4004	Hardware	The 4-bit CPU created by Intel in 1971 for $60
4095	Limits	Highest unsigned number with 12 bits, meaning that 4096 wraps to 0
4116	Hardware	Eight of these RAM chips were part of the lower 16 KiB of ZX Spectrum's memory
4340	Prices	The cost of the Apple III (Apple Computer, Inc.) was $4340 (1980)
4532	Hardware	Eight of these RAM chips were part of the upper 32 KiB of the ZX Spectrum's memory. These are 64 KiB chips, of which half are broken (and the computer simply uses the good half). This changed with the Issue 3, mark 5 board which used eight 64 KiB memory chips with half their capacity being left idle. This use of less-than-perfect components was repeated by Roland with the TR-808 drum machine and their use of faulty transistors
5000	Hardware	For connecting the Sinclair Spectrum to Prestel's Micronet and similar systems, one might use the Prism VTX 5000 modem. (Not to be confused the TTX2000, which used an identical case)
5000	Machine	Philips VG5000
5000	Random	Amount of dollars Jobs and Wozniak were *actually* paid for *Breakout* for Atari

Num	Category	Notes
5475	Prices	The cost of the DEC Rainbow (DEC) was £5475 (1982)
6000	Machine	IBM RISC System/6000 was a family of super-high spec, business-oriented desktop supercomputers from 1990s. It could also run *Doom*
6010	Machine	Minivac 6010 (memory)
6128	Machine	Amstrad CPC 6128 (memory)
6501	Hardware	Drop-in replacement chip for the 6800
6502	Hardware	The chip used in Bender, from *Futurama*
6502	Hardware	The assembler seen on the T-800's HUD in *The Terminator*
6502	Hardware	A MOS CPU which was similar, but incompatible to, the 6800
6502	Index	The WAIT instruction which triggered an Easter egg on the Commodore PET
6510	Hardware	A version of the 6502 with six additional IO pins
6522	Hardware	Commodore IC which included a timing bug that made the disk slow
6526	Hardware	Peripheral controller chip
6581	Book	Sound generation
6800	Hardware	Motorola CPU
6800	Machine	Southwest Technical Products produced the SWTP 6800, based on the Motorola chip of the same numeral
6802	Hardware	CPU used in the 1977 Oldsmobile Tornado
6803	Hardware	Motorola CPU, used almost exclusively in the Mantra Alice
6809	Hardware	Motorola CPU, featured in the Dragon and CoCo machines
6847	Hardware	Motorola video display generate chip (VCG)
6858	Random	Self destruct code in *Space Quest 1*
7001	Machine	Quantel DPB-7001 Digital Paintbox
7501	Hardware	Another MOS variant of the 6510
7861	Machine	Nissei Sangyo manufactured the Samurai KDS 7861 and has a 16-bit 8086 and so is sometimes known as the Samurai 16
7862	Random	A grease for unsticking floppies is called IPA 7862
8008	Hardware	The 8-bit CPU created by Intel in 1972 for $120, double the price and bit width of the 4004
8032	Machine	Commodore 8032-SK
8080	Hardware	Intel 8-bit CPU used in the Altair 8800 and since featured in Microsoft's phone number
8086	Hardware	The Intel CPU which spawned the x86 architecture
8088	Hardware	A modified 8080 with an external 8-bit data bus (akin to the 68000 vs 68008 from Motorola)
8271	Hardware	The Intel disk controller used in the BBC Micro
8800	Machine	Altair 8800b (CPU)
9000	Machine	Positron 9000, a very rare 6809 machine
9000	Machine	Victor 9000, an 8088-based PC, sold as the Sirius 1 in Europe
9345	Hardware	Video chip, EF9345, as used in the Alice 90 and Philips VG5000
9995	Prices	The cost of the Apple Lisa (Apple Computer, Inc.) was $9995 (1984)
10204	Random	Asteroid named for Turing
11341	Random	Asteroid named for Babbage

Num	Category	Notes
16384	Hardware	The start of 'contended memory' in the ZX Spectrum. The 16 KiB of lower RAM in the 0x4000–0x7FFF range would be processed slower since the ULA had priority access to it because the screen data was located in this area (and therefore the CPU would have to wait if it needed to read or write to it)
16509	Book	ZX81 1K Display
16514	Hardware	The start address for ZX81 machine code routines
22824	Random	Asteroid named for von Neumann
26429	POKEs	Spectrum, *Hungry Horace*, POKE 26429,0 gives infinite lives
31250	Book	MIDI
31337	Random	Hacker spelling of 'elite', or 'leet'
31337	Random	Port number of hacking tool, 'back orifice'
31900	Book	With prizes
32767	Limits	Highest signed number with 16 bits, meaning that 32768 becomes –32768
34483	POKEs	Spectrum, *Jet Set Willy*, POKE 34483,195 removes the copy protection
34785	POKEs	POKE 34785 sets the number of start lives in *Jet Set Willy* on the ZX Spectrum
35899	Book	PEEK and POKE
38911	Book	Bytes (free memory)
42183	POKEs	Spectrum, *Jet Set Willy*, POKE 42183,11 moves an inaccessible (and invisible) item to a room where it can be reached
47196	POKEs	Spectrum, *Knight Lore*, POKE 47196,201 gives immunity
49152	Book	PEEK 49152
49152	Book	SYS 49152
53272	POKEs	Commodore 64, POKE 53272,23 switches to lower case mode
56876	POKEs	Spectrum, *Jet Set Willy*, POKE 56876,4 replaces a wall with a floor so you can navigate the rooms
59901	POKEs	Spectrum, *Jet Set Willy*, POKE 59901,82 fixes the arrow position in The Attic
60231	POKEs	Spectrum, *Jet Set Willy*, POKE 60231,0 removes enemy from Conservatory Roof so the bottle to its right can be collected
64738	Random	SYS address to reset a Commodore 64
65495	Book	Going faster
65535	Limits	Highest unsigned number with 16 bits, meaning that 65536 wraps to 0
65816	Hardware	Motorola CPU in the Apple IIgs
68000	Hardware	Motorola CPU released 1979, eventually found fame in the Amiga and Atari ST
68000	Random	The opening text of *Alien Soldier* referenced the Motorola chip with 'Now is the time to the 68000 heart on fire'
68008	Hardware	Motorola CPU with an 8-bit data bus, but 32-bit registers internally. Came with 20- or 22-bit addressing modes
262144	Hardware	The factorisation run by Manchester Baby in June 1948 (instead of 8616460799)

Num	Category	Notes
270835	Random	The only motherboard registration of the Spectrum +3 to *not* have sound issues
524287	Limits	Highest signed number with 20 bits, meaning that 524288 becomes -524288
1000000	Book	Sales
1000000	Random	Wrap score in *Donkey Kong*, so it's presented as 0
1048575	Limits	Highest unsigned number with 20 bits, meaning that 1048576 wraps to 0
2455992	Book	The Cathode Ray Tube
3333360	Book	*Pac-Man* Hi Score
6031769	Random	The cheat code for *Manic Miner*, taken from Matthew Smith's driving licence
8388607	Limits	Highest signed number with 24 bits, meaning that 8388608 becomes -8388608
16777215	Limits	Highest unsigned number with 24 bits, meaning that 16777216 wraps to 0
16777216	Limits	Floating point errors mean that this is the last sequential whole number. Adding one to it results in 16777216
16777216	Book	Colour
2147483647	Book	Seconds
2147483647	Limits	Highest signed number with 32 bits, meaning that 2147483648 becomes -2147483648
2222222222	Random	The user 'name' for the Prestel system. When combined with the default password of 1234 (Yes! Seriously!) it allowed Robert Schifreen and Steve Gold to hack into the entire Prestel system and read the Duke of Edinburgh's email (Probably has no connection to the fake phone number in the De la Soul song "Ring Ring Ring — Ha Ha Hey")
4294967295	Limits	Highest unsigned number with 32 bits, meaning that 4294967296 wraps to 0
8616460799	Hardware	The semiprime number used for WS Jevons factoring, which inspired early computer tests

Acknowledgements

Since this book was first envisaged, back in 2014, many people have come into my life. And left. My family has grown, and shrunk. The world has changed, and changed me. So much so that I barely recognise the person I was. This book is offered as a historical (and technical) account of out-of-date machines that did not (and cannot) have any of the issues associated with the current era, meaning we can treat retro computing as our comfort food in a world of anti-social media and divisive modern technology. Similarly, this acknowledgement is a reminder of resolute people who are both good and true!

To the uncountable number of family, friends and colleagues who got used to my enforced absence during the 'C'-nario of 2020–21, and endured it through my voluntary isolation whilst writing this, I hope this book serves as a suitable excuse!

For my supporters, thank you for believing! With little more than a title and some brief examples you understood what the book meant, and why it was important. You are named individually elsewhere in this book. Yet, despite the title of 'published author' I still live with imposter syndrome, as my spellchecker continues to re-write my biography of 'celebrity' to 'yet another media non-entity'. An extended thank you to the supporters who encouraged other supporters to join us on this journey – especially Javier Pedreira, Pete Golding, Tony Jewell and Ian Mansfield.

To my new family at Unbound – Mathew, DeAndra, Isobel, Justin, Lena and everyone else I never met – who are scurrying behind the scenes to make me appear possible competent! I'm glad you all redirected my rule-bending and geeky antics into /dev/null to give me delusions of adequacy.

Thanks always to the good people, past and present, from the Centre for Computing History in Cambridge who've provided so much to this book's existence, including Jason, Katrina, Jeremy and Adrian.

And finally, to those that have a permanence in my life. I might not see you from one month/year/decade to the next, but when I do it's like we've never been apart. In no particular order I raise a distant glass of a suitable beverage to Lucas Grange, Darren Bolland, Justine Griffith, Jérôme Muffat-Méridol, Dave Wall, Mal

Lansell, Alan Troth, Ben Crossman, Kevin Toms, Mike Knight, the fabulous gang of Tracey, Andy and Betsy, Ian, Jane, Anne-Marie, Karl and Alex. To all the members of TULS, the Pentacle Club, FAB, Chaos Chaps, Mensa and whichever company is paying my day job salary by the time you read this – thank you! Never forgetting John Southern and Anne Mullane.

To those that know all about me – but seem to like me anyway – I'm glad my secrets are safe with you! Everyone else should send bribes to Phillip Hart, Frank Scott, John Grant, Phil Downer, Shane O'Neil, Bruno Baillorge & Josiane Baillorge Valverde, David Eade and Lily.

Of course and as always, to the family. Shirley, Juliette & Dean and George & Matilda, Melanie & Dan and Grace & Rose, Mum and Dad, Angela and Holly.

Unbound is the world's first crowdfunding publisher, established in 2011.

We believe that wonderful things can happen when you clear a path for people who share a passion. That's why we've built a platform that brings together readers and authors to crowdfund books they believe in – and give fresh ideas that don't fit the traditional mould the chance they deserve.

This book is in your hands because readers made it possible. Everyone who pledged their support is listed below. Join them by visiting unbound.com and supporting a book today.

Otto Benz
Rob Bernstein
Tim Berry
Denesh Bhabuta
Brad Bidnick
Brad Biglin
Andres Blanco
James Bland
Matt Bland
Robbie Blundel
John Blythe
Joanne Boal
Dimitrios "Taki"
   Bogiatzoules
Gavin Bollan
Keith Bond
Peter Borg
Paolo Borzini
David Boston
Katrina Bowen
Neil Bowers
Carolyn Braby
Edwin Brady
Jamie Brammer
Anna-Maria Bromley
Jeremy Bromley
Jason Brooks
John Brown
Joseph Brown
Kristina Amanda
   Coleman Brown
Brian Browne
Tim Buchalka
Adam Buckland
Andy & Mel Buntine
Stuart Bunyan
Andrew Burgess
Thomas Burggraeve
Dean Butcher

Paul Butler
Rob Butterworth
Blaine Buxton
Ged Byrne
Francisco Cabello
James Cadd
Yannick Cadin
Martin John Callanan
Esteve Camós
Geoff Campbell
Richard Campbell
Jorge Campos Coloma
Juan Campos Coloma
Paul Campy
Marco Cappellari
Håkan Carlsson
Jonathan Carpenter
Xisco Carrascosa
Adele Carroll
Dave Carroll
Charles Carsberg
Edison Carter
Les Carter
Stuart Carter
Jon Caruth
Richard Case
Stephen Cass
Derek Chandler
Jac Chandross
Jonathan Chapman
Heather Chappelle
Andy Charalambous
Chris Charla
Charles
Simon Chatterjee
Joanne Chittenden
Yeomanson Christopher
Michelle Chuang
Liam Clancy

Lee Clarke
Nicholas Clarke
Mathew Clayton
Mark Clerkin
Wayne Clipperton
Neil Coffey
Richard Cohen
Robert Cole
Jeffrey Coleman
Darren Coles
Richard Anthony Coles
Matteias Collet
Christopher Collingridge
Laurence Collins
Steve Collins
Kevin Conan
David Constable
Christopher Cook
Paul Cooney
Barry Cooper
J Cooper
Martin Cooper
Steve Cooper
Ray Cornwall
Andrew Cosgriff
Federico Costa
Iain Cowper
Matthew Craig
Katherine Crispin
Paul Crompton
David Cull
Jules Curran
d3la
Tom Dalby
Steve Dallape
Frederic Dang Tran
Professor James
   Davenport
Martin Davidson

Debbie Davies
Martyn Davies
Russell Davies
Kevin Davis
Theresa Davis
Wes Davis
Steve De George
Tonny de Jong
Vin de Silva
Todd Decker
Oscar Delgado Mohatar
Paul Deluce
Sencer Demir
William Depper
Dethwiff
Alan Devine
Guillaume Dewaele
Michele Di Paola
Antoine Diamant-Berger
Glenn Dietz
James Docherty
Dana Dominiak
Brendan Donahe
Greg Donald
Ben Dooks
Paul Douglas
Simon Douglass
Philip Downer
Gareth Downey
Kevin Driscoll
Norman Driskell
Dylan Drury
DSP
Nic Dunlop
Vivienne Dunstan
Jean-Michel Durand
Matthew Durkin
Chris "DeadFleshRetro" Dymond

Dave Eagle
Alex Eaton
Paul Edwards
Thomas Egloff
Nick Ellerby
Jayson Elliot
ELT
Brad Emerson
Louis Emmett
Matias Enroth
Ian Entwistle
Gergo Erdi
Jose Esteve
Denis Estevez
Cristian Estrada
Andrew Evans
Adam Fahn
Alf Fairweather
Paul Fearns
Nick Fellows
Krysia Fenwick-Loye
Nick Ferguson
Manuel Fernández Baños
Nigel Fernando
Jesus Fidalgo
Elliott Field
Andrew Fielder
Paul Fillery
Thomas Finnerup
Paul Fiscarelli
Andrew Fisher
Nick Fitzsimons
Sean Flannigan
G Foskett
Kevin Foss
Colin Foster
Alexander Fox
Stu Fox

Jason Freeman
Julian Freeman
Kevin Frei
Stephan Freundorfer
Jack Fuller
Steven Gailey
Andy Garden
Dave Gardner
David Gardner
Stephen Garland
Paul J. Garrett
Lynn Genevieve
Jonathan George
Keith George
Matheus Jose Geraldini dos Santos
Matthew Gerber
Cathie Gibbens
Colin Gibson
Tim Gilberts
Richard Gillin
Rodney Gitzel
Pete Golding
Ricardo Lucas Gómez
Laurence Gonsalves
Stephen Gow
Adrian Graham
James Grainger
Joe Grand
Thomas Grant
Liam Graves
Rory Graves
Kathryn Green
Tim Green
Lawrie Greenfield
Steve Gregory
Andrew Gregson
Griffin
Ben Griffiths

Ted Griffiths
Iain Grossart
Michael Grugel
John Gruver
Marcello Gualano
Mikołaj Gugała
Olivier Guinart (•_•)
Alby Guzman
Michael Gwyer
GypsyRose67
Jonathan Haddock
John Haines
Eileen Hall
Michael Hall
Danielle Hallett
John Halton
Rune Finstad Halvorsen
Steven Hamilton
Adam Hammond
Mark Hammond
Stephen Hampshire
Marc Hampson
Elizabeth Hanson
Simon Hardy
Lee Hardy Dydo
Robert Hargraves
Paul Hargreaves
Anthony Harker
Pat Harkin
Neil Harper
Paul Harrington
Sean Harrington
Bob Harris
Paul "HardwareHarry"
     Harris
Robin Harrison
Stephen Harrison
Thomas Harte
Dean Hartwell

Colin Harvey
Rosie Harvey
Kim Haverblad
Kim Hawtin
Todd Haynie
Neil Hazzard
Garry Heather
Rob Heaton
Dan Helderle
Mark Hemans
Robin Hemmings
Joaquín Herrero Pintado
Brandon S Higa
Stu, Katherine &
     Izzy Higgins
Mark Hinchcliffe
Lucien Hoare
JK Hollan
Iain Holmes
Alex Hopson
Tom Hostler
Mark Howlett
John "The Piggle"
     Howson
Francisco Javier Huerta
     Garces
Jeremy Huggett
Ken Hughes
Chris Hulbert
Adrian Humphris
Tracy Hunt
Juan Ildefonso S.G.
Ibon Iloro
Hew Ingram
Luke Ireland
Roger Isaac
Itgrrl
Daniel Jackson
Greg Jackson

Brian Jacob
Paul James
Jelte Jansen
Paul S Jenkins
Tim Jenness
Anders Jensen
Tony Jewell
Dylan John
Andrea Johnson
Brian Johnson
Graham Johnson
John Jones
Luke D. Jones
Mike Jones
Peter Jones
Lars Jonsson
Timothy Joransen
Alex Joseph
Tushar Joshi
Mike Jury
Nick Kaijaks
Nikos Karagiannakis
Maximilian Karasz
Steve Kearns
William Franklin Keck
Sloan Kelly
Kris Kennaway
John Kennedy
Alasdair G. Kergon
Tim Kerslake
Jean-Marie Kieliger
Dan Kieran
Thomas Kim
Matthew King
Linde Kirby
Ian Kirkpatrick
Eeku Koponen
Rainer Koschnick
Krascek99

Thomas Kristiansen
James Kruth
Jeffrey Kuhlmann
Brian Kumanchik
Rajasekaran Senthil
    Kumaran
D L
Pierre L'Allier
Al La Prade
Paul Labedan
Matthew Laker
Abhilash Lal Sarhadi
Gabriele Lana
Christian Langeland
Malcolm Lansell
Matt LaRussa
Robert Last
Ron Lauzon
Nick Lavalle
Andy Lee
Joost Leeuwesteijn
    (The Netherlands)
Andre Leiradella
Phillip Lemky
Mat Lemmings
Michael Leonardi
Andrew Lewis
John Lewis
Sean Michael Lewis
Stephen Lewis
Rupert Licht
Craig Linderoth
Mike Lindgren
Anton Lindholm
Orla Linehan
Nick Lines
Jessica Linnington
John Linnington
David Linsley

Jo Livingston
Jamie Lloyd
Edward Loach
Dunc Lockwood
Fabrizio Lodi
Pamela Loetterle
Chad Dylan Long
Chris Long
Donovan Loperena
Oddvar Lovaas
Gary Lucero
Chris Luke
Søren Lund
Tor-Eirik Bakke Lunde
Philip James Lunt
Graham Lutas
Phil Lutas
Elizabeth Lynch
Richard Lyne
Tom Lyon
Ricardo M
Ross M
Mike M.
Rob MacAndrew
Mack Macias
Ramon Macias
Andy MacKinnon
Mark MacLennan
Alasdair Macmillan
Macrospace
Andrew Maddison
Paula Maddox
Dariusz ZX Freeq
    Malczewski
Rick Mallen
Bob Mallett
Ava Mandeville
Herb Mann
Bruce Maret

Tobias Marquardt
Steve Mars
Barry Marshall
David Martin
Juan Martínez
Humberto Martínez
    Barberá
Doug Mason
Craig Massey
Joseph Mastromarino
Alexis Mather
Austin Matthews
Rick Matthews
William HB Mawhinney
Herman I May
mb
Brian McBarron
Barry McCauley
Peter McCowie
Laurence McDonald
Geoff McHugh
Allan McLeod
John McMullin
Andrew McVeigh
Mike Mee
Pierre Mengal
Rich "EchoDad" Merrett
Caroline Mersey
Andy Methley
Jim Methley
Evert Meulie
Donald Meyer
Thomas Michanek
Peter Milburn
Julián Miranda
Thor Mitchell
John Mitchinson
Andrew Moate
Xander Mol

José Manuel Molina
Dee Montague
Joshua Moore
Kim Moore
Terry Moore-Read
Manuel Morales Román
Billy Morgan
Andy Morrison
Joerg Mueller-Kindt
Michael Mulhern
Peter Edmund Mullins
Jay Mundy
Claus Munk
Colin Murphy
NackUK
Clive Naish
Naked Retro Gamers
Amador Navarro
Carlo Navato
Eric Neustadter
John Newcombe
Hugh Newsam
Kechong Nguyen
Mark Nias
E Nicholls
Gary Nicol
Fiona Nielsen
Kes Nielsen
Andy Nightingale
David Nightingale
Felix Nijpels
Noid
Noniq
Mikael Nordgren
Thorsten Nordholm
    Søbirk
Peter Norman
Conrad Nowikow
John O'Donnell

Mark O'Neill
Shane O'Neill
Chris O'Prey
Chris O'Regan
Ian O'Connor
Rik O'Hanlon-Smith
obliviosa
Simon Oliver
Claire ZX Claire
    Osborne
Ian Osborne
Magnus Överengen
Richard Owens
Simon J. Painter
Kevin Palser
pansycow
Paul Papathomas
James Pardey
Steph Parker
Steve Parker
Victoria Parkinson
Gareth Parry
Gary Partis
Shannon Partridge
Kevin Pascoe
Siobhan Peal
Alan Pearse
Fabrizio Pedrazzini
Javier Pedreira «Wicho»
David Pegg
Eva Pelayo
Simon Pennell
Ignacio V Perez
Chris Perkins
Graham Peyman
Peter Phipps
Felipe Aguilar Picazo
Simon Pilgrim
Justin Pinner

Mark Pinto
Andy Piper
Maurizio Pistelli
Hervé Piton
Playfish
PLOPPLOP62
Eric Poirier
Justin Pollard
Javi Polo - Panda Crew
Christophe Ponsard
John Porter
Chris Post
Les Pounder
lewis price
Robert Price
Sebastien Pujadas
Aaron Quigley
Mark Quiney
Mike Rachel
Jose Raez Rodriguez
Daniel Rafferty
Rebecca Rajendra
Todd Ramsey
Iain Randle
RC2014
John Read
Matt Reading
Philip Reagan
Simon Reap
Fiona Redmond
Nigel Reed
Ian Rees
Robert Rees
Simon Rees
Mads Regnar
Fasih Rehman
Bruce Rennie
RetroCollective.co.uk
Andy Ribaudo

Guy Richardson
Philip Richardson
Brandon Riley
Dan Riley
Craig Ritchie
RobertPayne556
Rod Robinson
Ed Robson
Nadia Rodgers
Kenn Roessler
Axel Roest
Paul Roff
Melanie Rogan
Gareth 'Gaz' Rogers
Pete Rogers
Dannyorker &
    Carlotus Rojas
David Rojo Gonzalez
Nicholas Rust
James Rye
Nandan Saha
Stephen Salmon
Daniel García
    Santamaría
Javier Santiago Mesa
Michael Sauers
Lee Savidge
Steven Savile
David Saxon
Ben Scarboro
Arthur Schiller
Dominik Schläpfer
Sebastian Schleussner
Boris Schneider-Johne
Rob Schofield
Don Schuy
Ryan Scoular
Philip Searle
Gregg Seelhoff

Richard Selby
Kevin Seltmann
James "Airshack"
    Shackel
Spencer Shanson
Mike Sharp
Remy Sharp
Xenon Sharp
Ben Sharpworks
Jeff Shaw
Michael Shaw
David Sheldon
Bob Shingler
Ken Shirriff
Bruno Silva
Dan Simon
Peter Simpson
David Sivés-Rutherford
Rebecca Sivieri
Phil Sivills
smilz18
Alexander Smith
D J Smith
Darren Smith
Fraser Smith
Gavin Smith
Kev Smith
Lionel Smith
Nic Smith
Simon C Smith
Stacy Smith
Adrian Smith
    (TheNinjaFinger)
Dave Snowdon
John Southern
Andy Spencer
Rob Spencer
Patrick Spicer
Dan Steadman

Terry Steege @
    RetroTechTime.com
Mark Steele
William Steele
Phil Steer
Matthew Stephenson
Anthony Stern
Simon Stewart
E Stockan
Dan Stormont
David Stradling
Henry Strickland
Lawrence Struzik
James Sutherland
Stephen Swindley
Matthew Sylvester
Kevin Symonds
Lee Symonds
Ian Synge
Tall Man with Glasses
Blax Tamborez
Wong Tang Fung
Anemic TANT
Iain Tatch
Christopher Taylor
Gary Taylor
Kevin Taylor
Michael Taylor
Riikka Teikari
Roy Templeman
George Terezakis
Terry
TheWatcher
Mark Thompson
Dominic Thoreau
Matthew Thredgold
Barry Tipper
TLi
Grigor Todorov

Howard Tomlinson
Malcolm Toms
Gene Toye
Sean M. Tracey
Robert Trangmar
Craig Treptow
Peter Tribble
Stephen Trotman
Jon Truran
Graham Turner
Bob Twells
Mike Tynan
Lewis Tyrrell
Yarek Tyshchenko
Ola Uleberg
Dr. Tim Urban
Rob van der Most
Jeroen van der Velden
Daaf van Oudheusden
Chris Vardy
Jon Veal
Mark Vent
Paul Vincent
Karl von Randow
Ingve Vormestrand
Vicky Waine-Riley
HD Walker
Sir Harold Walker
Steve Walker
Peter Walker-Birch
Dj Walker-Morgan

Joe Walnes
Joe Walter
Christopher Walton
Netty Wap
Ken Waters
Mike Watts
Chris Webb
Richard Webb
Larry Wedow
Jack Weeland
Jim Weil
Jase Wells
Clancy Wendt
Scott Wendt
Fabien Wernli
Mark Whaite
Mack Wharton
WhatHoSnorkers
Shawn Wheatley
Paul Whelan
Chris White
Jon White
Rabbit White
Dan Whitehead
John Whitworth
Andreas Wiklund
James Wilcox
Andrew Wilcox,
    @unclewilco
Peter Wilde
Vincent Willcox

Arnold Williams
Daniel Williams
Dennis P Williams
Gareth Williams
Ian R Williams
Kirsty Williams
Kevin Wilson
Matthew Wilson
Dilan Winter
Simon Wistow
Morten Wittrock
Krystian 'Tygrys' Włosek
Alex Il Buono Wolter
Matthew Wood
Peter Wood
David Woozley
Alec Worsfold
Michael Wright
Sam Wright
Simon Wright
Derek Wyatt
XYZprototype
Allain Yann
You lost the game!
    Signed: Yxuer
David Youd
Peter Young
Yvo Zoer
Tristan Zwalf
Неточка Незванова